D1068492

Pygmalion
in Management

Issues in Organization and Management Series
Arthur P. Brief and Benjamin Schneider, *Editors*

Pygmalion in Management

Productivity as
a Self-Fulfilling Prophecy

Dov Eden

Lexington Books
D.C. Heath and Company/Lexington, Massachusetts/Toronto

Library of Congress Cataloging-in-Publication Data

Eden, Dov
   Pygmalion in management : productivity as a self-fulfilling
prophecy / Dov Eden
      p.   cm.
   ISBN 0–669–12293–9 (alk. paper)
   1. Labor productivity—Management.   2. Employee motivation.
I. Title.
HD57.E28   1990
658.3'14   dc20   89–29576
                              CIP

Published simultaneously in Canada
Printed in the United States of America
Casebound International Standard Book Number: 0–669–12239–9
Library of Congress Catalog Card Number: 89–29576

The paper used in this publication meets the minimum requirements of
American National Standard for Information Sciences—Permanence of
Paper for Printed Library Materials, ANSI Z39.48–1984. ∞™

Year and number of this printing:

90 91 92 10 9 8 7 6 5 4 3 2 1

In memory of my parents
Mary and Isadore ("Al") Fine

Contents

Figures

Tables

Acknowledgments

I want to thank Art Brief and Ben Schneider for their invitation to contribute a book to their series, which I'm proud to be part of. Their editorial comments on my drafts have added to the book's quality. In particular, I want to express my special esteem for Art, who was two doors away during my two-year visitor appointment at the Graduate School of Business Administration at New York University. During that time, Art was not only my editor; he became my friend.

A grant from the Israel Institute of Business Research supported some of the work on this book.

Over the last decade, several students have worked with me on *Pygmalion* and other expectancy-related research. Some of their names appear throughout the pages of this book as collaborators in various Pygmalion experiments. These include Gadi Ravid and Abraham B. (Rami) Shani, who have gone on to complete their doctoral degrees and are now independent researchers in their own right. Other students are involved in expectancy research in progress, not yet published, and their names have not yet appeared. They include Arie Aviram, Taly Dvir, Abigail Greenwood, Joseph Kinnar, Mordecai (Moti) Liberman, Reuven Stern, and Michal Yefet-Michaeli. They are doing empirical field work testing practical Pygmalion applications. These students have been my partners in the quest to investigate manager-expectation effects in the field. I envy no colleague for having better students. Supervising people like these makes playing the Pygmalion role a piece of cake.

Researching this book has not always been a joy. It become onerous when some colleagues who did not like it did their best to make my life unbearable. During those tough times, there were several people without whose support, encouragement, and good advice I might not have made it through the crisis. These include Elisha Babad, Yair Orgler, Bob Rosenthal, Gabi Salomon, and Yitzchak Westman. They were there for me when I needed them, and I will never forget it.

Throughout the period of **Pygmalion** research, my wife, Nili, has been more than a source support and encouragement; she has been a behind-the-scenes partner. Her own career in nursing training and health-systems management has led her to many Pygmalion-relevant insights, which have continuously enriched my thinking and writing on the topic.

Foreword

Arthur P. Brief
Benjamin Schneider

Even a casual reading of management history suggests that many so-called innovations in management practice represent little more than rediscovery of some long-discarded practice. For example, some of the profit-sharing plans, matrix organizational designs, and concerns for quality of working life seen today as "innovations" also were popular in the late nineteenth century. Simply put, true innovations in the management of people are rare.

With the publication of Dov Eden's *Pygmalion in Management,* the conceptual and empirical evidence for such an innovation may be here. Eden articulates a creative way to view management that may capture the imagination of practicing managers—stimulating them to test out new behaviors that define a new role. The role Eden envisions for managers is that of a prophet.

According to Eden, managers as prophets expect certain things to happen and then act in ways to fulfill their expectations. In the role of prophet, he sees managers as capable of rehabilitating the chronically poor performer. More importantly, Eden advocates that organizations, not just individuals, can be turned around with a prophet at the helm.

In addition to speaking to managers, *Pygmalion in Management* has much to say to the scholarly community. Eden, primarily drawing on his own organizational research as well as work done in social and educational psychology, carefully details what is known about the self-fulfilling prophecy phenomenon. Moreover, he outlines a research agenda to fill gaps in our knowledge that we suspect will keep many organization scientists busy in the years ahead.

As a highly suggestive guide to practice and a superb piece of scholarship, we could not be more pleased to add *Pygmalion in Management* to our series. We are confident that the reader, whether his or her interests lie in the practical or academic world, will be intrigued by Eden's thesis and his data. We fully expect our goals for the book to be fulfilled!

Introduction

Scenario A

Janet Simms was an eager but cautious management trainee at a medium-sized Wall Street brokerage house. This was her first job since completing the requirements for her MBA degree seven months earlier at a respectable, but not outstanding, business school. She was still learning the ropes as a member of the small analysis team to which she had been assigned when she was summoned to the office of Hal Yardley, the department head to whom her current unit chief reported.

Mr. Yardley greeted her pleasantly but briefly and got right to the point. He explained that while her present role on the analysis team was fine for starters during an initial training period with the company, he had reviewed her progress and thought that she had already reaped the benefits that could be gained from that job and could now be replaced by someone less qualified. Yardley asked Janet if she would be willing to take upon herself an independent project that was important to the company, cut across several departmental lines, and had a four-month deadline. Doing this special project would afford her a chance to learn a lot and fast about how the company operated. The project required the specialized knowledge she had acquired in her MBA minor area, so it was a fortuitous case of the right person for the right job at about the right time. The project had been ordered by the division head's office, and would be closely watched. Yardley concluded by saying that he had checked her record carefully before deciding to offer her the project, and was confident that she would be able to handle it.

Janet could feel the butterflies in her stomach. This was the chance she had hoped for, but the added visibility meant that any foul-up would be detected immediately. What did he mean by "about the right time"? Probably a euphemism for "too soon," she thought. Besides, she was never sure she deserved the high grades she got in those three minor courses. She didn't think she had mastered that material, even though the professor had obviously been impressed. But this wasn't college, where the worst outcome can be a low grade. And where does one go for help?

Sensing her hesitancy, Yardley reassured her: "It's natural to be concerned about doing something like this for the first time. But I know you can do it, Janet. I've alerted Bromley in the contracts office that you'll probably be in to consult with him, since he knows the legal side of this cold, and I'll be here to help you. So go for it!" he encouraged her with an expectant nod.

Hearing the confidence in his voice, seeing his smile, and sensing the supportiveness of his mannerisms towards her, she felt her self-confidence start to well up as in the past when she had mustered her determination to tackle tough challenges. Overcoming her self-doubts, she accepted the project, invested enormous energy using all resources, both her own and those Hal Yardley made available to her, and gave it all she had. It was tough, but she successfully completed the project. This was the start of great things for Janet Simms, who went on to several more acclaimed successes, after which everyone in the organization, herself included, came to expect the best of her.

Hal Yardley played the role of "Pygmalion" in the above scenario. Because of his high expectations, he treated Janet in ways that aroused her own self-confidence and motivated her to use her talents more than she otherwise might have. He prophesied that she would succeed, and then acted in ways that made his prophecy come true. The payoff for manager, subordinate, and organization was better performance and higher productivity. Similar superior-subordinate interactions happen all the time in organizations, but not always with such salutary outcomes.

Scenario B

The Washington Redskins and the Dallas Cowboys were locked in a do-or-die struggle for Superbowl grandeur. Trailing and with the clock running out, the Redskins' offensive squad managed to scrimmage to within field-goal range. A field goal would win the game for Washington. Curt Knight, the Redskins' place kicker, had the best kicking record in the whole league under Vince Lombardi. Given this situation, the Redskins' George Allen, widely regarded as a top-flight coach, called a risky run for the end zone against the tough Cowboy defense. When it was all over, the press immediately jumped on George Allen, demanding to know why he didn't call a field goal. Allen responded, "I didn't think Curt Knight would make it." From that point on Curt Knight's kicking record plummeted. Said Knight, "Every time I get out there and miss I feel like I committed a federal offense, so all I ever do is think about missing."*

George Allen's low expectations of Curt Knight incurred an immediate cost—not using Knight's outstanding kicking potential in that playoff game. But the coach's low expectations also exacted a long-term toll in the poor subsequent performance of a kicker whose ability had been convincingly demonstrated in the past. Scenario B shows the down side of interpersonal expectancy effects; a manager's communicating low expectations can be devastating to a subordinate's performance. Allen prophesied poor performance and then behaved in a manner that fulfilled his own prophecy.

These scenarios depict a phenomenon that has been studied intensively by sociologists and by social and educational psychologists, and whose time has come in the study of management and organization. The expectancy effects illustrated in the scenarios are a type of self-fulfilling prophecy (SFP). An SFP is said to occur when one's belief concerning the occurrence of some future event (Hal Yardley expects Janet Simms to succeed) makes one behave in a manner (Yardley provides Simms with supportive, task-oriented leadership) that increases the likelihood that the expected event *will* occur (Yardley's support and leadership motivate Simms and facilitate her achievements).

Whether or not they know it, managers are prophets. They expect certain things to happen, and then act in ways that fulfill their own expectations. In many instances of SFP at work the manager does not know that his expectation was fulfilled by his own actions. Sometimes SFP in management is beneficial to the organization, as in Scenario A. Often SFP is detrimental, as in Scenario B. Each of us, managers, employees, shareholders, the public at large, indeed, everyone who stands to gain from increased productivity, has a stake in creating more positive SFP and eliminating negative SFP in the workplace.

SFP in management is the central theme of this book. In the course of researching, teaching, consulting, and thinking over the last several years about SFP, and in particular the Pygmalion effect, I realized that these expectancy processes address the core issues of managing the productive behavior of people in organizations. Accumulated research findings have established the crucial role of expectation in many of the interpersonal processes that comprise managerial leadership. As I came to see the role of expectation in leadership, motivation, and performance, I realized there was an important story to tell to those who want to understand organizational behavior, and to practicing managers who want to achieve excellence through their subordinates. This book is addressed to both.

---

*Retold by J. Sterling Livingston in the McGraw-Hill CRM management training film titled *Productivity and the Self-fulfilling Prophecy: The Pygmalion Effect*.

Chapter 1 defines SFP and gives examples from different spheres of social life. It focuses on the SFP notion as originally defined by Robert K. Merton, Robert Rosenthal's pioneering work on the experimenter effect in social psychology, and Rosenthal and Jacobson's seminal field experiment on Pygmalion in the classroom. Chapter 2 presents evidence demonstrating SFP among adults in organizations. It includes case studies, theoretical positions, and field studies that predated Pygmalion, as well as several field experiments that have demonstrated the Pygmalion effect among adult workers, soldiers, and trainees. Chapter 3 presents a theoretical model of SFP that explains the Pygmalion effect in management in terms of the expectancy theory of work motivation. Chapter 4 adds the manager's leadership role to the SFP model. It enumerates the sources of managers' expectations and explains just what it is that managers *do* to get their subordinates to conform to their expectations. In Chapter 5 SFP is viewed as an organizationwide process, as opposed to the interpersonal expectancy effect treated in previous chapters. Organizational culture is proposed as a major source of organizationwide expectations, and its far-reaching SFP implications are discussed. Chapter 6 is a compendium of practical applications that describes various ways SFP can be purposefully created and used to make organizations more productive. Some of these applications already have been successfully tested, and others are suggested in this book for the first time. They are proposed with the expectation that they will tickle the imagination of practitioners and field experimenters, hopefully triggering further SFP.

"Yes, by George: it's the most absorbing experiment I ever tackled."
—Henry Higgins, in George Bernard Shaw's *Pygmalion*

1
From Ancient Myth to Modern Reality: Rediscovery of the Power of Expectations

T he modern notion that expectations can influence behavior has its roots in ancient mythology. The renewed interest of social scientists in this theme was kindled by keen observation of social phenomena, and was intensified by serendipity. A mountain of social science research findings now forms a vantage point from whose peak we can review how our present understanding of self-fulfilling prophecy (SFP) has evolved, and from which we can look forward toward the largely uncharted future of practical applications in management to promote organizational effectiveness. The purpose of this chapter is to trace the evolution of the SFP concept from its inception forty years ago to its current status in social and educational psychology. The next chapter will review what we know about SFP in management.

Self-Fulfilling Prophecy Defined

The best starting point for understanding SFP is Robert K. Merton, the Columbia University sociologist who originated the concept in his seminal essay published in the *Antioch Review* in 1948. There Merton described SFP as a three-stage process beginning with a person's belief, false at the time that it is held, that a certain event will occur in the future. In the second stage this expectation, or "prophecy," leads to some new behavior that the person would not have performed were it not for his expectation. In the third stage the expected event occurs and the prophecy is fulfilled. The SFP concept has become a widely recognized phenomenon in all areas of social science, and is today familiar to educated people in many walks of life. As we shall see, Merton's original idea has led to the identification of many variants of SFP in social life and has had far-reaching practical consequences in the fields of research methodology and education. The SFP concept is similarly pregnant with implications for management theory and practice. The SFP process is depicted in figure 1–1.

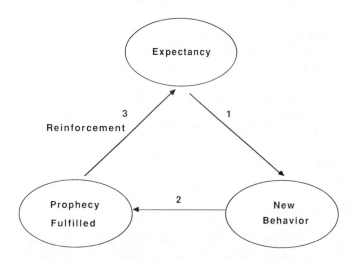

Figure 1–1. Model of SFP According to Merton

Merton's example of the failure of an initially solvent bank serves as an excellent illustration of SFP. The process begins with a belief, false at the time that it is held, that the bank is in trouble and may soon go bankrupt. This belief, or expectation, is the "prophecy." Arrow 1 depicts the influence of this expectation. It leads the person to perform some new behavior that is different from what he would have done were it not for the expectation. In the case of an anticipated bank failure, the new behavior is prompt withdrawal of all deposits from the bank. The inevitable end result of a large number of individuals' withdrawing their deposits is the fulfillment of their expectation, represented by arrow 2: the bank fails. *Any* bank will fail when rumor creates panic leading to a "run" on the bank. The bank goes broke because most of the money on deposit is out in the form of loans and cannot be called in immediately, and the relatively meager funds held on reserve are not enough to meet all the panicked depositors' withdrawal demands.

Ironically, in the case of an initially solvent bank, it is the panicked depositors who *by their own actions* bankrupt their own bank, without intending to do so, and, in most cases, without even being aware of their destructive role. The "prophets" serve as unwitting dupes in the SFP process. Feelings of relief and self-righteousness often arise in the aftermath of SFP, as witnessing the fulfillment of their expectations reinforces the prophets' initial (wrong) definition of the situation ("the bank's in trouble") and its concomitant expectations ("the bank is about to go broke"), and serves to justify the action they took to escape personal financial doom. "Had I not acted in time, I would have lost all my money." This psychological reinforcement, which gives the SFP a measure of closure from the prophet's standpoint, is represented by arrow 3 in figure 1–1.

The basic ingredients of SFP are an expectation, a new behavior, and an outcome that reinforces the expectation. Once the expectation is established, the likelihood that the prophesized outcome will result is increased by the expecter's intervening behavior. This occurs whether or not the individual expecter, or "prophet," is aware of the process.

The bank failures that Merton analyzed as tragic examples of SFP were not inevitable. They were a fact of life during the Great Depression, and they had many root causes, SFP being only one. Nevertheless, eliminating SFP could reduce the frequency of this particular type of economic disaster. Merton described the creation of the Federal Deposit Insurance Corporation, the now familiar FDIC, as an ingenious social invention that intervenes in the SFP process and disrupts it. By putting the prestige and treasury of the U.S. federal government behind the program, and essentially guaranteeing depositors that their money will be safeguarded regardless of what ill fortune may befall their bank, depositors are relieved of the threat of financial disaster. No longer anticipating personal losses, they do not rush to make panicked withdrawals upon hearing rumors of impending bankruptcy, and solvent banks are spared undeserved calamity; the prophecy is not fulfilled. Thus, SFP is not an immutable phenomenon that we can only observe and analyze, but one we can influence. We can willfully prevent destructive SFP and create productive SFP. This utilitarian aspect of SFP has been largely ignored by social scientists.

Examples of Self-Fulfilling Prophecy

Stereotypes

There are many fascinating varieties of SFP in everyday life (Jones 1977; Merton 1948). One of Merton's original examples is stereotypes. Gentiles who expect Jews to be clannish refuse Jews membership in their private clubs (arrow 1). Finding themselves excluded, the Jews establish new clubs that Gentiles choose not to join (arrow 2). Then the Gentiles point to the Jewish clubs as proof of Jewish clannishness (arrow 3). Expecting Jews to be clannish, the "prophets" treat them in such a manner (exclusion) that leads to the fulfillment of their own prophecy (Jewish clubs). Korman (1988) has shown the appalling extent to which Merton's example from forty years ago goes on unchecked in present-day corporate America.

Blacks, according to the racist stereotype, are believed to be lazy and stupid, and therefore are discriminated against in employment, barred from training programs, and excluded from membership in unions (arrow 1).

Because of this mistreatment, blacks do not get good jobs and do not advance vocationally (arrow 2). Whites then point to blacks' poor vocational achievements as proof that they are lazy and stupid (arrow 3). Thus, stereotypes trigger the SFP process inasmuch as they involve expectations that lead to overt behaviors whose impact on the targets of the stereotype makes their behavior conform to the stereotype, reinforcing the stereotype in the minds of those who believe in it. Experimental social psychologists have convincingly demonstrated in the laboratory how SFP can be triggered by a stereotype (Snyder, Tanke & Berscheid 1977).

Inflation

An economic SFP that our generation has witnessed all too often is inflation. Demand–pull inflation is caused by consumer expectations for higher prices. Expecting prices to rise, some consumers rush to beat the hikes by making their purchases earlier than they had planned. The resulting short-term increase in aggregate demand pulls prices up. Fleetfooted consumers who made their purchases before the price hike, rendered inevitable now in part by their own preemptive buying behavior, experience the satisfaction of knowing that they were among the last to buy at the lower price, and continue fueling the inflationary spiral by anticipating impending price rises to beat inflation. Thus, in certain instances SFP is a repetitive process, not merely a one-shot affair.

It should also be noted that price *stability* can also be an SFP. When consumers expect prices to remain constant over extended periods of time, they purchase only what they need. Expecting price stability, people forego the "hedge on inflation" and relieve the upward pressure on prices caused by excessive demand. By inspiring public confidence in future price stability, economic leaders can reduce that portion of inflation that is caused by SFP. Indeed, during periods of deflation, expectations of lower prices cause people to hold on to their money by deferring purchases, thereby reducing aggregate demand and causing prices to fall. Thus, price shifts in either direction are in part the product of SFP, fueled by expectations.

Marketplace Ups and Downs

Another economic SFP is evidenced by the impact of investor expectations on stock market fluctuations. Optimism and pessimism are positive and negative expectations that influence investors to buy or sell, resulting in bull or bear markets, respectively. Expecting the market to go up, they buy, pressuring prices up. Anticipating a decline, they sell and thereby contribute to the falling market that they anticipate. The same SFP process occurs in foreign currency and commodity exchanges. Moreover, the business cycle itself is in part an

SFP caused by businessmen's increasing orders for capital goods and build-up of inventories in anticipation of an expansion, and cutting orders and inventories when they expect a decline in demand for their goods and services. Their actions in increasing or decreasing their investments contribute to the expansion or decline, respectively, that they expect.

The self-fulfilling nature of the public's expectations for the economy is evidenced by the ongoing success of the University of Michigan's Index of Consumer Sentiment. Based on the Institute for Social Research's (ISR) monthly Surveys of Consumer Attitudes, the index has been used since 1946 to forecast subsequent indicators of the health of the U.S. economy, including consumer spending and saving (Curtin 1976). The consumer expectations component of ISR's Index of Consumer Sentiment is currently being included by the U.S. Department of Commerce's Bureau of Economic Analysis as one of the ten components of its composite Index of Leading Indicators.

Thus, the crucial role of expectations in determining economic outcomes is widely recognized in economic and political circles. Most macroeconomists today accept the validity of the "theory of rational expectations," which was originally advanced by Lucas (1972) and subsequently "popularized" by Sargent and Wallace (1976). When economists throw up their hands in frustration over the failure of their theories to make accurate predictions, and lay the blame on what they call "psychological factors," often it is the SFP at work. At any rate, the tactic of having the U.S. president broadcast an optimistic speech designed to inspire public confidence in the future of the nation's economy is recognition of the importance that political economists attribute to expectations in determining the health of the consumer-driven American economy. SFP can make—or break—a recovery or an expansion.

Placebo

SFP can foil medical scientists as well. The placebo effect is an annoying SFP for research on the therapeutic value of new medicines. The placebo effect occurs when either a pharmacologically inert substance or a nonspecific treatment, dubbed "placebo," induces a recovery from an ailment. The placebo derives its healing power from its being expected to cure the ailment (Critelli & Neumann 1984; Shapiro 1971). Recovery rates among subjects treated with a placebo are higher than among untreated control subjects. So powerful and ubiquitous is the placebo effect that drug researchers are required to show that a new remedy works better on experimental patients who actually *got* the drug than on a control group of patients who received an inert placebo such as sugar or starch, which is known to have no healing effects. It is furthermore necessary that patients in neither group know whether they were given the drug or the placebo, and that the person(s) dispensing the treatment not know which patients are receiving the experimental drug and which the placebo.

This is because simply *expecting* a treatment to heal a malady has therapeutic effects. So powerful is the SFP in healing that this double-blind procedure, in which neither experimenter nor subject, physician nor patient, knows who is getting the real treatment, is required in order to overcome it! Recovery among placebo-treated patients can "merely" be an SFP, and the experimental treatment must be shown to do better than that.

The experimental procedures for eliminating, or at least controlling, the placebo effect are appropriate for medical *research,* but not for medical *practice.* What for the researcher is a nuisance variable (Bernstein & Neitzel 1977) can be of use for the practitioner and his client. In their discussion of the changing meaning of the placebo effect, Critelli and Neumann (1984) emphasized "the undisputed point that placebos do have real, empirically demonstrable, therapeutic effectiveness. . . . placebo mechanisms also need to be understood and utilized more effectively. . . . Pragmatically, the best available treatment should be recommended, regardless of whether it operates through placebo or nonplacebo mechanisms" (p. 35). In other words, if physicians can use the placebo effect to promote healing, they should. We would harshly judge the clinician who abstained from producing a placebo effect that could aid a patient's recovery. If smiling supportively, nodding affirmatively, and saying reassuringly, "Take the medication I've prescribed and I'm *sure* you'll feel better" can augment the drug in promoting the healing process, then the physician should add these placebo interventions to his treatment repertoire. As the FDIC is a *constructive disruption* of a destructive SFP process, so the purposeful generation of the placebo effect by a clinician is a *constructive creation* of an SFP created in the service of human betterment.

For some clinical psychologists, the deliberate creation of placebo effects as part and parcel of psychotherapy is standard practice. Coe (1980) cites evidence that one of the most important determinants of the success of therapy is the therapist's belief in the client's capacity to improve. "It seems quite likely that therapists subtly communicate their optimism or pessimism to their clients, and thereby affect their clients' expectations of a positive or negative outcome" (p. 426). The same would seem to be true of managers and subordinates. Thus, there is a point at which expectancy effects cease being an annoying distraction or complication, and become useful in the solution of social problems. This point is usually overlooked. In this book we will focus on managerial parallels both to healers' use of the therapeutic placebo effect and to FDIC-type constructive disruptions of negative SFP.

War and Peace

The most destructive SFP is war. Allport (1950) called the SFP process in the bringing on of war the "principle of expectancy." Each of two nations suspects the other of hostile intentions. Acting in its own self-defense, each side engages in actions intended to avert its enemy's attack. Each side's acts of deterrence are perceived by the other as acts of provocation in a mirror-image process that escalates the stakes and increases the likelihood of miscalculation or error. This kind of SFP process has brought on countless conventional wars no one wanted. If unchecked, the ultimate prophecy of doom may yet be fulfilled. Realization that the total annihilation of our world in a nuclear conflagration may come about as an SFP (Klineberg 1984) ought to kindle ample motivation for us to understand the SFP process and attempt to gain some measure of control over it.

What is often overlooked is that *peace* may also be brought about by an SFP process, albeit a more difficult one to initiate and nurture along to fulfillment because of mutual distrust and the enormous stakes involved. Mutual nuclear disarmament is the crux, as each side will seek to maintain its own offensive arsenal as a deterrent as long as it feels threatened by the other side's weapons. Short of mutual trust, some means besides further arms build-up will have to be found to relieve each side of its feelings of being threatened with annihilation by the other before the nuclear SFP process can be fruitfully disrupted. There is a business parallel to the nuclear standoff in which two competing firms are locked into a protracted conflict in which both sides are held prisoner in an ongoing, mutually costly SFP process.

Management

In this book we shall examine in detail the managerial and organizational parallels of these SFP processes. We shall enumerate the counterproductive acts on management's part that bring on unintended declines in worker output. We shall propose steps management can implement to improve productivity, within the framework of the SFP process. Managers *are* prophets. They initiate SFP every day. It is sometimes a boon to productivity. However, SFP can also be wasteful of human resources and fatal to organizational effectiveness. Whether positively or negatively, managers usually are involved in SFP without any awareness of their role in the process. Reading the following chapters will increase awareness of SFP in management, and suggest ways of gaining control over the process. The aim is to manage SFP instead of passively letting it take its course for better or for worse.

It is important to understand that SFP is somewhat of a misnomer. The prophecy does not fulfill *itself;* it is a mental abstraction that cannot "do" anything. It is the *prophet* who, acting under the influence of the prophecy, behaves in a manner that molds events to conform to his expectations. This suggests that SFP is not an inevitable process. Like accidents, SFPs don't just happen. Planned interventions can prevent them or make them occur.

Interpersonal Expectancy Effects

Being a sociologist, Merton analyzed SFP mainly as a societal phenomenon, and his early examples involved fairly large numbers of people. One person does not make a stereotype, a lone depositor cannot break a bank, and a single consumer cannot pull up prices. In these examples, it is the behavior of a large number of individuals who share an expectation, each acting independently but simultaneously with others, that fulfills the prophecy. Miller and Turnbull (1986) have termed this type of SFP "coaction" effects. Psychological approaches to SFP have been focused more on "interaction" effects; that is, how one individual's expectations influence another individual's behavior. The interaction approach to SFP is exemplified by studies of expectancy effects in one-on-one relationships and in the relationships between an individual experimenter, teacher, or manager and a group of subjects, pupils, or workers. Such research is often referred to as the study of interpersonal expectancy effects. Of the several possible outcomes of SFP studied in this context (see Jones 1977; Miller & Turnbull 1986), the focus in this book is on job performance and productivity as dependent variables influenced by the process. Understanding how one person's expectations influence another person's achievement can be used to enhance productivity on the job.

There are several dictionary definitions of expectancy, only one of which is involved in SFP. *Webster's New Universal Unabridged Dictionary* (1983) defines *expect* as "to look for as likely to occur or appear." It is this likelihood-of-occurrence sense of expectancy that triggers SFP. *Webster's* also defines *expect* as "to look for as due, proper, or necessary; as your bill is due and immediate payment is *expected.*" This is a normative definition of expectancy. The object of normative expectancy is what *ought* to occur in the future. This is not the type of expectancy that produces SFP; it is rather the stuff of which role expectations and other normative concepts are made.

These two meanings of expectancy—likelihood of occurrence and normative—are sufficiently different that they can be contradictory. If the boss tells a subordinate that he *is expected* (in the normative sense) to report in on time, but in his heart he actually *expects* (in the probability sense) the subordinate to be late, it is the latter expectation, not the normative one, that will be unwittingly communicated and initiate an SFP that may result in tardy behavior on the part of the subordinate. Thus, it is expectancy in the sense of that which the expecter *believes is likely to occur,* rather than that which a person believes *ought* to occur, that leads to the behavior that fulfills the prophecy. In particular, the present use of "performance expectations" refers to the level at which the manager believes the subordinate is likely to perform.

SFP in the Laboratory: The Experimenter Effect

All the previous examples of SFP have been part of the human condition for time immemorial. Recently, modern behavioral science gave birth to a new kind of interpersonal SFP that has come to be known as the *experimenter effect*. The emergence of experimental SFP occurred in the mid-1950s as an outgrowth of an experimental accident. Through a combination of serendipity, intellectual curiosity, and research ingenuity, Robert Rosenthal, now professor of psychology and social relations at Harvard University, succeeded in turning an imminent academic failure into a long line of fascinating research. The resulting studies spawned significant improvements in our experimental methodology and pointed the way to revolutionizing classroom teaching to improve pupils' learning performance. An aim of the present book is to carry over this revolution to the realm of managerial leadership to promote organizational effectiveness by improving workers' job performance.

The accidental discovery of the experimenter effect has been retold by Rosenthal (1985). The saga began with his doctoral research in clinical psychology at the University of California at Los Angeles. He was studying the defense mechanism of projection among three groups of subjects using a standard before–after experimental design. The study had been designed to test whether experimentally induced experiences of success or failure would affect how subjects subsequently judged the degree of success or failure of persons shown to them in photos. The 108 subjects were divided into "success," "neutral," or "failure" conditions. Then, in the first of three experimental stages, Rosenthal had each subject rate the degree of success or failure of persons shown to them in photos. After this pretest, each subject was given an experience of either success, failure, or neither, in a structured task that simulated a standardized intelligence test. In the third, or posttest stage, the subjects were again asked to give success/failure ratings of a set of photos that was equivalent to those rated in the pretest. Rosenthal had hypothesized that subjects who experienced success in stage 2 would increase their success ratings from pretest to posttest, whereas those who had experienced failure would see more failure in the photos than they had seen before the failure experience. That is, Rosenthal hypothesized that individuals "project" their experiences of success and failure onto others.

In analyzing his data, Rosenthal compared the amount of before–after *change* among subjects in each of the three experimental conditions, which might have sufficed to test his hypothesis. But Robert Rosenthal was not one to make do by satisfying minimal requirements! In what he retrospectively has called "an attack of studently compulsivity" (1985, 39), he also compared the projection scores obtained *before* he had manipulated the independent variable. At this preexperimental stage there should have been no difference between the three groups of subjects, for they had been assigned to the three experimental conditions at random, a standard procedure used to establish preexperimental equivalence.

But the groups were different!

Worse, these significant pretest differences were in the direction that facilitates confirming the experimental hypothesis. This was not only an unexpected finding; it was inexplicable. No systematic difference had been deliberately introduced at this stage; indeed, meticulous care had been taken to assure equivalence among subjects in the three conditions in keeping with the experimental logic of comparing how *similar* subjects respond to *different* treatments. How could they differ after being made comparable, but before receiving different treatments? This anomaly sparked the systematic study of that special case of SFP dubbed "the experimenter effect." Seeking a deeper understanding of projection, Rosenthal unearthed an intriguing phenomenon that neither he, nor most other researchers, had any idea existed.

Rosenthal contemplated the quandary implied by the unexpected pretest differences and came up with the only possible explanation barring chance or crass mistakes: since the only conceivable difference between the groups after the pretest but before the treatment was his research hypothesis, he must have somehow unintentionally influenced his subjects to respond in a manner that confirmed his expectations. Expecting his subjects to respond differently, he somehow *made* them respond differently.

But how? He was not aware of any discriminating behavior on his part; on the contrary, he had used all the conventional procedures, such as standardization of instructions, to assure equal treatment of his subjects to prevent any influence of his biases on the findings. *But scientists' hypotheses are expectations.* Rosenthal reasoned that an SFP had taken place. In some way unbeknownst to him at the time, he must have treated subjects in different conditions differently in ways that facilitated hypothesis confirmation *despite* the precautions he had taken to avoid this.

Clearly he had uncovered a failure of conventional experimental methodology. The standard procedures were not adequate to safeguard an experiment's validity against the biases of an honest researcher. How many previous experimenters had "confirmed" their hypotheses in like manner? How are experimenter expectations communicated? How large is this effect? How can it be prevented? These intriguing questions led Rosenthal to embark on a long-term research program in which he systematically elucidated the experimenter effect.

The flavor of the research on the experimenter effect can be savored by reviewing a typical early experimenter-effect study. The research strategy is to get subjects to believe they are serving as experimenters, to inform them about certain hypotheses, and then have them conduct the experiment by carrying out the prescribed experimental procedure on the subjects and collect the relevant data. The experiment is rigged so that the only independent variable that can actually influence the results that these "experimenters" obtain is the hypothesis they think they are testing. When the data show that the experimenter's hypothesis, and it alone, produced confirmatory results, the experimenter effect has been demonstrated.

To illustrate, Rosenthal and Fode (1963) had psychology students serve as "experimenters" in what was introduced to them as a study of maze learning among laboratory rats described as having been bred to be either maze-bright or maze-dull. The students were told that rats designated maze-bright could be expected to perform well in the maze-running task, whereas those labeled maze-dull should perform poorly. However, the only difference between the rats designated bright and dull was the designation itself; in reality there was no systematic difference in innate maze-running ability as the rats were distributed to the experimenters at random.

The only initial difference between the subjects was the expectation implanted into the minds of the experimenters. Half were told that their rats were maze-bright and half were told that their rats were maze-dull. They had been led to expect differential performance from equivalent subjects. Each "experimenter" got five rats. The experimenter effect was evidenced by results showing that the "bright" rats outperformed the "dull" rats by a statistically significant amount. The rats designated as bright outperformed their controls beginning with the first day and continuing through the fifth and last day of the experiment. Furthermore, when asked to rate their own attitudes and behavior toward their subjects, experimenters who had been told that their animals were bright rated them as brighter, more pleasant, and more likable, felt more relaxed with them, reported behaving toward them in a more pleasant, friendly, enthusiastic, and less talkative manner, and reported handling them more and in a gentler manner. The experimenter effect had been demonstrated. The experimenters had unwittingly influenced their subjects' performance. As prophets who fulfill their own prophecies, the experimenters got their animal subjects to fulfill their expectations.

Many experiments on the experimenter effect have since been conducted using animal and human subjects. Rosenthal (1976) has summarized these findings convincingly. The existence of interpersonal expectancy effects has been supported by seven metanalyses that cover 388 studies. Metanalysis combines the results of a large number of studies and estimates the magnitude and significance of the overall effect found. There remains no reasonable doubt that the experimenter effect is a real phenomenon. This body of research is often referred to as the social psychology of the psychological experiment. It was a major step along the path toward SFP in management.

The experimenter effect presents a clear and present threat to the validity of many types of experiments, and its reduction or elimination is essential. Uncontrolled experimenter effects cloud the causal relationships of interest in the experiment and render its results equivocal. Rosenthal (1976) has proposed several safeguards for controlling experimenter effects and has summarized ten of them (1985, table 3.3). These techniques for the elimination of unwanted expectancy effects from the psychological experiment provide further examples of "constructive disruption" of SFP and should inspire us to seek new ways to avert SFP in other arenas of human endeavor where its effects are harmful.

From Laboratory to Classroom: The Rebirth of Pygmalion

After publishing an article summarizing a dozen experimenter-effect studies (Rosenthal 1963), and wondering in print whether similar interpersonal expectancy effects might occur among physicians, psychotherapists, employers, and teachers, Rosenthal was approached by Lenore Jacobson, the principal of an elementary school. She invited him to conduct a teacher-expectation experiment in her school. This was a logical extension of the experimenter-effect research inasmuch as in both situations the effects of one person's expectations concerning the performance of others are manipulated in a controlled experiment to determine if such expectations per se influence performance. The notable differences are a change in personnel, as teachers replace experimenters and pupils serve as subjects, a site switch, as the experiment is conducted in a natural classroom rather than in a contrived laboratory setting, and the time perspective of the study and its participants, as the classroom far outlives a short-term laboratory experiment and may have a past as well as a present and a future.

The transition from experimenter effects to teacher effects marked the beginning of experimentation on interpersonal expectancy effects in a field setting with important practical implications. The 1968 publication of Rosenthal and Jacobson's book on this experiment, titled *Pygmalion in the Classroom,* gave expectancy effects a new dimension of publicity and fired the imagination of a generation of researchers who have lavished enormous attention on the topic. But it was still to be a while before management scholars would realize the implications of expectancy effects for managers and workers and begin exploring the phenomenon in the workplace.

The Pygmalion experimental paradigm employed the same strategy already described for the experimenter-effect studies, substituting hypotheses concerning experimental subjects' performance with expectations for pupils' classroom achievement. As a prelude to raising teacher expectations, near the end of a school year Rosenthal and Jacobson administered Flanagan's (1960) Tests of General Ability (TOGA) to all pupils from kindergarten through fifth grade. Though actually a nonverbal intelligence test, the TOGA was presented to the teachers as the "Harvard Test of Inflected Acquisition." It was described as a diagnostic instrument valid for identifying "late bloomers." Late bloomers were defined as pupils who till now have not fully used their native abilities, but who should bloom intellectually during the coming year.

At the beginning of the following academic year, purportedly on the basis of scores on the "Harvard Test," the experimenters designated at random 20 percent of each teacher's new pupils as late bloomers. Since the designation was random, at the beginning of the experiment the "late bloomers" in each class could not differ in any way as a group from the remaining 80 percent of their classmates, except in the achievement expectations implanted in the teacher's mind. Rosenthal and Jacobson made no further interventions. They did not tell the teachers how to treat the pupils in any way. Any subsequent differences detected in the behaviors or attitudes of either the teachers or the pupils, as well as any differences in classroom performance, would have to be the direct or indirect effects of the initially manipulated expectations.

The results confirmed the expectancy hypothesis. Readministration of the TOGA at the end of the school year revealed that pupils who had been designated as late bloomers had gained four points more in IQ than had their control classmates. Raising teachers' expectations regarding pupil performance had initiated an SFP process in which teachers unwittingly acted in different ways toward different pupils and thereby fulfilled their prophecies.

Rosenthal and Jacobson coined the term "Pygmalion effect" to refer to this phenomenon. They borrowed the label from George Bernard Shaw's (1957) play in which Professor Henry Higgins trained a simple, uneducated flower girl from the streets of London to exquisite mastery of the English language. Confident that he could do it, Professor Higgins persisted in his efforts and Eliza Doolittle was seemingly miraculously transformed. Shaw was inspired by the Pygmalion of Greek mythology, a celibate prince of Cyprus who sculpted a maiden of ivory and fell in love with his inanimate masterpiece. Aphrodite brought the statue, named Galatea, to life, and they lived happily ever after. The common theme in all these phenomena, mythological, literary, and scientific, is that one person, inspired by a vision, desire, prophecy, or expectation, persists in his relationship with another person, ultimately transforming that person in accord with the vision.

Mediating Mechanisms in SFP

Recall that prophecies do not fulfill themselves. It is the *prophet* who, acting under the influence of his own prophecy, behaves in a manner that molds someone else's behavior to conform to the prophet's expectations. Rosenthal and Jacobson only imparted the expectations for high performance; the teachers did the rest.

But what did they do?

Till now nothing has been said about *how* interpersonal expectancy effects occur. How does one person's expectation influence another's performance? Without addressing this crucial and perhaps most interesting aspect of interpersonal SFP, the process seems eerily magical. Specifying the mechanisms by which expectations influence behavior demystifies the phenomenon, making it understandable both scientifically and commonsensically.

In the wake of Rosenthal and Jacobson's demonstration that the Pygmalion effect occurs, many subsequent studies sought to reveal the interpersonal processes that mediate the effects of expectations on performance. Much of this research has been based on classroom observation of teacher-pupil interaction. The research strategy has been to compare teacher behavior toward pupils about whom they have high and regular or low expectations. Many discriminating teacher behaviors have been found. Rosenthal (1973) has summarized these mediating behaviors according to a four-factor model, and Brophy (1985) has reviewed subsequent relevant research. Rosenthal's four mediating factors are:

Socioemotional climate, which is defined as teacher behaviors that are nonverbal, and mostly subconscious, that convey positive or negative feelings toward pupils. Teachers have been found to smile more at pupils of whom they expect a lot, to maintain eye contact with them more frequently and for longer duration, to get physically closer to them, and to convey greater warmth, acceptance, and approval to them by various forms of posture and body language, such as touching and nodding approvingly. Most of this emotional communication occurs without any awareness on the teacher's part. The resulting "good feeling" that characterizes the relationships between teacher and pupil facilitates learning. Rosenthal (1981) and his colleagues (Rosenthal, Hall, DiMatteo, Rogers & Archer 1979) have undertaken quantitative analysis of the subtle, nonverbal, interpersonal communication processes that mediate expectancy effects.

Feedback is an indispensable ingredient in any learning process. Teachers give more feedback and more varied feedback to pupils of whom they expect more. This surely flies in the face of both conventional wisdom and sound principles of pedagogy, according to which teachers *should* give more feedback to those expected to fail, for they need it more. Nevertheless, classroom studies have documented that teachers give more feedback to those expected to excel.

Input, in the form of teaching more material and harder material, is provided more to those expected to do well. This mediating factor may serve to challenge these pupils and spur them on to greater achievement. It may also be a means of communicating high expectations to pupils. Pupils expected to fail are ignored and deprived of input. Consequently, they learn less.

Output is defined as producing a learning result as in answering a question in class. Teachers give pupils opportunities for producing output by assigning them challenging projects or by calling upon them to do something extra, beyond the minimal requirements. Getting the chance to produce output is an important factor in pupils' learning. Research has uncovered a tendency for teachers to provide greater output opportunities for pupils expected to achieve more, and to withhold such opportunities from those deemed unlikely to deliver.

The combination of all four factors points to a straightforward explanation of the Pygmalion effect: high expectations work their "magic" by making teachers more effective instructors for those they expect to do well. The four mediating factors comprise good teaching behavior. The SFP process appears deceptively simple: teachers expect some pupils to perform well, treat those pupils to the best teaching behaviors they can muster, and consequently those pupils do well. Observing their fine achievements reinforces the teachers' high expectations (arrow 3 in figure 1–1) and primes them for another round of ongoing SFP. Rosenthal's integrative summary of the four factors clarifies the interpersonal SFP process and explains it with no recourse to magic.

SFP in Science: The Matthew Effect

Merton (1968) described the increased likelihood of success of an already successful scientist, compared to an equally talented but unknown novice, and dubbed this special case of the SFP "the Matthew effect in science." As the First Gospel tells us, the rich get richer and the poor get poorer. Merton illustrated how, among scientists, advantages accrue to those who have accumulated past accomplishments. Publications and patents, tangible evidence of productivity, create visibility in the scientific community. Reputation based on previous work, or lack thereof, influences the expectations of those serving on grants and awards committees. When two equally sound proposals are submitted for funding, the one written by the more renowned scholar has better chances of being funded. Being granted the means for doing research, the grantee has an advantage over those whose proposals were not funded. The "prophets" win again.

Many young faculty members at research universities tell stories that paint a vivid picture of the Matthew effect and how it is making their careers difficult at their pretenure stage. However, the Matthew effect is not limited to the scientific community. Certainly reputation bears on who in a business enterprise gets the chance to tackle challenging projects that give people the exposure they need to impress others with what they can do and land more such opportunities. Depriving a talented young, starting executive of the chance to "show what he can do" retards his progress. Many an athlete sat through game after game on the bench waiting for the chance to show talent that exceeded that of teammates whom they ultimately replaced.

Such things should not be left to chance. The Matthew effect is wasteful of human talent because opportunities are not made available to people in proportion to their actual ability. Giving the "poor" and the "rich" in past accomplishments equal access to opportunities to use their ability to be productive would wipe out the distortions of the Matthew effect. We have not managed to accomplish this since Biblical days. Some recommendations geared toward alleviating the Matthew injustice will be provided in a later chapter.

The Notion of Pygmalion in Management

Studying the educational literature to gain a deeper understanding of the Pygmalion effect, I had a déjà vu experience. The teacher behaviors found to mediate the Pygmalion effect in the classroom had a familiar ring. Though the terminology is a bit different, Rosenthal's four factors virtually overlap the kinds of behaviors that organizational psychologists define as leadership. The high-expectancy teacher is described in terms that are hardly distinguishable from those used to characterize the effective manager. Teachers and managers actually do have quite a bit in common. Both have authority over other persons whose activities they direct and for whose well-being, accomplishments, and future they assume considerable responsibility. Both have tasks they must complete, accountability to superiors for output, and "people" problems with subordinates, colleagues, and superiors. Both often act as though they were obsessed with the problem of control and how to motivate others for greater achievement. Given these similarities, it should come as no surprise that there are "manager expectancy effects" that parallel teacher expectancy effects. Would raising manager expectations boost worker productivity, just as raising teacher expectations enhances pupil performance?

Although social and educational psychologists have been studying teacher expectations for two decades, and organizational psychologists have been studying expectations in the workplace even longer, the possibility of Pygmalion effects in management has only recently begun to be explored. At first glance, as Rosenthal (1963) alluded early on, there is no reason to doubt the existence of the Pygmalion effect in management. I have often wondered how the course of industrial–organizational psychology, organizational behavior, and management would have been altered had an industrial psychologist approached Rosenthal twenty-five years ago with the proposition to do an experiment on manager-expectation effects in his plant. Delving into Pygmalion in management rewards one with a sense of pioneering, since managing is after all not identical to teaching, and, notwithstanding the Pygmalion-at-work research reviewed in the next chapter, much virgin ground still remains to be tilled. The potential payoff in terms of productivity increments is huge, and the capital investment required to reap this benefit is virtually nil. The remainder of this book lays the foundation for unleashing some of the dormant energy in the workforce by harnessing the Pygmalion effect and other SFP processes in work organizations.

2
Productivity as Self-Fulfilling Prophecy: The Research Evidence

U nlike the huge and ever-expanding volume of research conducted on the experimenter effect and on Pygmalion in the classroom, the number of studies that have directly investigated interpersonal SFP among adults in work organizations is small. This relative neglect may be caused in part by a tendency not to attend to SFP *because* it is so ubiquitous and so deeply embedded in the social fabric at work. We often fail to notice phenomena that pervade our everyday lives. To the extent that SFP at work is part of the organization's culture, to become cognizant of it we must "uncover the mundane as well as the more vivid aspects of the reality-construction process. And sometimes these are so subtle and all-pervasive that they are very difficult to identify" (Morgan 1986, 131).

According to Weick, the frequency with which expectation effects occur "may be underestimated because of the inflated image implied by the phrase *self-fulfilling prophecy*. The image of a prophecy suggests . . . a major activity preceded by considerable fanfare and, consequently, rare. The more appropriate image would be that in everyday/anyday life people expect, anticipate, foresee, and make mundane predictions all the time" (1979, 164). Thus, the ubiquity and importance of SFP effects in management are not proportionately reflected in the quantity of research conducted on them in work organizations to date. Most observers have simply missed them.

In this chapter we shall briefly trace the development of the idea of SFP in work organizations from its early inclusion in pre-Pygmalion human-relations theories, through the first management-oriented work to have been inspired by *Pygmalion in the Classroom,* to the field experiments among adults in work organizations that demonstrate that raising expectations improves performance and boosts productivity. We shall see that, although relatively new to management thinking, the Pygmalion idea is not at all alien to it.

Pygmalion Presaged

Douglas McGregor's SFP

Douglas McGregor's (1960) influential Theory X and Theory Y approach to management predated the Pygmalion research in invoking SFP as an explanatory concept in understanding supervisor–subordinate relations. Theory X and Theory Y are two different sets of assumptions about human nature that managers hold. Theory X assumptions are that people are naturally lazy, hate work, shirk responsibility, have to be controlled and coerced into exerting effort on behalf of organizational goals, and are concerned primarily with security. In contrast, Theory Y assumptions hold that work is as natural as play or rest, that people can learn to accept responsibility and to be resourceful, creative, and imaginative at work, that workers exert great efforts to achieve goals to which they are committed, particularly when attaining those goals leads to a sense of ego fulfillment and self-actualization, and that current organizational arrangements engage only a small part of their members' productive potential.

McGregor described the circular SFP process by which managers' assumptions (expectations) determine how they treat their subordinates, which in turn affects how the subordinates respond, which reinforces the managers' assumptions. A manager acting on the basis of Theory X assumptions treats workers with mistrust, uses close supervision, and abstains from delegating authority to subordinates. Treating workers this way leads to fulfillment of the manager's prophecy, as workers so treated react by investing less effort in the job and showing less commitment to the organization. These worker reactions reconfirm the manager's Theory X assumptions. Workers treated this way would also be less productive, according to McGregor.

In contrast, belief in Theory Y assumptions leads the manager to trust subordinates with authority, to rely on their sense of commitment to perform their jobs competently, conscientiously, and creatively, and to establish and maintain open relationships with the subordinates. Theory Y thinking also makes the manager seek ways of achieving greater integration between individual and organizational goals, which leads to greater productivity. Thus, McGregor considered managers' expectations to be a determinant of productivity via an SFP process, a Pygmalion-like idea that predated the Pygmalion experiments.

Rensis Likert's High-Expectation Manager

Another influential theorist of the human-relations tradition who laid early groundwork for expectation effects in management was Rensis Likert (1961, 1967). In Likert's theory of the human organization, managerial leadership is a major causal variable that determines the level of intervening variables. The intervening variables are social–psychological in nature and include such crucial determinants of organizational effectiveness as subordinates' loyalty, identification, sense of responsibility, motivation, and production norms. These intervening variables in turn influence the end results that the manager obtains through his subordinates, including quantity and quality of output. The term *intervening* denotes the role of these variables as mediators of the effects of the causal variables on the end results. By establishing a high level of causal variables, the manager indirectly raises the intervening variables, which in turn produces improvements in the end results.

Likert included the communication of high performance expectations by managers to subordinates as an important component of leadership behavior. Describing the highly effective manager who has the most productive subordinates, Likert wrote: "His confidence in his subordinates leads him to have *high expectations* as to their level of performance. With confidence that he will not be disappointed, *he expects much,* not little" (1961, 191, italics added). Likert had the foresight to postulate a management expectation effect before the publication of any Pygmalion research.

Thus, the major thrust of the present book was presaged by some of the foremost management scholars of a generation ago. But manager expectation effects and SFP were not their central focus. Their humanistic bent led them to emphasize more the building of mutual trust and respect in superior–subordinate relations, the supportiveness of the "supervisory climate" (Roethlisberger & Dickson 1939), the nature of the work group, and the fulfillment of higher-order needs at work (Maslow 1954, 1965). They stopped short of making performance expectations the centerpiece of the human relations approach.

Labeling in the U.S. Air Force

Published in the same year as *Pygmalion in the Classroom,* Schrank's report (1968) on his study of labeling did not include the SFP concept or any Pygmalion terminology. Nevertheless, his findings can be interpreted as adult interpersonal expectancy effects. Schrank began his field experiment by informing approximately one-hundred enlisted airmen at the United States Air Force Academy Preparatory School that he was conducting a "study related to organizational procedures." These freshmen were then assigned at random to five class sections. He designated the sections with the numbers one through five, and informed the instructors that the sections had been formed on the basis of ability levels. He conceived of his study as an investigation of the "labeling effect," which he defined as "the effect upon academic achievement of giving ability labels to groupings of pupils" (1968, 51). The labeling effect is a variant of SFP since different labels create expectations for different levels of achievement.

Schrank found that in each of eight subsequent marking periods "the difference between the means of the highest-label section and the lowest-label section was found to be significant" (p. 52). Furthermore, he reported that in almost every comparison between adjacent ability-level sections, the higher section obtained a higher mean score than did the lower one. Thus, Schrank found that merely labeling airmen "high-quality" resulted in higher achievement, when in fact on average these men were no different in initial ability from their classmates. Schrank's results demonstrate that expectancy effects are obtainable with adults by simply conveying credible information about subordinates' ability in the form of mere numerical labels. Labels produce expectations that in turn trigger SFP. Schrank's study also demonstrates how easily SFP can be willfully created.

To anticipate a later chapter, consider the practical implications of Schrank's labeling findings. Organizations use labels profusely. It seems as though personnel departments just couldn't get by without them. Many labels strongly imply positive or negative performance expectations: "Management potential." "Low performers." "Stars." "Security risk." "Fast trackers." "Hardcore unemployed." "Achiever." "Yuppies." "Burned out." "College boys." "Whiz kids." These and many other labels arouse performance expectations and thereby initiate unintended SFP processes, some of which are counterproductive. Labeling people in organizations needs to be brought under rational control.

Korman's Laboratory and Field Studies

Korman (1971) reported the results of two laboratory experiments and three small-scale field studies under the title "Expectancies as Determinants of Performance." Korman derived his hypothesis from his own earlier theorizing about the role of self-esteem in work motivation (Korman 1970) and cited previous cross-sectional findings as supportive evidence. Berlew and Hall (1966) had conducted a longitudinal study of managerial socialization of forty-nine college graduates hired on as management-level employees at AT&T. They had found a strong relationship between the level of performance the company had initially expected of these new hires and evaluations of their contributions to the company during the next five years. Stedry and Kay (1966) had also found a relationship between managers' expectations and subordinates' performance.

Korman made no mention of the Pygmalion research. He accepted the relationship between superiors' expectancies and their subordinates' performance as an established finding. He conducted his five studies with the aim of showing that manipulating expectancy *causes* performance differentials, a conclusion not justified on the basis of nonexperimental, cross-sectional, or correlational research. Furthermore, Korman sought evidence that the source of the performance expectancies need not be a person of superior status, but that peers' expectations can have similar performance effects.

The subjects in the laboratory experiments were college students who were asked to perform various creative tasks. In each group, they were told that the same tasks had been taken by other college students who had been asked to indicate what they considered to be an appropriate level of performance for college students on those tasks. Actually, the expectancy levels indicated were chosen on the basis of previous research with the same tasks among college students. The results were that subjects given high peer expectancies consistently outperformed those given low peer expectancies. Splitting the sample in the second experiment into those of high intelligence and those of medium intelligence revealed that the peer expectancy effect was replicated across intelligence levels.

Korman's field studies were done on three samples of workers chosen for their diversity to establish the generality of the expectancy effect: low-level office employees in a federal government office, high-level technical employees at a large university data-processing center, and clerical employees in a branch of a large bank. A questionnaire was developed to measure the extent to which employees felt that they were being expected to engage in meaningful behavior and the extent to which high performance was expected of them. The resulting expectancy scores were analyzed in relation to performance evaluations obtained from superiors in the first two field studies, and to self-reported work motivation in the third field study. The results consistently supported Korman's conclusion that "expectations from others are related to performance, regardless of the source of the expectancy or the characteristics of the receiver of the expectancy" (p. 220).

In discussing his results, Korman wrote:

> One interesting implication of these findings is that high expectancies can be established in an organization by working through the medium of work group norms and group values, as well as through the medium of leadership influence directly. This opens the door for a greater variety of ways by which the motivation to work may be increased by organizational leadership (p. 221).

In these few insightful sentences, Korman foresaw many of the leadership and cultural issues developed later in the present book.

Pygmalion's Debut on the Management Stage

The Unheard Prophet

Fresh in the wake of *Pygmalion in the Classroom,* Livingston (1969) was the first to publish a discussion of Pygmalion in management. Although it appeared in the *Harvard Business Review* and provided cogent arguments for the applicability of Pygmalion concepts to managements, bolstered by rich case material, response in the management literature was slow in coming. Livingston was a prophet whom few seemed to hear.

Livingston drew his case material from his experience working with several organizations, including the Metropolitan Life Insurance Company, a large West Coast bank, and Ford dealerships in New England. Based on these cases and other research evidence, Livingston concluded and colorfully illustrated the following points:

- What a manager expects of his subordinates and the way he treats them largely determine their performance and career progress.
- A unique characteristic of superior managers is their ability to create high performance expectations that subordinates fulfill.
- Less effective managers fail to develop similar expectations, and, as a consequence, the productivity of their subordinates suffers.
- Subordinates, more often than not, appear to do what they believe they are expected to do (p. 82).

One of Livingston's case examples was an "organizational experiment" undertaken by the manager of a district office of the Metropolitan Life Insurance Company. Noticing that outstanding insurance agencies grew fastest and that new agents in outstanding agencies performed better than new agents of similar ability who had been assigned to less successful agencies, this district manager regrouped the assistant managers and agents into the three agencies in the district on the basis of ability. He assigned the six best agents to work with the best assistant manager, average agents to an average manager, and the low producers to the assistant manager considered least able. The district manager then set a very difficult goal for the best agency, which began to call itself the "super agency." This agency's sales soared in the first twelve weeks. When district expansion mandated the addition of a new agency, staff assignments were again based on ability, and once more a so-called "super staff" excelled. At the same time, the productivity of the men expected to do poorly declined, and attrition among them increased. "The performance of the superior men rose to meet their managers' expectations, while that of the weaker men declined as predicted" (p. 82).

The "average" unit performed in a manner unanticipated by the district manager. Its productivity increased significantly despite the average expectations. This was attributed to the average unit's manager, who maintained his belief that both he and his men had greater potential than the "super-staff" personnel. This assistant manger challenged his agents to outperform the super-staff, with the result that every year it posted higher percentage increases in productivity than did the super-staff.

The lessons from this case have far-reaching practical implications. First, expectations can be created and transmitted in many ways. Though it appears from Livingston's account not to have been the creation of the district manager, the emergence of the high-expectancy label "super-staff" undoubtedly served as an aid in building and maintaining high expectations. But a superior's expectations must be credible and accepted to influence productivity. The district manager's prophecy regarding the mediocrity of the "average" staff's future performance was blocked by the assistant manager's countervailing expectations that his staff would excel. The expectations of the assistant manager, who must have been in daily personal contact with the agents and certainly was closer to them, held sway over their productivity.

Second, a manager's belief in his own capacity to lead his subordinates to outstanding performance, in this case the assistant manager's self-confidence, is important in determining how he plays Pygmalion's role. An assistant manager with lower self-confidence might have yielded to his superior's expectations and sufficed with mediocre productivity. Livingston stated this point succinctly:

> Superior managers have greater confidence than other managers in their own ability to develop the talents of their subordinates. Contrary to what might be assumed, the high expectations of superior managers are based primarily on what they think about themselves—about their own ability to select, train, and motivate their subordinates. What the manager believes about himself subtly influences what he believes about his subordinates, what he expects of them, and how he treats them. If he has confidence in his ability to develop and stimulate them to high levels of performance, he will expect much of them and will treat them with confidence that his expectations will be met. But if he has doubts about his ability to stimulate them, he will expect less of them and will treat them with less confidence (p. 85).

Third, conveying low expectations to the "wrong" people can backfire. Both the assistant manager and the agents who had been dubbed "average" may have resented the implied putdown. Their escalating productivity may have been a form of "We'll show you who's average around here!" Reactance on the part of persons expected to fail can be productive. Conversely, there may be a potential for counterproductive reactance on the part of persons expected to excel. This kind of SFP backfire also must be considered and prevented. We must guard against negative unintended consequences.

Besides his own rich personal experience in management consulting and the cases, Livingston drew upon Berlew and Hall's (1966) longitudinal study at AT&T. Livingston emphasized the effects of the expectations of the young manager's own first manager during the critical early period of his apprenticeship on his first job after college. He also discussed the negative impact of low expectations, invoked the theory of achievement motivation to explain expectancy effects, and spoke of self-esteem as mediating the relationship between expectations and performance. In this early article Livingston thought through much of what has since been corroborated by experimental findings.

Pygmalion-at-Work

The First SFP Experiment in Industry

The first field experiment in civilian industry that explicitly invoked the Pygmalion paradigm was reported by King (1971). He replicated the Pygmalion effect in a training program for disadvantaged persons using the Pygmalion approach pioneered by Rosenthal and Jacobson. He designated four pressers, five welders, and five mechanics as "high aptitude personnel," leading the instructors to expect outstanding performance from these individuals. In reality, each of the four or five had been chosen at random from among a training group numbering about twenty. Therefore, those designated as high were in reality equivalent in aptitude to their cotrainees. The designations produced the hypothesized SFP. The trainees who had been designated as having high aptitude obtained significantly higher scores on objective achievement tests, higher supervisor and peer ratings, and shorter learning times, confirming the operation of the Pygmalion effect among these young industrial trainees. They also had lower dropout rates, which is a very important criterion of success in a training program of this type. Pygmalion thus graduated from grade school to early adulthood.

King sought to reveal the subtle and unintentional ways in which supervisors transmit differential expectations to their subordinates. He used the relationship between positive affect and pupil dilation. When a person eyes someone whom he holds in positive regard, his pupils dilate without his being aware of it. King resourcefully used this autonomic response to uncover a subconscious mediator of the Pygmalion effect. In postexperimental interviews he showed the trainees in the welder program two pictures of their supervisor. The pictures were identical except that in one the size of the pupils of the supervisor's eyes had been made much larger. The welding trainees were asked if they saw any difference between the two photos, and were asked which photo "shows how you usually see the supervisor looking at you" (p. 376). None of the trainees noticed any difference between the two photos. Most could not articulate any reason for choosing the one they did. Nevertheless, all five of the welding trainees who had been designated as having high aptitude selected the photo with the enlarged pupils, whereas five of the seven control welders chose the other picture. King concluded: "Clearly, eye contact in face-to-face relations is likely to serve as an unintentional, but nevertheless remarkable indicator of the attitude, interest, and expectations supervisors hold for subordinates. Most likely, expectations are communicated without any awareness by either supervisor or subordinate" (King 1971, 376–377).[1] Subsequent research has shown that such subtle interpersonal communication can be measured reliably and that it operates over many channels (Rosenthal 1981). Thus, King was not only the first to demonstrate experimentally that the Pygmalion effect can be created among adult civilians in industry, but he also opened a window to the subtle interpersonal processes that mediate the effect.

The best known of King's Pygmalion experiments is the one with the welder trainees because it was described in greatest detail in his published report, along with the pressers and mechanics (King 1971). However, in his unpublished doctoral dissertation (1970), King reported the results of five small-scale experiments. The two experiments not described in the published report were among trainees for jobs as electronics assemblers and nurses. It may be significant that these two groups of trainees were comprised wholly or mostly of women, and yielded negative findings.

Rosenthal (1973) reanalyzed the data in King's dissertation to remove the supervisors' subjective ratings from the composite performance ranks that King had used to quantify trainee performance. In Rosenthal's reanalysis there was still a significant Pygmalion effect in four of the five samples. The only sample for which the results were not statistically significant was the nursing trainees, comprised of women only. Rosenthal concluded that the effect was largest for the two samples that were comprised almost entirely of men, much smaller in the two samples comprised mostly of women, and nil among the exclusively female nursing sample. While this evidence, by itself, is not conclusive, it raises the possibility that women are less subject to Pygmalion effects than men. We shall return to the issue of gender differences later.

Pygmalion in the Israel Defense Forces

The next three field experiments using the classical Pygmalion research design were carried out by my students and me in the Israel Defense Forces (IDF). The first IDF experiment (Eden & Shani 1979, 1982) was designed to replicate the basic Pygmalion research design in a culture and an age group different from nearly all previous Pygmalion studies. Successful replication in highly dissimilar circumstances would establish the Pygmalion effect as a robust phenomenon that is not culture-bound. Broadening its scope should enhance its appeal and pave the way for SFP applications.

An additional aim of our IDF experiments was to treat the mediating variables that had been revealed in classroom research in a way that would render them applicable to management. We assumed that Rosenthal's four mediating factors of climate, feedback, input, and output operate in adult superior–subordinate relations. They should therefore be detectable using a managerial leadership questionnaire. There was a precedent for using an adapted version of a standard measure of managerial supervision in investigating college instructors' behavior (Dawson, Messe & Phillips 1972). King (1971) had concluded his Pygmalion article calling for "a serious reexamination of the process of leadership behavior and specifically of the role of supervisors and managers in organizations" (p. 378). He then quoted Likert's description of the effective manager as maintaining high performance expectations to corroborate his own experimental evidence. Thus, both Likert and King had hypothesized a relationship between expectations, leadership, and performance, but neither had tested it experimentally. Likert had measured leadership without manipulating expectations, and King had manipulated expectations but had not measured leadership.

We therefore hypothesized that the manager's leadership behavior mediates the Pygmalion effect. Confirmation of this hypothesis would make it possible to achieve an integration of Pygmalion and leadership, and, in a larger sense, of educational and organizational psychology. Rosenthal (1974) had originally described the four mediating factors in classroom terminology. Leadership is conceptualized in terms that organizational psychologists and managers comprehend more readily. The Pygmalion literature could be enriched by leadership concepts, and the leadership literature could be enriched by Pygmalion concepts.

We also sought to uncover why many previous attempts to create the Pygmalion effect in educational settings had failed. We did not want to increase their number by one! Reviewing the Pygmalion literature, we discovered that most of the successful replications were conducted among newly formed teacher-pupil relationships, whereas most of the failures occurred when experimenters attempted to produce the effect after considerable prior contact between teachers and students. Retrospectively, it seemed foolhardy to expect expectations to change much after they arose naturally out of prior teacher–pupil interaction and crystallized in the teachers' minds. We reasoned that, in the IDF at least as much as in the American classroom, it would take more than a five-minute experimental treatment to raise instructor expectations of trainees whom they had already gotten to know pretty well. We therefore took pains to time our expectancy manipulation before any instructor–trainee acquaintance.

Subsequent research has borne out our suspicion. Raudenbush (1984) metanalyzed the results of eighteen teacher expectancy experiments in which IQ was the dependent variable and length of prior teacher–pupil acquaintance varied. He found that among the ten studies in which prior acquaintance was two weeks or less, eight obtained teacher expectancy effects that exceeded the median effect size, whereas only one of the eight studies in which prior acquaintance exceeded two weeks obtained a teacher expectancy effect above median. This difference was both dramatic in its proportions and statistically significant. In short, Raudenbush showed that, as we had suspected, prior acquaintance mitigates the Pygmalion effect in experiments using the "five-minute manipulation."

Pygmalion Goes to Boot Camp: The Combat Training Experiment

The setting for the first IDF experiment (Eden & Shani 1979, 1982) was a combat training base. The trainee sample included 105 soldiers, all men, who had been selected into a combat command course on the basis of ability and motivation. All had had at least eleven years of schooling. Their instructors were four experienced training officers, each aided by an assistant instructor. Each pair instructed a group of about thirty trainees. This was an intensive course that involved an average of sixteen hours of instructor–trainee contact daily for fifteen weeks.

Procedure. Four days before the trainees' arrival at the base (to preclude any prior acquaintance between the instructors and their trainees), we induced differential expectations in the instructors and their assistants by convening them and informing them as follows:

> The army is undertaking a large-scale project to evaluate training methods. We will be studying this course and collecting information of various kinds. We have compiled considerable data on the trainees, including psychological test scores obtained at time of their induction into IDF, sociometric data from the previous course, and performance ratings by previous commanders. Based on this information we have predicted the command potential (CP) of each soldier. Experience in previous courses has shown that course grades predict CP in 95 percent of the cases. Based on CP scores, we have designated each of your trainees as having either high, regular, or unknown CP, the latter due to incomplete records. When we're not sure, we don't guess. Soldiers of all three CP classifications have been divided equally among the four training classes.

Each instructor was then given a list of his trainees in which about a third were designated with an asterisk to indicate high CP, a third were unmarked to indicate regular CP, and a third were marked with a question mark indicating that they were unclassifiable due to insufficient information. The instructors were asked to copy each trainee's CP into his personal record and to learn their trainees' names and predicted CP scores before the trainees arrived. Unbeknownst to the instructors, the assignment of trainees both to the four training groups and to the three CP conditions was random.

There were two reasons for using the unknown category. First, previous

Pygmalion research had always used two categories, high and regular or no expectations, and we were curious as to how the instructors would relate to the unclassified trainees. Second, we wanted to strengthen the credibility of the information we were conveying to increase the likelihood that the instructors would acquire the expectations we intended to convey. By admitting uncertainty in some cases, we appeared convincingly professional in what we said. Subsequent postexperimental debriefing revealed that this succeeded; the instructors never doubted the validity of the information given them.

The above procedure replicated Rosenthal and Jacobson's classroom experimental paradigm as closely as was feasible in this military situation. Like Rosenthal and Jacobson, we manipulated the instructors' expectations but abstained from intimating in any way how they should relate to their trainees. Except for collecting data on attitudes and performance, we made no further interventions of any sort. Any subsequent differences in attitude, behavior, or performance, among either the instructors or the trainees, could have been caused only by the induced expectations.

The first measure was a "manipulation check" to verify that the information we had conveyed did influence instructor expectations as intended. One week after the course had begun, the instructors rated their trainees' CP on a nine-point scale. The mean ratings were significantly different, indicating that the experimental manipulation "took." We created the expectations we had intended to create. The instructors expected better performance of trainees designated as having high CP.

From among dozens of performance measures available in the course records, we omitted all those that had any subjective, judgmental component. Grades in the four subjects chosen for analysis were determined absolutely objectively. The first three were basic studies, topography, and theoretical specialization. Achievement in these subjects was assessed by means of multiple-choice examinations in which there is no room for leniency or giving the trainee the "benefit of the doubt." To remove any possible threat to objectivity, these exams were graded by someone other than the trainee's own instructor. The fourth subject, called practical specialization, was evaluated by an impartial examiner from corps headquarters who arrives at the training base near the end of each course to test the trainees' proficiency in the operation and maintenance of weapons they have been trained to master. This is a hard-nosed, individual performance test. The external examiner is charged with the responsibility of assuring the corps' high professional standards, knows no one on the base, and is impervious to any attempts to influence his evaluations. The examiner knew nothing about the experiment. Thus, grades in all four subjects were entirely free of any instructor-expectancy bias.

Performance. The mean performance grades shown in table 2–1[2] confirm the SFP hypothesis. Those designated as high in CP outperformed their classmates

Table 2–1
Effect of Instructor Expectancy on Trainee Performance

	Instructor Expectancy		
Performance	*High*	*Unknown*	*Regular*
Basic studies	77	71	65
Topography	81	73	66
Theoretical specialty	80	73	66
Practical specialty	81	73	64
Performance Index	80	72	65

Source: Eden & Shani 1979, 1982.

by substantial amounts in each of the four objectively graded subjects. Those whose CP had been designated as unknown scored about midway between those in the other two expectancy conditions. These differences in performance evidence a Pygmalion effect of substantial size—about fifteen points on a conventional one-hundred-point grade scale. Analysis of the overall Performance Index obtained by combining the scores in the four subjects showed that the experimentally induced instructor expectations caused nearly three-quarters of the differences among the trainees in performance, a high proportion by any standard.

Attitudes. We assessed attitudes by having each trainee fill out a self-report questionnaire that included three questions about the extent to which he would recommend the course to a friend or desired to go on to the next course, and the extent of his overall satisfaction with the course. The attitudinal results are shown in table 2–2. Trainees in the high-expectancy condition expressed more favorable attitudes toward the course as evidenced by higher scores on each of the three items as well as a significantly higher mean on the summary attitude scale formed by averaging the responses to the three items. Further statistical analysis revealed that the instructor expectations caused two-thirds of the variation among the trainees' scores in the Attitude Index. This is not only evidence that these trainees enjoyed the course more; it also portends a more positive attitude toward training in the future ("desire to go on to the next course"). The next experiment bears more directly on the future implication of exposure to the Pygmalion experience.

Leadership. We measured leadership as a potential mediator of expectation effects. Each trainee described his instructor's leadership behavior using items borrowed from the University of Michigan's Survey of Organizations (Taylor & Bowers 1972). These items operationalize the four factors of leadership conceptualized by Bowers and Seashore (1966) on the basis of their review of several approaches to leadership. The factors, listed in table 2–3, are support,

Table 2–2
Effect of Instructor Expectancy on Trainee Attitudes

	Instructor Expectancy		
Attitude	High	Unknown	Regular
Recommend course to a friend	4.61	3.90	3.29
Desire to go on to the next course	4.36	3.59	3.00
Satisfaction with the course	4.64	3.78	3.03
Attitude Index	4.55	3.76	3.11

Source: Eden & Shani 1979, 1982.

Table 2–3
Effect of Instructor Expectancy on Mean Instructor Leadership

	Instructor Expectancy		
Instructor Leadership	High	Unknown	Regular
Support	3.79	3.38	3.07
Interaction facilitation	3.12	3.13	2.68
Goal emphasis	4.22	3.78	3.39
Performance facilitation	4.28	3.50	3.27
Leadership Index	3.97	3.57	3.23

Source: Eden & Shani 1979, 1982.

interaction facilitation, goal emphasis, and work facilitation. In the combat experiment we used the ten-item version of these items that Eden and Leviatan (1975) had translated into Hebrew and Eden and Daniely (1979) had adapted for use in research in the IDF. The summary means of instructor leadership revealed that trainees regarding whom we had induced high expectations in the instructors rated their instructors' leadership significantly more positively. Induced expectations accounted for 28 percent of the variation in the scores on the Leadership Index. Examination of the rows of means in table 2–3 shows that this pattern of leadership differences was replicated with a high degree of consistency for each of the four factors of leadership.

Conclusions and Implications. These leadership findings support two relatively new and very important ideas about managerial leadership. The first is that leadership mediates the Pygmalion effect. The leadership evidence is consistent with the conclusion that high expectations cause improved leadership, which in turn augments subordinates' performance. Supervisory leadership is comprised of behaviors that are very similar to those summarized by Rosenthal's four factors of teacher behavior. Both Bowers and Seashore's four factors and Rosenthal's four factors facilitate subordinate performance. Thus, manager expectations work their "magic" on subordinates by inducing supervisors to provide better leadership to the subordinates they expect to perform well. Other things being equal, better supervisory leadership promotes higher performance. Leadership is indeed a means by which supervisors fulfill their prophecies regarding their subordinates' performance.

The second implication of the leadership results is that managers allocate leadership to their subordinates in accord with their expectations. Livingston (1969) had understood this. He considered the manner in which supervisors' expectations influence the way they *treat* their subordinates to be of paramount importance in the Pygmalion effect. Recall that each of the four instructors in the combat course had a mix of high- and control-expectancy trainees in his class. We designed the experiment this way to control instructor effects. At face value, what the trainees were telling us in their leadership ratings is that *different trainees got different leadership from the same instructor.* This translates King's pupil dilation finding into concrete, familiar leadership behavior.

This is not the way management scholars have traditionally thought about leadership. Accepted measurement practice has been to summarize a number of subordinates' questionnaire descriptions of a manager's leadership in terms of mean scores, and to regard the within-group standard deviations on these measures as statistical "error" or as inconsequential differences of opinion among the subordinates who rated the managers. However, this averaging may be a way of unintentionally disregarding rich data about leadership behavior that go undetected in a means analysis. Alternatively, Graen and his colleagues have pioneered the "leader–member exchange" approach to leadership (Dansereau, Graen & Haga 1975; Duchon, Green & Taber 1986; Graen & Schiemann 1978; Scandura, Graen & Novak 1986). They have demonstrated the usefulness of analyzing the data indicative of the relationships *within each leader–follower pair* separately. According to this approach, a manager treats subordinates differently based on his judgment of their competence and motivation, and the degree to which he trusts them. Liden and Graen (1980) have called those who get treated best "in-group" subordinates and the others "out-group." There can be little doubt that supervisors expect better performance from in-group subordinates. In light of the findings in the IDF combat experiment, the superior performance on the part of the in-group subordinates in the studies of Graen and his colleagues may be interpreted as a Pygmalion effect.

Both Pygmalion and leader–member exchange research thus reveal that averaging across subordinates' descriptions of a manager obscures some of the truth. The reality that is lost by averaging is that *managers do not treat all their subordinates the same!* Different ratings of the same manager by different subordinates are neither errors nor trivial differences of opinion. Our findings in the combat experiment show that managers are discriminating when it comes to allocating their leadership resources; they bestow their best leadership upon those they expect to perform best. This implies that one way to improve leadership is to raise managers' expectations.

In the combat course, and undoubtedly in other management situations, the same supervisors were simultaneously very good leaders and not such good leaders. They were very good leaders for those of whom they expected a lot, but not such good leaders for those of whom they expected less. The differences in leadership reported by high- and control-expectancy trainees when describing the behavior of the *same* supervisors indicate that the supervisors were not *using* their best skills when commanding subordinates not expected to excel. Evidently, *high expectations bring out the best leadership in a manager.* This suggests the hypothesis that if managers would treat *all* their subordinates to the same quality leadership they lavish upon those of whom they expect the most, all would perform better.

This interpretation differs from Likert's (1961) view of the role of expectations in leadership. Likert did not consider the possibility of *raising* managers' expectations as a means of improving their leadership. Rather, Likert conceived of high performance expectations as integral to a highly effective management style. For him, managers who get the best results do so in large measure because of a subordinate-centered leadership style that upholds the "principle of supportive relations," part of which entails conveying high performance expectations to subordinates. We shall return to the issue of interrelationships between leadership, expectations, and performance in the next chapter.

The role of leadership in the Pygmalion effect as described before is one interpretation of the findings in the combat course, but not the only possible interpretation. This ambiguity is because the trainees filled out the leadership questionnaires *after* knowing the results of several tests and other evaluations of their performance. There is evidence that evaluations of leaders' effectiveness influence how their leadership behavior is rated (Phillips 1984; Phillips & Lord 1982). Thus, the trainees' ratings of their instructors' leadership behavior could have been influenced by how the trainees evaluated their instructors' effectiveness, which in turn might have been influenced by how the instructors had rated the trainees' achievements before the trainees filled out the leadership questionnaire. Our leadership results would have been more conclusive had the measures of leadership been made before the feedback to the trainees of any information about their performance.

Despite the ambiguities involved in interpreting the mediating processes, what can be concluded unequivocally from the combat-training experiment is that raising expectations triggers some process that culminates in high performance. The cynical adage that "managers get the subordinates they deserve" should be replaced with a wiser one: *Managers get the performance they expect.* The practical upshot is that we need to develop practical ways of getting managers to expect more. This conclusion is the basis for the discussion of the Pygmalion Leadership Style in a later chapter.

Pygmalion and Galatea: The IDF Adjutancy Experiment

In the combat experiment we learned how raising expectations affects the supervisor: his leadership improves. But what goes on in the trainee's mind? What intrapsychic mechanism gets him to perform better? Another study was necessary to extend our understanding of the Pygmalion effect by examining *intra*trainee factors. One possibility is that when a manager expects much of a subordinate and communicates his high expectations to the subordinate, a likely response on the part of the subordinate is to raise the level of his own performance expectations. King (1971) had made a similar interpretation of the process: "Indirectly, supervisors' expectations likely benefited the HAPs [high aptitude personnel] by influencing group-made norms, perceptions, and evaluations of their behavior. Such collective predictions could serve to reinforce the HAPs' individual motivations for achievement and *raise their individual expectancy for success*" (p. 377, italics added).

This line of reasoning enables us to link manager expectancy effects to the expectancy theory of motivation (Lawler 1973; Vroom 1964), which postulates that the more an individual expects to succeed in performing a task, other things being equal, the greater the effort he exerts in performing it. We invoked expectancy theory and hypothesized that self-expectations mediate the Pygmalion effect; the manager communicates high expectations to the subordinate, who then raises his own level of self-expectations, resulting in higher motivation, greater effort, and enhanced performance. We tested this hypothesis in the second IDF experiment by comparing trainees' self-expectations before and after inducing high expectations in the instructors.

On further reflection, it seemed that if they key to the Pygmalion effect were the subordinate's own self-expectation, the manager may be tangential to the core phenomenon. It should be possible to short-circuit the SFP process by directly raising the subordinate's level of self-expectations, bypassing the supervisor. If self-expectations mediate the Pygmalion effect, then raising a person's level of self-expectations directly as part of an experimental manipulation should be as effective a way to enhance performance as by raising his expectations indirectly, through the supervisor.

It is incredible that, despite the voluminous theory stressing the importance of performance expectations for work motivation and job performance, there had been no previous reports of expectation raising as a motivational technique. Therefore, in the second IDF experiment we hypothesized that directly inducing subordinates to expect more of themselves enhances their performance. If obtained, such performance enhancement would be dubbed the "Galatea effect," after Pygmalion's sculpture, since it would result from working directly on the statue itself, so to speak.

Sample. The second IDF experiment (Eden & Ravid 1982) was conducted in a different training base with different instructors and different trainees. This experiment involved two simultaneous seven-week adjutancy courses. One course included twenty-eight trainees divided randomly into two training groups. The other course had thirty-three divided at random into three training groups. Each course was commanded by an officer. The five instructors were sergeants and corporals aged eighteen and nineteen. The trainees were eighteen-year-old privates and PFCs in their first half year in the army. These men were above average in mental aptitude but were either physically unfit for combat or were only sons or sons of bereaved families who were therefore exempt from combat duty.

Procedure. The procedure used in the adjutancy experiment was similar to that employed in the combat course, except that there were four experimental conditions instead of three. Only about 25 percent of the trainees were described to the instructors as having high potential (Pygmalion condition) and 25 percent were designated regular (Pygmalion-control condition); 50 percent were described to the instructors as having unknown potential because of incomplete information. This unclassified category was further split in two and assigned to two trainee-expectancy conditions, Galatea and Galatea-control, each comprising 25 percent of the trainees. Thus, there were four experimental conditions, each having about a quarter of the trainees. All these assignments were random. The four experimental conditions are shown in the column headings in table 2–4.

   The instructors were told the same background story as in the combat experiment, and their expectations regarding trainee performance were manipulated in the same manner. The trainees also received information about their potential according to the experimental conditions to which they had been assigned. The Galatea trainees were given the following five-minute personal interview by a military psychologist:

> Shalom! My name is _____. I'm a psychologist. I wanted to get to know you on your arrival at the base. We interview all new trainees. Please tell me a few details about your military service up to now, such as length of service and courses you've had.
> [Trainee answers.]
>
> How do you feel about your arrival here for this course?
> [Trainee answers.]

Thank you. To conclude, I wanted to tell you that, in light of prior information we've gathered about trainees with the aid of the military psychology unit, you have high potential for success.
[Psychologist dismisses trainee.]

The Galatea-control trainees were similarly interviewed, except that they were told at the end, "You have regular potential for success." The interview with the trainees in the Pygmalion conditions ended without the last sentence; that is, their self-expectations were not manipulated.

The Impact of Expectation Raising on Reported Self-Expectancy. We measured trainee self-expectations by means of a paper-and-pencil questionnaire that included an item asking the trainee to indicate whether he expected to do better than (1) 20 percent, (2) 40 percent, (3) 60 percent, or (4) 80 percent of the other trainees in the course. This question asks the respondent to indicate his expected performance quintile, omitting the lowest quintile. Trainees completed this self-expectancy measure three times: a) preinduction, on the day they arrived on base before any contact with their instructors and before the self-expectation interviews, b) in the fourth week, and c) in the seventh and final week of the course. Mean reported self-expectancy scores are presented in table 2–4.

Comparing the preinduction mean levels of reported self-expectations for trainees in the four expectations conditions in the first row of table 2–4 reveals that the initial levels of self-expectations were very similar. This reflects the effectiveness of random assignment in creating preexperimental equivalence among the trainees assigned to different experimental conditions. These scores evidenced a very realistic level of initial expectations. The means were all just above 2.00. This represents an average percentile expectation of between forty and sixty, that is, the middle quintile. On average, the trainees expected to attain average levels of performance.

Statistical analysis of the data summarized in table 2–4 revealed a pattern of substantially rising self-expectations among trainees in both the Pygmalion

Table 2–4
Mean Self-Expectancy Reported by Trainees

Occasion	Instructor Expectancy		Trainee Expectancy	
	Pygmalion	Control	Galatea	Control
Preinduction	2.17	2.15	2.12	2.07
Fourth week	2.89	1.92	3.06	2.21
Seventh week	3.28	1.77	2.88	1.93

Source: Eden and Ravid 1982.

and the Galatea conditions throughout the course, in contrast to relatively stable or slightly declining expectations among the controls. The increase in self-expectancy among the Pygmalion trainees confirmed the hypothesis that raising the manager's expectations of certain subordinates causes those subordinates to expect more of themselves. This is consistent with the conclusion that raising the manager's expectations results in elevated self-expectations among subordinates, which in turn generates the motivation that fuels the effort that results in higher achievement.

For the trainees in the Galatea condition, the changes in self-expectancy could not have resulted from manipulation of the instructors' expectations, as trainees in both the Galatea and the Galatea-control conditions had been designated to the instructors as unclassifiable. Rather, these results serve as a manipulation check of the induction of self-expectations among the Galatea trainees and show that the five-minute personal interviews did raise self-expectancy as intended.

Effects of Expectancy Raising on Performance. Performance in the adjutancy course was measured both by examinations administered at the end of each week and by weekly ratings of trainee performance. Instructors rated trainees on a one-hundred-point scale. They were asked to base their ratings on their overall impression of each trainee during the past week, considering discipline, cleanliness, and orderliness, besides the week's exam score. This was the standard rating procedure used in previous courses. Analysis of scores on both performance measures in the four experimental conditions across the seven weeks of the course revealed that raising instructor expectations and raising trainee self-expectations influenced performance significantly and substantially.

The mean weekly exam scores are displayed in table 2–5. Statistical analysis revealed significant effects for expectancy. Between a quarter and a third of the variation in exam scores was attributable to the expectancy manipulations. The trend *across* the seven weeks revealed a high degree of stability in performance *within* each of the four conditions. Comparing adjacent columns in table 2–5 across the weeks, it is clear that the gap between each high-expectation condition and its relevant control was evident by the end of the first week and was sustained for the duration of the course. This pattern replicates Rosenthal and Fode's (1963) findings in their study of the experimenter effect on rats tested on five consecutive days, in which the performance differences between the "bright" and "dull" animals were evident on the first day and were maintained throughout the remaining four days. Comparing the summary means, both the twelve-point Pygmalion effect and the seventeen-point Galatea effect were significant. However, the two effects were not significantly different from each other, indicating that Pygmalion and Galatea were equally potent in this experiment.

Table 2–5
Mean Weekly Exam Scores for Trainees in Both Adjutancy Courses

Week	Instructor Expectancy		Trainee Expectancy	
	Pygmalion	Control	Galatea	Control
1	85	74	82	68
2	80	70	76	60
3	80	71	81	63
4	82	68	79	62
5	82	74	79	61
6	79	59	73	56
7	75	66	71	53
Mean across 7 weeks	81	69	77	60

Source: Eden & Ravid 1982.

Similar analysis of the instructors' ratings revealed the same confirmatory pattern as the exam scores. When the ratings were averaged across all seven weeks, each high-expectancy group outscored its control group by fifteen points. Both fifteen-point differences between high and control summary ratings were significant, replicating the Pygmalion effect and confirming also the Galatea hypothesis. It is noteworthy that both expectancy effects were again equivalent in potency—fifteen rating points.

Self-Sustaining Prophecy: Second-Generation Pygmalion. The performance ratings in one of these two parallel adjutancy courses are particularly interesting because of the unscheduled replacement of the instructors after the third week. The original instructors in this course were sent on very short notice to participate as trainees in an officer-training course at a different base. This afforded us an opportunity to capitalize on their abrupt replacement as a "natural experiment." When we first got word of the impending instructor substitution, we considered "refreshing" the command potential information with the relief instructors. However, we decided that we could learn more by letting nature take its course at that point.

Table 2–6 displays the mean weekly performance ratings of the trainees by the original instructors and by the relief instructors in Course B. Examination of each column reveals that the ratings changed little in any of the four conditions when the instructor substitution occurred. The effects of the initial expectancy induction carried over to the relief instructors, whose expectations had not been manipulated experimentally.

The spillover of the expectancy effects to the relief instructors underscores the potency of interpersonal expectancy effects and supports the idea that expectations can produce *self-sustaining*, as well as self-fulfilling, prophecies (Salomon 1981). The manner in which the spillover occurred seems obvious. The relief instructors were not hermetically insulated from the original

Table 2–6
Mean Weekly Ratings of Trainees by Original and Relief Instructors,
Course B

Week	Instructor Expectancy		Trainee Expectancy	
	High	*Control*	*High*	*Control*
Original				instructors
1	89	75	78	68
2	88	77	79	64
3	86	76	82	65
Mean across 3 weeks	88	76	80	65
Relief instructors				
4	89	79	82	61
5	87	79	80	65
6	88	75	79	58
7	89	77	80	60
Mean across 4 weeks	88	78	80	61

Source: Eden & Ravid 1982.

expectation induction. The information provided to the original instructors during induction had been copied into the trainees' records, which were used by the relief instructors for the duration of the course before going into "dead storage" at the base at the end of the course. Furthermore, there was a brief period of overlap—several hours—during which each original instructor transferred his affairs, including his trainees' records, to his replacement. At this time they described their trainees as they had come to know them. If in these transfer discussions instructors passed along the expectations we had created three weeks earlier, it would indicate that expectancy effects are contagious. Expectations must have been passed on from instructor to instructor, as they evidently are passed from instructor to trainee. This would be a case of one instructor passing a Pygmalion effect on to another instructor. A similar transfer of information about pupils is said to take place in teachers' rooms in schools and about employees in discussions, performance reviews, and "bull sessions" among managers. This "second-generation" Pygmalion effect may also be sustained beyond the termination of the course. The near-disruption of the adjutancy experiment caused by personnel exigencies is typical of field experiments, and simulates organizational reality. There is little doubt that the spillover of expectancy effects in the adjutancy experiment also simulates everyday management actualities.

This spillover interpretation, being based on the transfer of experimentally induced *instructor* expectations, cannot explain the stability of the Galatea effect because the Galatea trainees had been described to their original instructors as unclassifiable. Consequently, the instructor replacement could not have had any differential impact on these trainees. Therefore, an alternative explanation for the stability of performance over time is necessary. It is likely that both the Pygmalion and the Galatea effects are self-sustaining because of *intratrainee* factors. Once aroused to high performance expectations by a manager with high expectations or by a psychologist, a subordinate may maintain high performance under subsequent supervisors, regardless of the latters' initial expectations. The subordinate's subsequent high performance may be sustained by the high *self*-expectations that he has internalized, and not by the expectations of his new supervisor. This interpretation focuses on the subordinate as the prophet who fulfills his own expectations after initial exposure to a manager with high expectations.

Another possibility is that, over time, the Galatea effect eventually converts into a Pygmalion effect. To begin with, high self-expectations produce high performance; that is, a Galatea effect. In the next stage, observing a subordinate's high performance or being told about it by the previous supervisor produces high expectations of that subordinate on the part of the new supervisor, and we have the makings of a Pygmalion effect. The interplay among the different types of expectancy effects and the consolidation of expectancy effects over time will be treated in the next chapter when we discuss the distinction between stable trait-expectancy and labile state-expectancy.

The Mediating Role of Self-Expectations. Having demonstrated that expectation raising leads to both higher self-expectations and higher performance, we wanted stronger evidence of the mediating role of the subordinate's self-expectations in these SFP processes. Therefore, we analyzed the performance measures by means of a statistical procedure, called analysis of covariance, that estimates the effect of expectation raising on performance after controlling self-expectations by statistically removing their effects from performance. The results of this analysis showed that most, but not all, of the effect of expectation-raising on performance operates via subordinates' self-expectations. Holding self-expectations constant reduced the proportion of variation in performance scores, which was explained by expectation-raising from 32 percent to only 6 percent. We can therefore conclude that the subordinate's self-expectations *do* serve as a mediating mechanism in the Pygmalion effect.

Thus, subordinate self-expectancy is a key in the SFP process. We have demonstrated statistically that it mediates the Pygmalion effect and experimentally that it can be directly raised to produce similar performance gains in what we call the Galatea effect. The common denominator shared by these SFP effects is the subordinate's self-expectations. Figure 2–1 portrays the mediating role of self-expectations in both effects. Credible high expectations communicated by an authority figure, whether an experimenter, a manager,

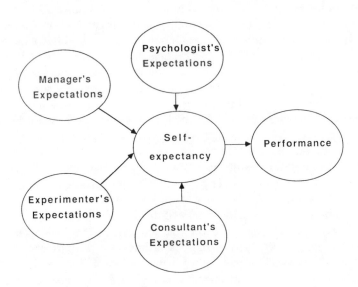

Figure 2–1. The Mediating Role of Self-Expectancy in the Pygmalion and Galatea Effects

or a staff psychologist or other consultant, lead subordinates to expect more of themselves and consequently to perform better.

However, Galatea is not Pygmalion. In the Pygmalion condition, the supervisor *unwittingly* treated subordinates differently in accordance with his expectations. In contrast, in the Galatea experiment, the psychologist imparted his "expectations" to the trainees *knowingly.* Following the five-minute interviews, the psychologist had no further contact with the trainees. Therefore, he could not have fulfilled his own prophecy by means of his own behavior. Calling the psychologist a prophet in this situation misses the point. In this sense the Galatea effect is not an *inter*personal expectancy effect. Raising self-expectations relies on the subordinate's capacity to mobilize his *own* resources to perform better. In the Galatea effect, the *subordinate* is the one who functions is a prophet. He fulfills his own prophecy. Getting managers to believe in subordinates' potential is one way, an important way, but not the only way, to raise the subordinates' self-expectations and boost their performance. Later chapters will discuss other ways to raise the expectations of organization members.

The distinction between a Pygmalion effect and a Galatea effect is not always unequivocal. The Pygmalion effect is named after the expecter, whereas the Galatea effect is named after the expectee. When a person in authority has high expectations of a subordinate and treats the subordinate accordingly, with a productive outcome, we speak of a Pygmalion effect. In instances of expectancy effects in which it is not clear whether the effect should be credited more to the expecter or to the expectee, it will not be clear whether it should be called a Pygmalion effect or a Galatea effect. Nor will it be very important. What is important is that the subordinate's self-expectations be raised, by whatever means, and no matter what the label.

Equity: A Motivating Mediator in the Pygmalion Effect. While planning the adjutancy experiment, we were considering additional intrapsychic mediating mechanisms that seemed worthwhile testing. In addition to self-expectations, we included a measure of equity as a potential mediator. Livingston (1969) had opened his pioneering article on Pygmalion in management with the famous quotation from Shaw's *Pygmalion* in which Eliza Doolittle explains to Colonel Pickering after Professor Higgins' experiment was over that "the difference between a lady and a flower girl is not how she behaves, but how she's treated." Considering our findings in the combat experiment, that trainees of whom more was expected enjoyed better leadership and were more satisfied with the course, it seemed to be more rewarding for a subordinate to be managed by a supervisor who expects more of him than by one who expects less. Such rewarding benefits are called outcomes in equity theory (Adams 1965). According to equity theory, individuals who receive more outcomes than others investing equivalent inputs should experience dissonant feelings of overpayment. Such feelings should motivate them to invest greater effort in order to restore equity, resulting in higher performance.

Random assignment of trainees to conditions had rendered them initially equivalent on input variables, such as experience, aptitude, motivation, and commitment. We therefore hypothesized that being in the high-expectation conditions, and thereby benefiting from higher outcomes, produces feelings of overreward and that getting lower outcomes arouses feelings of underreward among trainees randomly assigned to control conditions. We also hypothesized that any differences in equity that expectancy raising might arouse would mediate its effects on performance.

We devised a measure of equity by presenting each trainee with a list of twenty-three outcomes given by instructors and asking him to indicate whether the amount of each outcome he received was "(a) a little, relative to the effort you have invested compared to what others in your group have invested and received, (b) appropriate for the effort you have invested compared to what others in your group have invested and received, or (c) a lot, relative to what others in your group have invested and received." We defined the first alternative as underpayment, the midpoint as equity, and the last answer as overpayment. Illustrative outcomes are the relative amount of consideration, patience, encouragement, punishment, threat of punishment, backing, perks, attention, chance to prove yourself, criticism, and muzzling that the trainee felt he had received from his instructor.

Table 2–7
Mean Equity

Item	Instructor Expectancy		Trainee Expectancy	
	High	Control	High	Control
Mean	2.34	1.71	2.29	1.61
Standard deviation	.32	.34	.31	.40

Source: Eden & Ravid 1982.

The equity results are shown in table 2–7. Each high-expectancy mean was significantly higher than the mean equity score in its control condition. These differences confirm the hypothesis that trainees in different conditions felt that they were treated differently—indeed, inequitably. Trainees in both high-expectancy conditions reported overpayment and the controls felt underpaid. These results were remarkably symmetrical. Each mean for high-expectancy trainees was one standard deviation above the scale midpoint, 2.0, indicating overpayment, and each control-expectancy mean was one standard deviation below the midpoint, expressing underpayment.

To test whether equity mediated the effects of induced expectancy on performance, we computed an analysis of covariance on the seven-week mean exam scores in which the effect of equity was statistically controlled. This analysis showed that removing the significant effect of equity on examination scores reduced the impact of the expectancy induction on the scores to a non-significant level. This confirms what Eliza Doolittle said: it's how one is treated that makes the difference. When a manager expects a lot, he treats the subordinate more favorably, thereby arousing inequitable feelings of overpayment. The subordinate needs to justify the overpayment. He does this by investing greater effort and consequently he performs better.

We found two different psychological mediators of the Pygmalion effect in the same study (self-expectations and equity) and another mediator (leadership) in another study. This underscores the fact that there is no single variable that deserves being called *the* mediator. A multiplicity of mediators gives the practitioner a range of options in applying SFP. We shall explore these options in a later chapter.

An Ethical Epilogue. There was some after-the-fact concern over the possibility that being in a control group in an expectancy experiment may be harmful to participants. The foregoing performance results show that those in the high-expectancy conditions performed better than those in the control conditions. However, lacking an absolute standard of comparison, it is conceivable that the experimental trainees gained nothing, whereas the control trainees lost something. A statistically significant difference between high and

Table 2–8
Comparison of Course Grades in the Adjutancy Experiment with Grades
in Seven Previous Groups in Same Course

Grades in Previous Groups
73
72
72
72
71
70
70

Means of Present Courses, by Course

Course A	76
Course B	78

Means of Present Courses, by Experimental Condition

Instructor Expectancy		Trainee Expectancy	
Pygmalion	Control	Galatea	Control
84	70	78	67

control groups is consistent with both interpretations. So how do we know whether rasing expectations facilitated achievement among the experimental trainees, or whether being in the control condition hindered learning performance among control trainees?

Fortunately, summary course grades were retrievable from records stored at the base for seven previous groups that had been through the same adjutancy course during the two-year period before the beginning of the two courses we studied. We computed the mean grade for each of the previous groups to contrast their achievements with those of our trainees. The relevant means are displayed in table 2–8. The first part of the table lists the seven previous means in descending order. They range between 73 and 70. In contrast, the means of the two courses we studied were 76 and 78, showing overall performance above the means of the previous groups. However, the most relevant comparison for the question at hand involves contrasting the seven previous means to the means for trainees in the four different conditions in our experiment, shown at the bottom of table 2–8. Taking the upper limit of the grade distribution in the previous groups, 73, as a standard of comparison, our experimental manipulations produced average grades of 84 and 78, which were higher by 11 and by 5 points in the Pygmalion and Galatea conditions, respectively. Comparing the control means to the grade distribution in the previous groups, the Pygmalion-control mean of 70 is within the range of the previous groups. The Galatea-control mean of 67 falls three points short of the previous range. However, the 95 percent confidence interval for this mean of 67 is ± 6. That is, because of sampling error, the likely true value of the mean in the Galatea-control group ranges anywhere between 61 and 73. Thus, it includes the entire range of the means of the previous groups, and is significantly different from them. The apparant three-point shortfall is negligible.

To summarize, the means in table 2–8 provide evidence that being in a high-expectancy condition in a Pygmalion or Galatea experiment can have beneficial effects on performance, whereas being in a control condition is inconsequential. The comparison of the performance of the trainees in our adjutancy experiment to their predecessors in previous groups is not a rigorous one, for it lacks randomization. Random assignment of trainees to the four experimental conditions in our tightly controlled experiment is the source of our confidence in their having been equivalent at the outset. No such confidence is justified when comparing across trainees who entered the course at different times. It is possible that from time to time the qualifications of trainees entering the course differ. This possibility renders the comparison of present trainees to previous trainees susceptible to additional interpretations. However, it was the best we could do in the present study—after the fact—to shed light on the issue of the contrast between relative gains and losses among experimental and control participants. More rigorous evidence that the benefits gained by those in a Pygmalion condition are not reaped at the expense of their comrades assigned to a control condition had to await an additional experiment on "Whole-group Pygmalion," described later.

Pygmalion and Galatea among Women: A Failure to Replicate

We (Eden & Ravid 1981) replicated the design of the adjutancy experiment in a clerical course conducted at the same base and at about the same time. The chief difference between the two adjutancy courses and the clerical course was that both the instructors and the trainees in the clerical course were women. The clerical course lasted four weeks, and the trainees were tested at the end of each of the four weeks. The procedure for manipulating expectations to create the Pygmalion and Galatea effects was exactly like the one used in the adjutancy experiment. Initial analysis of the data confirmed the Pygmalion and Galatea hypotheses. Table 2–9 compares the mean weekly performance scores of the women in the four conditions. Each high-expectancy group outperformed its control group substantially and consistently across the four weeks. If that were the end of the analysis, we would have concluded that the replication succeeded and that we now had data showing SFP effects among women.

However, despite random assignment of trainees to the four experimental conditions, we undertook a postexperimental, precautionary check to reassure ourselves that randomization had resulted in preexperimental

Table 2–9
Mean Weekly Exam Scores for Women

| | Instructor Expectancy | | Trainee Expectancy | |
Week	Pygmalion	Control	Galatea	Control
1	72	64	75	53
2	77	69	77	66
3	82	77	78	56
4	72	64	68	59

equivalence. To our astonishment, this comparison revealed that the women who had been assigned to the high-expectancy conditions had significantly higher aptitude. A similar equivalence check among the men in the adjutancy courses detected no such preexperimental differences.

Randomization *ought* to produce preexperimental equivalence among subjects assigned to different treatment groups, and it usually *does*. However, even in a truly randomized experiment, a significant preexperimental difference can be obtained. Using the conventional .05 level of statistical significance, such differences are to be expected about 5 percent of the time. When detected, pretest differences require an analysis that removes any effects they may have had on the dependent variable. A difference in aptitude would certainly be expected to account for differences in learning performance. Therefore, in reanalyzing the exam scores among the women in the clerical course, we held aptitude constant by recomputing scores adjusting for differences in aptitude. This was done using a statistical procedure that estimated the effect of aptitude on performance and removed its effect. The residual, or adjusted, scores are free of any effect of aptitude and can be interpreted as the exam scores that the trainees would have gotten had they all been equal in initial aptitude. The adjusted exam scores are presented in table 2–10.

Comparing the adjusted exam scores in table 2–10 to the original, unadjusted scores in table 2–9 reveals what the adjustment procedure does. It reduces the difference between experimental and control trainees by an

Table 2–10
Adjusted Mean Weekly Exam Scores for Women

| | Instructor Expectancy | | Trainee Expectancy | |
Week	Pygmalion	Control	Galatea	Control
1	70	65	72	58
2	75	70	74	71
3	80	79	75	62
4	70	65	66	61

amount attributable to the differences between them in aptitude. The means in each pair are more similar after adjustment. Despite the consistent direction of the weekly differences between each high-expectancy group and its control, none of these differences in mean adjusted test scores was significant. Consistency in the direction of the differences "survived" the adjustment, but the magnitude and statistical significance of the differences did not survive. Therefore, the conclusion must be that this replication failed to produce either a Pygmalion effect or a Galatea effect. This negative finding among IDF women is consistent with King's (1971) (non)findings among women.

Seeking *post hoc* explanation for our failure to replicate, one possibility was that the instructors in the clerical course were more experienced instructors than were the instructors in the adjutancy course. Perhaps the more experienced instructors were less prone to accept the information we supplied about trainee potential as part of the expectancy manipulation. Subsequent research has indeed shown that more experienced teachers are less inclined to accept background information about pupils than are novices to the teaching role (Carter, Sabers, Cushing, Pinnegar & Berliner 1987). Another possibility is that the training the women in the clerical course received was much less interesting, challenging, and worthy of their best motivated efforts than was training in the adjutancy course for the men. Why get excited about being trained for a clerical job, even if the instructor *is* Pygmalion-like?

Certainly, this is not the final word on expectancy effects among women. It is methodologically displeasing to obtain the effect and then have it wiped out by a *post hoc* statistical adjustment. Although the rules of statistical inference dictate not rejecting the null hypothesis that there is no effect, the results from our clerical study should best be regarded as inconclusive. Scientific prudence counsels suspension of judgment. There is simply not enough evidence available to dismiss the validity and applicability of the Pygmalion concept to women. Common sense and intellectual curiosity impel one to look further. In short, all considerations point to the need for more research on Pygmalion among women.

Whole-Group Pygmalion Controlling Contrast Effects: The IDF Squad Leaders Experiment

Virtually all previous Pygmalion research was conducted using an experimental design that does not control contrast effects. This is true of the SFP-at-work research reviewed before, as well as all the research reviewed and referenced in the previous chapter. Since Rosenthal's earliest experiments on the experimenter effect, the procedure has always been to designate some members of a group as worthy of high performance expectations. The remaining individuals in the same group are in a control condition for the sake of comparison to those in the high-expectancy condition. Although the researcher says nothing to deprecate the control subjects, it is possible that conveying information about the high potential of their experimental peers implies that nothing has been said about them because they are of lower potential. Thus, it is possible that raising expectations toward some is paramount to lowering expectations toward others.

This experimental design raises several important questions. First, there is the methodological issue of contrast effects. Can the Pygmalion effect be produced without a control group? Positive SFP effects had been produced experimentally only in contrast to control subjects who were members of the same class or training group. It was possible that comparison of "high potential" subjects to some of their classmates who are not designated as having high potential is necessary for the effect to occur. The comparison between subjects assigned to experimental and control conditions, which is inherent in the experimental design, may be a substantive factor that interacts with raising expectations and creates the Pygmalion effect. It was conceivable that raising expectations toward some without contrast to a control group would not produce SFP effects. If interpersonal expectancy effects were to boil down to a mere artifactual contrast effect, then our entire perspective on SFP in management would have to change. It would not seem as important or as applicable an effect.

The second question concerns productivity. If the Pygmalion effect requires a control group, is it worthwhile economically? Our efforts would be better spent seeking management innovations that raise the productivity of all subordinates simultaneously, rather than only some of them. Worse still, suppose the experimental subjects gained at the expense of their counterparts in the control group. If that were the case, it would be hard to justify deliberately creating expectancy effects in the name of organizational effectiveness. Managerial action that makes some individuals more productive and others less productive is equivalent to the proverbial "robbing Peter to pay Paul." In such a redistribution of productive potential in which some individuals gain and others lose, the organization profits nothing in aggregate. However, some individuals are aggrieved.

This grievance is the third, but not least important, reason for concern about contrast effects. Is it fair to the control subjects? If it were to be shown that expectancy effects come at the expense of individuals randomly assigned to the control group, it would be unfair to those individuals. Even if being relegated to the control group does not detract from their performance, being outperformed by others who happened to have been chosen at random for the experimental treatment in itself may create relative deprivation. This is an ethical dilemma posed in the American Psychological Association's *Ethical Principles in the Conduct of Research with Human Participants* (1982) under the heading, "Withholding Potential Benefits from Control Participants."

Peering through the mists of these ethical ambiguities, it seemed crystal clear that the Pygmalion effect would be hard to disseminate as a practical management technique if it were dependent upon contrast effects. Establishing its feasibility goes beyond showing that control subjects are not actually harmed. If creating the effect required discrimination of any sort, it would be distasteful to researchers and managers alike.

Because of these considerations, there was need of an additional experiment in which contrast effects would be eliminated. However, the classical experimental paradigm is based on contrasting subjects who have been exposed to an experimental treatment to comparable others who have not been so exposed. How can one make the contrast without creating contrast effects? Campbell and Stanley (1966) provided the answer in their discussion of randomization. Random assignment of subjects to experimental conditions is used to assure the preexperimental equivalence required for a high degree of internal validity. However, sometimes it is not feasible to assign individuals to conditions at random. This difficulty arises in experimental research on intact work groups in organizations. Campbell and Stanley proposed that in such cases preexperimental equivalence be achieved by assigning *whole groups* to conditions at random. In the case of the Pygmalion effect, the whole-groups design requires randomly assigning a number of *managers,* each in charge of a group of subordinates, to experimental conditions. Each manager and his entire group are assigned to a condition. The relevant contrast for hypothesis testing involves the comparison of means of group means. No distinction is made among individuals within groups, nor is any comparison of individuals within groups made. Therefore, there can be no contrast effects among individuals within groups. This requires a sufficiently large sample of comparable groups to allow for statistical inference testing, for the number of degrees of freedom for statistical hypothesis testing is based on the number of groups, not the number of individuals in the groups. The randomized whole-groups design was used in a Pygmalion experiment in the IDF School for Squad Leaders.

Sample. Company-sized units are brought to the IDF School for Squad Leaders for combat and command training. Each company is comprised of three platoons, and each platoon is trained by its own instructor. The platoon is the natural training group in the school. The platoon was therefore adopted as the unit of analysis in this experiment. The platoons were assigned at random to experimental and control conditions. Once the platoon was assigned to a condition, all its members were assigned with it. Ten companies were included in the present experiment. One of the three platoons in each company was chosen at random for the Pygmalion condition, and the other two platoons were assigned to the control condition. One company had only two platoons, which were assigned to conditions at random. Therefore, we had ten experimental platoons and nineteen control platoons. The trainees were all men aged nineteen or twenty who had graduated high school. They were of average or above-average aptitude as measured by an IDF battery. They had been through basic training.

Procedure. This school has a military psychologist[3] on its permanent staff, and instructors are accustomed to working with a psychologist on various problems that arise during a course. One day before each company arrived at the school to begin its course, the psychologist met individually with the instructor of each experimental platoon for a conversation designed to raise the instructor's expectations toward the men in his platoon. In this conversation, the psychologist conveyed the following information:

> The IDF is conducting a large-scale research project to investigate the effectiveness of different training methods. The aim is to improve how we train soldiers. Among other goals, we are trying to find out whether there are certain training methods that are appropriate for certain groups in certain courses.
>
> As part of the project, I will follow your course closely. I'll be checking on several aspects of the training and I'll gather data also from the trainees during the course. I want to make it clear that any recommendation I may make will be applicable only in regard to training methods employed in future courses.
>
> One of our assumptions is that there is a relationship between the training method used and the trainee's ability and his success as a commander. As you know, the school uses experiential methods of training. For you to know the trainees who will be arriving tomorrow better, I checked out the following aptitude information: aptitude test scores; sociometric evaluations from their basic training; and ratings by previous commanders.
>
> On the basis of this information, we can predict the command potential of the soldiers. Comparing the mean command potential scores of the men in the platoon you're getting tomorrow with other groups, it is evident that the average command potential of your trainees is appreciably higher than the usual level.
>
> Research on previous courses has shown that there is a great deal of correspondence between our evaluation of trainee's command potential and their actual achievements. It was found that command potential could predict the level of success in 95 percent of the cases. Therefore, you can expect unusual achievements from the trainees in this group. Throughout the course you will be asked to complete an instructor's questionnaire in which you will be asked to evaluate your trainees. The trainees will also be asked to complete questionnaires.

The psychologist also met individually with the instructor of each control platoon and described the research in a similar manner, except that nothing was said about the command potential of their soldiers. The random assignment and conversations with the psychologist thus created two groups of platoons that were comparable in everything except the information provided to the instructors concerning the command potential of their soldiers. This procedure created an experimental group of ten platoons whose commanders were in a Pygmalion condition and a control group of nineteen platoons whose commanders' expectations were not manipulated.

Manipulation check. To check whether the brief introductory conversations achieved their aim of raising the expectations of the experimental commanders, all twenty-nine commanders were asked to rate their soldiers on a nine-point scale ranging from low to high command potential. The commanders of the Pygmalion platoons rated their trainees 6.72, 6.85, and 6.94 on the three rating occasions, compared to 6.02, 6.16, and 6.11 in the control platoons. The difference between the two conditions is statistically significant ($F = 27.89, p < .0001$) and consistent across occasions. It indicates that the manipulation succeeded in creating higher expectations among the instructors of the Pygmalion platoons than among instructors of the control platoons, as intended.

Results. Table 2–11 displays the mean achievement scores in two objectively assessed performance areas among the Pygmalion and control platoons. These subjects were taught by the platoon's own instructor. This is the commander whose expectations the base psychologist manipulated. In the theoretical material, trainees were administered multiple-choice examinations that were scored anonymously. Such examinations are free of subjective errors such as halo and leniency. A higher score could only result from the examinee's knowing more material. The practical specialty scores were determined by a series of performance tests in which each trainee progressed from station to station on a testing line manned by all the instructors. At each station the trainee was asked to perform a particular operation using weapons or other equipment. The instructors at the station graded his performance. Most of the instructors determining these grades were not the trainee's own instructor, and their expectations had not been manipulated. Therefore, these are also performance scores that are free of expectancy bias.

We also compared performance of experimental and control platoons in

Table 2–11
Comparison of Mean Performance of Trainees in Pygmalion and Control Platoons

Occasion	Pygmalion	Control
Theoretical specialty	70.70	64.68
Practical specialty	78.70	71.63

two objectively assessed "control subjects" that were not predicted to be influenced by the instructor's expectations. Physical fitness was assessed by a physical education specialist who drilled the men from time to time to keep them in condition during the course. This specialist was given no information about the experiment and had no reason to assess the potential of the men in the different platoons differently. Sharpshooting was not even drilled in this course. It was included in the course records as a performance dimension because of its generic importance in the military. There was no reason to expect spillover of the effects of the platoon instructor's expectations to performance in areas over which he has no influence. Thus, we analyzed the last two subjects as control subjects that were not predicted to be influenced by the expectancy manipulation.

The means in table 2–11 show that the experimental and control platoons differed in the first two subjects as predicted. Commanders who were told that their subordinates as a group had high potential led their men to higher achievement than comparable commanders of comparable subordinates. The Pygmalion effect was evident for both the theoretical specialization and the practical specialization. As predicted, there was no significant difference between Pygmalion and control platoons in physical fitness or in sharpshooting. These findings confirm the hypothesis that the Pygmalion effect is not dependent upon the contrast effect. SFP in management is not a methodological artifact. This means that supervisors do not create SFP for the benefit of some at the expense of the rest. Raising managers' expectations toward all their subordinates boosts those subordinates' average performance. These results open the way for whole-group SFP applications.

Pygmalion-at-Sea: Expectation Training in the U.S. Navy

Predating the IDF experiments, Crawford, Thomas, and Fink (1980) at the United States Navy Personnel Research and Development Center in San Diego took a very different approach to Pygmalion. They undertook a bold and creative SFP intervention aimed at improving the productivity of low performers. They identified a number of chronically low-performing sailors on a combat ship with a total crew of about 230 men. These unproductive sailors had come to be labeled "dirtbags." They were targeted for remedial treatment in a three-track training and development program designed to improve their motivation and performance. While the experimental ship was docked, supervisory personnel in the command were given a one-and-a-half-day motivation and leadership workshop intended to change their negative expectations toward the problem sailors. Second, fifteen senior enlisted supervisors, who had been carefully selected to serve as shipboard role models and mentors for the low performers, were given a one-day workshop in counseling and guidance skills designed to train them to enhance the low performers' self-concept and expectations. Finally, twelve low performers participated in two separate three-day workshops. The first was devoted to personal growth and self-improvement. This was followed by three one-day workshop meetings a week apart dealing with issues raised by the low performers themselves.

The low performers' first workshop was introduced by the ship's commanding officer. He informed the men that although they "were indeed problem sailors, the command felt that they had the potential to improve their performance" (p. 491). Thus, the low performers were told outright at the outset that they were expected to improve. In addition, the CRM McGraw-Hill training film titled *Productivity and the Self-fulfilling Prophecy: The Pygmalion Effect* was screened and discussed at length in the workshops with both the supervisors *and* the low performers.

It is impossible to isolate the effects of each of the several independent variables manipulated by these workshops. However, it is clear that the communication and cultivation of high performance expectations—among both the supervisors and the subordinates themselves—were the hallmark of this intervention. Thus, the Pygmalion-at-Sea program can be regarded as an attempt to create both the Pygmalion and the Galatea effects in the interests of boosting productivity. One of Crawford et al.'s underlying assumptions was that if the low performers could be made aware of the role of *negative* expectations in depressing their performance, they would be able to prevent or overcome these negative SFP effects and improve their performance. Thus, the Pygmalion-at-Sea program can be seen as an attempt to "immunize" these men against the debilitating effects of low expectations.

It is important to keep in mind that the high expectations aroused among the supervisors were buttressed by behavioral skill building. Crawford and his colleagues described the training segment for supervisors as consisting of "teaching the principles of behavior modification and then brainstorming actions that would constitute positive reinforcers in the eyes of the low performers. The supervisors were thus given some specific tools to back up their newly acquired positive expectations" (p. 489). This procedure is not only sensible, it is essential. It is unfeasible to convince managers to expect more of their subordinates by merely lecturing to them, showing them a film, and exhorting them to expect more. An expectation-raising program needs solid moorings.

The impact of the intervention was evaluated after the ship returned from a seven-month deployment at sea. The low performers on the experimental ship were compared to thirty-four of their shipmates and to twenty comparably low performers on four other ships. These comparisons revealed significant improvements in the experimental low performers both in overall performance as rated by their supervisors and in discipline.

Crawford et al. supplemented their quantitative results with postintervention interviews. The low performers themselves attributed the program's success to the fact that "someone had taken an interest in and believed in them," and for some this "had been their first positive encouragement since joining the Navy" (p. 497). The commanding officer "was extremely pleased with the outcome of the intervention." He "also stressed the importance of changing the negative expectations of the LPs" (low performers). The authors concluded from the interviews that "the apparent success of the intervention centered on changes in the self-fulfilling prophecies engendered in the LPs and their supervisors" (p. 497). Crawford and his colleagues pioneered in practical application of interpersonal expectancy effects. Their example is worthy of emulation.

A noteworthy point about the navy study was raised by Seiz (1982). He was appalled, as was I, by the report that low-performing sailors were dubbed "dirtbags" in ship parlance. No matter what the reasons, this is an abhorrent way to denigrate citizens enlisted in the service of their country. Moreover, this should be considered in the context of the Air Force labeling study. What kind of performance would a supervisor expect from a man called a "dirtbag"? How would a "dirtbag" be treated?

The Golem Effect

SFP is a double-edged sword. Until now, we have considered the positive effects of raising expectations on performance. However, there is evidence that *low* expectations have negative performance effects. For obvious ethical considerations, Pygmalion researchers have been understandably reluctant to impart low performance expectations. Nevertheless, there have been studies of the effects of naturally occurring low expectations. Such studies are causally ambiguous because they lack the rigorous control achieved in randomized experiments in which the experimenter manipulates expectations. Nevertheless, we can infer from such research what effects low expectations must have on performance. Since no experimental research on low expectations among adults in work organizations has been reported, the debilitating effects of low performance expectations are best illustrated by a study of schoolteachers.

Babad, Inbar, and Rosenthal (1982b) studied expectation effects among physical education student-teachers by comparing the effects of manipulated high expectations and naturally occurring low expectations on pupil performance. They found that pupils about whom they imparted high expectations to the instructors performed best. However, they also found that pupils toward whom the teachers harbored naturally low expectations performed significantly worse than those regarding whom they had high or intermediate natural expectations.

Babad and his colleagues dubbed the debilitating effect of low expectations on performance the "Golem effect." They borrowed this name from the legendary Golem of Prague. According to a sixteenth-century Jewish legend, a desperate rabbi constructed an automaton of the dust of the earth, brought it to life, and called it the Golem. His aim was to use the Golem to protect the Jews from anti-Semitic violence bred by the medieval blood libel. The Golem ultimately became an uncontrollable monster, turned on its creator, and wreaked havoc on the community. The word "Golem" is used in modern-day Yiddish and in Hebrew slang to denote a dumbbell. Thus, SFP is a double-edged sword that can either boost or depress performance, depending on the level of the expectations fueling it.

It should be noted that, like the Galatea effect, the Golem effect is named after the expectee. The difference between the two effects is that one is productive, whereas the other is destructive. In present usage, the expecter who produces a positive expectancy effect is called a Pygmalion. There is no separate label for the perpetrator of a Golem effect. Perhaps he should also be dubbed a Golem for doing something so dumb!

It is important to note that Babad and his colleagues studied physical task performance. Their criteria included sit-ups and push-ups, broadjumping, and running speed. This broadens the scope of generalizability of adult interpersonal SFP effects to nonintellectual spheres of performance. King's trainees were learning welding, and the performance measure called "practical specialization" that we used in the IDF combat experiment included such job behaviors as calibrating, dismantling, reassembling, and operating heavy weapons. Thus, SFP effects are not limited to academic performance.

The mission for anyone bent on profiting maximally from application of SFP in management is therefore twofold. It entails purposefully reducing Golem effects as well as deliberately creating positive Pygmalion and Galatea effects. For example, because of the initially low expectations toward the low-performing sailors, the Pygmalion-at-Sea project should be seen as an intervention undertaken to overcome a Golem effect. The distinction is not merely semantic. Eliminating Golem and creating Pygmalion are appropriate for different situations, and call for different interventions.

Organizationwide Expectation Raising

Expectations and Innovations in Factories

King (1974) reported very important experimental findings that demonstrate the impact of expectations on plantwide productivity. He had obviously been inspired by his own previous Pygmalion research, which had an individual focus. Like the classroom studies, King's previous experiment had dealt with the expectations of a supervisor toward individual subordinates. Having successfully replicated the Pygmalion effect among adult industrial trainees, King next broke new ground by shifting his focus from the individual subordinate to the entire organization as an object of SFP. He hypothesized that managers' expectations regarding the productive outcomes of organizational innovations could produce effects on those outcomes that are independent of the effects of the innovations themselves. His aim was to show that when we intervene in an organization with an innovation intended to increase its productivity, the expectations aroused by the intervention can produce performance effects that outweigh whatever productivity gains result from the intervention itself.

King conducted his expectations-and-innovation experiment in four Midwestern folding-and-packaging plants of a multiplant company that manufactured clothing patterns. The machine operators in each factory were organized in ten six-man crews who had loading, operating, and takeoff duties. With the collaboration of the firm's top management, King had the firm's director of manufacturing present the same changes differently to management in each of the four factories. King chose job enrichment as the organizational innovation he introduced into the plants. He defined enrichment as having two levels. The "high" level was job enlargement, which entailed increasing the number of operations each worker performed. The low level was job rotation, in which workers merely rotated their positions from time to time, but when in each position each worker performed only one operation.

King had management introduce job enlargement as the enrichment innovation in two plants and job rotation as the enrichment innovation in the remaining two plants. He simultaneously imparted high productivity expectations to management in one enlargement plant and in one rotation plant. By design, productivity expectations were unmanipulated, and therefore at "no-change" control levels, in the two remaining plants. Managers in the two no-change plants were told that the reason for the innovation was to improve labor relations, but that productivity should be expected to remain unchanged. This scheme resulted in four comparable plants' getting different treatments: a high-expectation job-enlargement plant, a high-expectation job-rotation plant, a no-change job-enlargement plant, and a no-change job-rotation plant. This design permitted a test of the independent effects of job enrichment and of expectations.

King's results are shown in table 2–12. The analysis of average monthly output in the four plants showed that enrichment had no effect but that expectations *did*. Over the twelve-month follow-up period, both high-expectation plants, shown in the upper half of the table, increased their monthly output by similar amounts irrespective of whether they had gotten enlargement or rotation, whereas output in the no-change plants, shown in the bottom half of the table, remained unchanged. Viewing the data within expectation condi-

Table 2–12
Average Daily Pattern Folding Output/Machine Crew

Manager Output Expectations	Months	Enlargement	Rotation	Total
		Plant 1	*Plant 3*	
	1	18,453	18,565	
	2	18,675	18,795	
	3	18,904	19,000	
	4	19,352	19,153	
	5	19,421	19,270	
	6	19,608	19,375	
Increased output	7	19,480	19,760	
	8	19,870	19,894	
	9	19,940	19,890	
	10	20,102	20,175	
	11	20,200	20,150	
	12	20,050	20,005	
Subtotal		234,055	234,032	468,087
		Plant 2	*Plant 4*	
	1	18,275	18,325	
	2	18,300	18,500	
	3	18,408	18,302	
	4	18,392	18,130	
	5	18,463	18,432	
	6	18,491	18,443	
No change in output	7	18,572	18,236	
	8	18,674	18,350	
	9	18,631	18,423	
	10	18,400	18,192	
	11	18,004	18,337	
	12	18,670	18,124	
Subtotal		221,280	219,494	440,774
Total		455,335	453,526	908,861

Adapted from King 1974, table 4.

tions, enlargement and rotation plants had similar levels of output. *If managers' expectations were raised, productivity improved regardless of which intervention was introduced.* If expectations were not raised, productivity remained unchanged regardless of which change program was installed.

Job enlargement and job rotation, which were compared in this experiment, either had similar positive effects on productivity or had no effect on productivity, depending on expectations. King concluded that, "Led to expect higher productivity as a result of these organizational innovations, the managers increased their plant output during the experiment period" (p. 221) and that "the results provide further evidence that managerial expectations concerning performance resulting from an innovation may serve as a self-fulfilling prophecy. When managers expected certain changes in jobs to result in greater productivity, those changes did result in greater output" (p. 229). King did not address the question of *how* the managers raised productivity to confirm their expectations.

Interpretations. There is some uncertainty as to how King's findings should be interpreted. The ambiguity derives from the manner in which he manipulated the managers' output expectations. His intention was to manipulate these expectations by creating two levels—raised and unchanged. However, the explanations that the manufacturing director gave in the two "unchanged" expectation plants may have actually *lowered* managers' expectations in those factories. Four "limitations" on the expected outcomes of the innovation were communicated to managers in the two no-change plants. In these two factories he followed a brief description of the contributions to more favorable labor relations that enrichment was expected to make with the statement that "several limitations can be expected to arise, however." He then enumerated four specific limitations. These included such phrases as "workers may become less proficient in performance of elements making up job tasks" and "workers may become less capable of eliminating wasted and ineffective motions" (King 1974, 223, table 1). The presentation was concluded in these two factories by telling the managers that, because of these limitations, productivity should be the same but industrial relations should improve.

King's choice of words is unfortunate. Their meaning was so equivocal that his high-expectancy manipulation conveyed a double message. They could easily have been interpreted by the managers in the two "no-change-in-output" plants as strongly implying that performance may slip. Enumerating four "limitations" that clearly spell out added difficulties that are going to challenge managers having to cope with implementation of the innovation is not the best way to insure unchanged output expectations! It is quite possible that King's "no-change" manipulation actually *depressed* output expectations. Thus, it is unclear whether his treatment raised expectations in the high-expectation plants, depressed expectations in the no-change plants, or both.

Therefore, two different, but not contradictory, substantive interpretations of King's results are equally tenable. The first is King's; that is, that raising expectations boosted output. The second is that when the commonsense practice of accompanying an intervention with assurances to the client that productivity can be expected to improve was replaced with (too) well-justified expectations for unchanged productivity, the beneficial effect of both otherwise productive enrichment interventions was thereby nullified. King may have unintentionally produced a plantwide Golem effect with his no-change manipulation that overpowered the productive impact of enrichment and negated it.

No matter which interpretation one may prefer, King's experiment did convincingly demonstrate that changing managers' performance expectations, be it by raising or by lowering them, can trigger a collective SFP that influences the productivity of an entire organizational unit. He thereby provided us with evidence that expectancy effects can be produced not only in one-on-one supervisor-subordinate relationships, but also at higher levels. This should inspire us to seek plantwide applications. However, this type of organizationwide SFP is neither an interpersonal expectancy effect nor a Pygmalion effect. No information about particular subordinates was used as a basis for imparting high expectations to managers. A later chapter will present a process model of organizationwide SFP and propose practical ways of raising expectations organizationwide to capitalize on SFP.

It should be noted that, although King's plantwide expectation experiment and Crawford et al.'s Pygmalion-at-Sea project both produced positive expectancy effects, they tested two very different expectancy-raising interventions. King got managers to believe in the productive potential of an organizational innovation, whereas Crawford et al. got managers to believe in the productive potential of individual subordinates. King convinced managers to expect productivity gains or not to expect such gains in a *five-minute* procedure in which they were not informed that their expectations were being manipulated. In contrast, Crawford and his colleagues enlightened supervisors and subordinates about SFP and related issues by investing a total of *eight-and-a-half days* in expectation raising and skill training. Crawford et al. thereby presumably raised supervisors' expectations concerning both their subordinates' potential to improve and their own potential to get their subordinates to improve their performance. Unfortunately, expectations were not measured in either experiment, and the performance measures are not readily comparable. King's five-minute expectation manipulation, coupled with enlargement or rotation, increased actual daily output by about fifteen-hundred units, or between 7 percent and 8 percent plantwide in two plants, whereas at best the Navy's eight-and-a-half days of intervention and training raised supervisors' subjective assessments of eight (seven of the original fifteen low performers who began the program were discharged from the Navy before the posttest measurement was conducted) subordinates' performance by a statistically significant amount. Thus, King's experiment seems to have had a much greater impact on productivity at a fraction of the cost of the Navy program. The difference between these two approaches is reminiscent of Lewin's (1951) principle that it is easier to change individuals' behavior by changing group norms than by trying to change each individual's attitudes. King's plant-level intervention may have capitalized on that principle.

The Forward Treatment Center: An Organization Designed to Shape Expectations

A different approach to organizationwide expectancy effects was applied in an entirely different setting with remarkable results. Noy, Solomon, and Benbenishti (1983) compared the relative effectiveness of forward- versus rear-echelon treatment centers to which Israeli soldiers diagnosed as combat psychiatric casualties were evacuated during the 1982 conflict in Lebanon. Noy and his colleagues were attempting to test the effectiveness of treatment principles that had been learned from earlier war experience of the British, French, and American armies. The key elements in the treatment of combat reactions are "immediacy, proximity, and expectancy," according to which treatment should begin immediately, in close geographical proximity to the battlefield, and should foster and maintain expectations of a quick return to the front. The ultimate criterion of success in treating combat reaction is the proportion of evacuees that return to their units to resume combat duties. In the Lebanon conflict, IDF casualties of equivalent severity were evacuated to forward or rear centers solely on the basis of "local tactical and technical conditions" rather than medical considerations. Therefore, the effectiveness of the two types of treatment centers could be compared.

The differences were dramatic. The forward treatment centers succeeded in returning 59 percent of those treated to their units compared to a return rate of only 39 percent in the rear treatment centers. As the authors pointed out, "proximity is not merely geographic. It is also a state of mind, a part of the expectancy set" (p. 7). In the forward treatment centers, the positive expectancy that the soldiers will return to their units is maintained in the minds of both the professional workers and the soldiers they treat by their proximity to the battlefield and by other props that keep their minds near the front. The forward treatment centers are army compounds in which all personnel wear uniforms, have daily reveille at dawn, bear arms, guard the perimeter of the base, maintain military discipline respecting the chain of command, and in general carry on their daily activities in accordance with all the familiar accouterments of military routine. In contrast, the atmosphere in the rear treatment centers resembles that of a civilian medical facility and is more conducive to the maintenance of illness behavior. Personnel don civilian garb, use no military ranks, and have little to remind them of their actual status as soldiers.

Noy and his colleagues provided an especially dramatic example of the manner in which atmosphere, organizational climate, or a "culture" of expectancy can influence success. Two IDF treatment units located in the northern part of Israel were situated only two-hundred meters apart geographically, but very far apart psychologically. One was a rear-echelon treatment center and the other was established next to the first as a makeshift forward treatment center for soldiers airlifted from the front. Although the soldiers sent to both centers had comparable symptoms, the one defined as a forward treatment center returned a much higher percentage of evacuees to their units, as expected. Thus, since the geographical propinquity of the two centers to each other and their equal distance from the front could not account for the difference in success rates, the inescapable conclusion is that the expectations conveyed by the staff and the various symbolic arrangements in the organizational environment profoundly influence the ultimate success of the treatment center in accomplishing its mission. When staff, style, symbols, and routine all join in creating an atmosphere that conveys a particular expectancy, its effects can be overpowering. In later chapters we will explore more examples of organizationwide expectancy effects and the high-expectancy culture that mediates them.

Pitfalls on the Way to Raising Expectations

Not every attempt to raise performance expectations will succeed. Particularly, when supervisors have personal knowledge of subordinate competence and productivity, their expectations become resistant to change and require information that is especially convincing and credible. Sutton (1986) recently reported an unsuccessful attempt to produce a Pygmalion effect among retail sales personnel. The fact that she did not obtain confirmatory findings highlights some potential pitfalls in willfully creating expectation effects.

Sutton herself was introduced to the sales managers in two department stores as being from corporate headquarters. She presented a personality test described as "similar to those used successfully by insurance companies to identify individuals with exceptional sales potential." She told them that "the test had been used by a limited number of retail stores, with a 93 percent success rate in identifying employees with high sales potential," and that headquarters "was attempting to validate the test for use in its retail chain" (pp. 53–54). Though intended to raise managers' expectations toward randomly selected subordinates purportedly identified by the test as having exceptional potential, some of the details Sutton provided could have aroused doubts in the managers' minds regarding the usefulness of the information. Many laymen (as well as psychologists) are wary of personality tests. Sales managers might be skeptical about information derived from personality tests found useful by insurance companies but by only a "limited number" of retailers, especially when their own company implies doubt by saying that it is currently trying to validate the test. For the layman, if it needs validation, it might not be any good.

Sutton provided a hint that doubts did indeed arise in the managers' minds: "During the meeting with this researcher, a few sales managers expressed surprise at the names on their list of associates with exceptional potential, and a few asked for information about the test" (p. 54). This remark alludes to an additional pitfall. Apparently, the managers had gotten to know the sales associates before Sutton's attempt to manipulate their expectations. Sutton did not state precisely when she imparted the information concerning "exceptional potential." We know only that the relevant information was given to the sales managers "after the initial hiring was completed" (p. 53), but we do not know *how long* afterward and how much opportunity the managers had had to form their own initial expectations of their subordinates. There is evidence that performance expectations are formed on the basis of very limited acquaintance, can become resistant to change, and then require more than the five-minute test-result manipulation to change them (Brophy 1983; Dusek, Hall & Meyer 1985; Eden 1984; Eden & Shani 1982; Jussim 1986). Finally, Sutton delayed her manipulation check until the *end* of her experiment, and although the independent variable was expectations, none of the four items in the manipulation-check measure directly assessed expectations. For all these reasons, it is doubtful whether Sutton actually did raise her managers' expectations. If expectations were not raised, the Pygmalion hypothesis was not tested.

To summarize, conveying information based on personality, purportedly useful in a different industry and in need of validation, after managers have had direct personal acquaintance with their subordinates, and using delayed, indirect measures of expectations, may each or in combination explain the failure to detect a Pygmalion effect among these sales personnel. One can only concur with Sutton's conclusion that, on the basis of her study, it would be premature to regard the Pygmalion effect as irrelevant for business organizations. Rather, her work is useful for mapping out some of the boundary conditions that must be respected in our attempts to create the effect.

Limitations

The basic message of this book is that raising performance expectations is worthwhile because it boosts output. However, as with every good thing, it has its limits. Like any improvement, if overdone, raising expectations can do more harm than good. Some obvious limitations are discussed briefly below. Others are described in chapter 6, which deals with applications.

Expectation Effects among Women

Beyond the possible reasons for the negative results of Sutton's experiment suggested above, Sutton herself provided an explanation in terms of gender. The salespersons in her experiment were mostly women. There are now experimental findings from three different studies showing that interpersonal expectancy effects are weak or nonexistent among women. Besides Sutton's, these include King's findings in his five miniexperiments as reanalyzed by Rosenthal (1974) and those of our (Eden & Ravid 1981) unsuccessful replication among IDF women, reviewed earlier. Since these negative findings appear to contradict previous findings that women are *more* influenced than are men by the expectations communicated by others, especially in achievement settings (Lenney 1977; O'Leary 1977), it would be prudent to suspend judgment about whether the effect takes place among women. We need more research to learn what conditions limit the effect among women.

We do know that women have lower self-assessed ability and lower performance expectations than men in academic situations, even when they are equally competent (e.g., Vollmer 1986). Knowing this, one would think that women would benefit *more* than men from experimental manipulations or practical interventions designed to raise their self-expectations or self-efficacy. It is possible that raising self-expectancy would indeed promote achievement among women as among men, but that previous attempts to do this failed to boost self-expectancy as intended. The sex difference might be in women's greater resistance to positive information about self-efficacy. It may require a stronger manipulation to get women to raise their expectations. Another possibility is that women as instructors do not discriminate among subordinates on the basis of competency information as men do. Thus, even if the instructors accept the credibility and validity of the information about their trainees' competence, and do expect more, they may not translate their expectations into differential treatment.

Therefore, future SFP research among women should include especially meticulous manipulation checks, as well as measures of instructors' behavior in the eyes of their trainees. If the SFP process is being blocked among women, we should be able to discover where. This knowledge would be useful in two ways. First, we could seek ways of circumventing the blockage to bring the benefits of positive SFP to women. Second, we might uncover a blocking mechanism that would be useful in preventing cases of negative SFP.

It is probably indicative of gender bias that both in the ancient Greek myth and in Shaw's modern play the expecter was a man and the expectee was a woman, and *she* ultimately succumbed to *his* expectations. The problem of the generalization of research findings from males to females is not new to motivation or unique to expectancy effects. Stein and Bailey (1973) have shown that findings from voluminous research on achievement motivation, mostly collected from men, do not readily generalize to women. With the entrance of growing numbers of women into the workforce and into management roles, more research is necessary to examine motivational issues among women, particularly in light of evidence that what we know from past research might not generalize to women. Specifically with regard to SFP at work, we need more studies of women in the role of manager and in the subordinate role, as well as mixed-gender studies.

How Much Should We Expect?

We are no closer to a precise answer to this question now than we were when Korman (1971) wondered "how far we can reasonably push the expectancy effect. It is clear that an asymptote will be reached, but where? How high?" (p. 222). For sure, raising expectations has its limits. High expectations improve performance when they motivate greater effort; too-high expectations are liable to erode the credibility of the source of those expectations, will not raise productivity, and may trigger indifference and even scorn. Unattainable goals can produce demotivating feelings of failure and frustration. What Locke and Latham (1984) wrote about unattainable goals applies as well to unrealistic expectations: ". . . a goal could be perceived as so hard that an individual would not only give up trying to reach it, but would even give up trying to get close to it. Total apathy could result" (p. 23). In Livingston's (1969) early and insightful words, "Managerial expectations must pass the test of reality before they can be translated into performance. . . . Subordinates will not be motivated to maximize productivity unless they consider the boss's high expectations realistic and achieveable. If they are encouraged to strive for unattainable goals, they eventually give up trying and settle for results that are lower than they are capable of achieving" (pp. 84–85). Making the same point in somewhat more general terms, Bandura has stated that "the efficacy judgments that are most functional are probably those that *slightly exceed* what one can do at any given time. Such self-appraisals lead people to undertake realistically challenging tasks and provide motivation for progressive self-development of their capabilities" (1986, 394, italics added). Thus, scholars who have considered the upper limit of effective expectations agree that there is a ceiling above which further raising of expectations would be ineffective or detrimental.

This limitation would seem to hold for any form of expectation raising. It is fruitful to expect people to perform at higher than current levels, for most people know that they can. Yankelovich and Immerwahr (1983) reported that only 27 percent of the workers they surveyed claimed that they were working to the best of their ability. It is reasonable to expect people to use their ability. A high level of expectations is legitimate, and even expected of managers by subordinates. However, it is *not* reasonable to expect people to perform at levels that far exceed their ability. Unattainable expectations do not arouse motivation. Moreover, people should not be expected to put forth supreme effort and do their best all the time. Managers who communicate sky-high performance expectations do so at the risk of losing credibility in the eyes of their subordinates. Thus, in any expectation-raising effort, expectations should be raised to a level that is high, challenging, and difficult to attain, but realistically within reach of the individuals or organizational units so challenged.

Summary

This concludes the review of research on SFP among adults in nonschool organizations. The empirical evidence marshaled shows that positive expectancy effects can be achieved by the following means:

1. Labeling
2. Conveying high expectations to managers
3. Conveying high expectations directly to subordinates
4. Training managers and subordinates in SFP and expectancy effects
5. "Piggybacking" on organizational changes
6. Using physical and psychological props to create a high-expectancy atmosphere

The evidence shows that raising manager expectations culminates in performance gains by improving supervisory leadership and by raising subordinates' levels of self-expectations and motivation. Although the number of studies reviewed is not overwhelming, there is sufficient evidence to justify generalization of what has been found in hundreds of studies of interpersonal expectancy effects in other areas of psychology to the behavior of members of organizations in general. Most of the confirmatory research reviewed above was conducted with military personnel (Babad et al.'s and King's two studies were not) and with trainees (Pygmalion-at-Sea and King's plantwide expectations experiment were not). Nevertheless, there is little reason to doubt that the underlying causal processes that produced SFP effects in these studies operate among personnel in a variety of civilian organizations, Sutton's unsuccessful replication notwithstanding. The psychological processes that underlie SFP at work, and the research that elucidates them, are described in the next two chapters.

There has been a tendency to restrict generalization of Pygmalion. The studies reviewed earlier break the artificial age barrier that has needlessly confined most Pygmalion research to young schoolchildren. Rosenthal and Jacobson had explained why the Pygmalion effect was strongest among the youngest children they studied in terms of their malleability. Livingston invoked the same concept as the basis for his argument that the Pygmalion effect should be strongest among young management trainees. He obviously did not intend to imply the sequitur that young managers are more malleable than the fifth and sixth graders among whom Rosenthal and Jacobson did not find the Pygmalion effect! Babad and his colleagues (Babad 1979, 1980; Babad & Inbar 1981; Babad, Inbar & Rosenthal 1982a) have found personality traits that predispose teachers to accept biasing information and to act on it. However, susceptibility to expectation effects among adults might be as much a function of circumstance as of the expecter's personality or the expectee's maturity. A question that must be answered by further research is, under what circumstances do individuals become more or less susceptible to expectancy effects?

Livingston's argument that susceptibility is especially high when people are just joining the workforce is convincing as far as it goes. Indeed, all of the

Pygmalion-at-Work studies reviewed above involved expectees who were at or close-to the beginning of their careers and at or close to the lowest-level entry points in their organizations. However, this may simply be because it is easier for researchers to gain access to lower-level employees. Moreover, not expecting to find expectancy effects at higher levels in the organization, researchers have not looked there. Where we don't look, we don't find. This is unfortunate. Restricting the search on the basis of research findings to date is premature. Susceptibility to expectations is likely high at critical career junctures beyond the new-employee stage. Furthermore, significant changes in the ebb and flow of organizational events can unfreeze members' expectations. King's plantwide expectations experiment illustrates this. Expectations rise and fall whenever anything of sufficient import happens than can unfreeze them. Such events include being promoted, passed over for promotion, demoted, laid off, fired, or transferred to another team or department; getting a special commendation, citation, or award; switching jobs; experiencing a major change in the technology used on the job; getting a new boss; or getting a special assignment. In short, expectations can be altered by any of the "organization-change events" (Adams 1978) or "critical job events" (Eden 1982, 1990) that have been shown to arouse acute stress. Unfortunately, the direction and degree of change in expectations in the wake of such events is commonly left to chance.

Moreover, off-the-job occurrences, such as critical life events (Dohrenwend & Dohrenwend 1974; Holmes & Rahe 1967) and such major transitions as midlife crisis and midcareer crisis that punctuate many adult lives (Levinson 1978), can also influence job performance expectations. Switching organizations may be a way for a person to break the shackles of crystallized negative expectations, both one's own and those of one's superiors, and get a fresh start with a clean "expectancy slate." The performance decrements that accompany aging might be, at least in part, SFP. Burnout (Freudenberger & Richelson 1980; Jones 1981; Maslach 1982; Pines & Aronson 1981) may be the result of a negative SFP in which a cycle of failure, frustration, despair, and depression fuels, and is fueled by, low self-expectations. Knowing when to expect changes in performance expectations can be of practical value, for being able to anticipate natural changes in expectations might aid managers and consultants in taking preemptive action to prevent performance decrements.

Much past Pygmalion research has cast disadvantaged persons in the role of Galatea. Some seized upon Rosenthal and Jacobson's research as exposing why so many minority schoolchildren perform below their intellectual potential. A particularly appealing practical application of SFP would be to use Pygmalion as a remedial intervention to counteract the cumulative negative effects wrought by the low expectations of teachers and other mentors upon disadvantaged persons (Clark 1963), thereby needlessly, albeit for the most part unintentionally, impeding the full realization of their potential. It is this kind of remedial use of expectation effects that is most frequently contemplated in the education literature. Teacher training efforts have been directed toward this goal (Banuazizi 1981; Greenfield, Banuazizi & Ganon 1979; Nicholsen 1982; Kerman 1979; Terry 1985).

It is no accident that in the first serious attempt to apply the SFP concept at work, the Pygmalion-at-Sea project was designed to improve the motivation and productivity of poor performers with problematic records. Perhaps it was the same remedial impulse that moved both King (1971) and Crawford et al. (1980) to focus their efforts on disadvantaged persons with a history of employment difficulties and poor performance. However, Schrank's (1968) airmen had obtained an average range of scores on the College Entrance Examination Board aptitude test for mathematics, and Livingston's (1969) case material was based on experience with average sales representatives who became outstanding when managed by a supervisor who believed in their ability to excel. Furthermore, Babad's subjects and the trainees in the IDF experiments were above average in aptitude. Thus, although positive expectations *can* be used to compensate for past negative effects, in part to right past wrongs, available evidence shows that individuals who have average and above-average performance records can reap performance gains from raising expectations. Therefore, SFP applications should not be limited to remediation.

We need more research on SFP effects among workers at different career stages, different levels in the organization, and different ages to know what limitations should govern generalizability. Meanwhile, we do know that both the Pygmalion and Galatea effects can be easily produced, and that there can be very substantial effects, both in terms of proportion of variance explained and scale points. The major limitation to raising productivity via deliberate SFP is our imagination. After weaving a conceptual framework to explain SFP in the next three chapters, we shall consider practical ways of creating productive SFP and blocking counterproductive SFP.

3
Expectations, Motivation, and Performance: Why Do Workers Achieve What They Expect?[1]

This chapter and the next present a conceptual model of SFP based on the research reviewed in chapter 2 and on other research findings that aid in understanding the linkages among the variables that play a role in the SFP process at work. The SFP model portrays the psychological processes that underlie interpersonal self-fulfilling prophecies as largely motivational in nature. Understanding these processes is important for appreciating how SFP operates and for contemplating how we might gain control over it. The model is further intended to demythologize SFP by explaining it in terms of plausible processes among familiar variables. Understood in such terms, SFP applications to improve organizational effectiveness become feasible. A brief overview of the model follows. Each part of the model will then be elaborated on in greater detail.

Overview of the SFP Model

The SFP model depicted in figure 3–1 encompasses five interrelated variables enclosed in lettered circles. The circles are connected by seven numbered arrows. The arrows represent the psychological processes that mediate the relationships between the major variables. The process represented by each arrow will be explained next in a separate section.

That special case of SFP known as the Pygmalion effect begins with the manager's performance expectations (circle A). In Pygmalion experiments we know that this is the starting point in the process because the experimenter manipulates manager expectations after controlling all other variables by means of randomization. Expecting a high level of performance from a subordinate, the manager decides, consciously or subconsciously, to allocate (arrow 1) better leadership (circle B) to that subordinate. Better leadership and other managerial behaviors communicate high expectations to the subordinate, who in turn gets the message and is influenced (arrow 2) to raise his own level of self-expectations (circle C). The resulting high level of

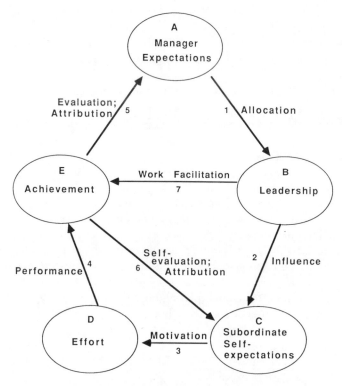

Figure 3–1. A Model of Self-Fulfilling Prophecy at Work

self-expectancy motivates (arrow 3) the subordinate to exert a great deal of effort on the job (circle D). Investing greater effort enhances performance (arrow 4), culminating in high achievement (circle E). Achievement, if visible, has expectancy implications for both the manager and the subordinate. The manager evaluates (arrow 5) the subordinate's achievements against the yardstick of his original expectations, completing the SFP cycle for him. High subordinate achievement justifies the manager's high initial expectations, reinforces them, and fortifies his decision to continue treating the subordinate to the positive leadership with which he favors high achievers, thereby sustaining the productive SFP process. The reinforcement of original expectations and the initiation of another SFP cycle are especially likely to occur when the manager attributes the subordinate's success to the subordinate's ability. Arrow 5 in figure 3–1 corresponds to arrow 3 in figure 1–1. Both represent the reinforcement, or closure, that the prophet gets from seeing his prophecy fulfilled.

Simultaneously, the subordinate perceives his own high achievement, since he assesses the achievements resulting from his performance (arrow 6). If he thinks he has done well, his high self-evaluation reinforces his own high self-expectations, particularly if he attributes his success to his own ability. Reinforcement of his own high self-expectations sustains his motivation and contributes to the perpetuation of the positive SFP process.

SFP at work can transpire independently of the subordinate's motivation. Arrow 7 represents the direct impact of the manager's leadership on subordinate achievement. The triangle formed by circles A, B, and E embodies the variables involved in managerial SFP that does not operate via subordinate motivation. This is the "Pygmalion triangle." For example, by devoting more time and attention to a subordinate expected to do well, a manager facilitates that subordinate's performance *irrespective of any motivational response on the part of the subordinate.* There are innumerable ways in which managers facilitate their subordinates' performance that can be understood without recourse to explanations in terms of subordinate motivation: by instructing subordinates in labor-saving methods, proper tool operation and maintenance, effective sales tactics, and analytical skills; by careful scheduling, planning, and removal of unnecessary obstacles that hinder performance; by quickly solving operational problems that arise so as to prevent them from diverting subordinates' efforts from doing their jobs; by "running interference" to buffer subordinates from actions by the surrounding bureaucracy that might otherwise impede the subordinates' performance; by serving as a shock absorber in handling changes from outside the unit in ways that reduce their distracting reverberations on the work of the subordinates. In short, by giving those expected to do well the best the manager can muster in terms of the administrative and technical aspects of his job, he is being instrumental in promoting their effectiveness more than that of subordinates not expected to do so well.

These effective manager behaviors are the supervisory leadership behaviors labeled "work facilitation" by Bowers and Seashore (1966). Items used to measure work facilitation in Bowers and Seashore's leadership scale include "Shows you how to improve your performance," "Helps you plan ahead," and "Offers ideas for solving problems on the job." Work facilitation was one of the leadership factors that we found mediated the Pygmalion effect in the IDF combat experiment. Arrow 7 is therefore called the work facilitation process, and the triangle formed by the supervisor's expectations, leadership, and achievement is dubbed the Pygmalion triangle.

The same relationships hold for the case of negative SFP, or the Golem effect, except that it begins with initially *low* manager expectations. Low manager expectations cause the manager to provide less favorable leadership and to communicate low expectations to the subordinate. As a consequence, the subordinate expects less of himself, develops a lower level of motivation, exerts less effort, performs at a lower level, and achieves less. Observing these low achievements reinforces the depressed performance expectations of both manager and subordinate and sustains the Golem effect. This negative SFP is more likely to occur when both the manager and the subordinate attribute failure to stable, internal traits of the subordinate—for example, low ability.

The "Galatea triangle" is formed by circles C, D, and E in figure 3–1. It depicts the Galatea variant of SFP. In a controlled experiment, the Galatea effect begins with high subordinate expectations. All other variables are neutralized as potential causes of the outcomes of the experiment by random assignment of subjects to expectancy conditions. Raising subordinates' self-expectations motivates intensification of effort, which enhances performance and yields high achievement. High achievement reinforces the subordinate's self-expectations and sustains the SFP process.

The processes encompassed by the Galatea triangle operate whether or not the manager transmits expectations to the subordinate. Even an unsupervised worker is exposed to performance expectations from a variety of sources. Besides the subordinate's knowledge of his own level of achievement and feedback from his immediate supervisor, there are other cues, not shown in the SFP model in figure 3–1, that impinge upon the subordinate and influence his self-expectations. These influences emanate from co-workers, clients, the organization's culture, and other sources that will be detailed in chapter 5.

Figure 3–1 thus depicts two variants of SFP at work; that is, the Pygmalion effect and the Galatea effect. However, although they can be distinguished analytically, in practice the two effects usually become inextricably intertwined. This is because they trigger each other. Initiating a Pygmalion effect by raising a manager's expectations toward a subordinate sets in motion the process represented by the Pygmalion triangle. Eventually, because of the effect of the subordinate's performance on his own self-expectations (arrow 6), the subordinate will be drawn into the process and the entire SFP model depicted in figure 3–1 will be operative. Then the SFP can become self-sustaining, as the process encompassed by the Galatea triangle can assume a momentum of its own, without further impetus from the manager. This is the self-sustaining phenomenon we found in the Pygmalion condition in the adjutancy experiment when the original instructors were replaced and the expectancy effects spilled over to the relief instructors whose expectations were not manipulated. Similarly, initiating a Galatea effect by raising subordinate self-expectancy can eventuate in a Pygmalion effect as well, because of arrow 5. Witnessing the impressive achievements of a subordinate whose self-expectations have been raised draws the manager into the process. At this point, both the manager and the subordinate have high expectations regarding the subordinate's performance, and a double-barreled SFP is operating.

The Galatea triangle represents basic psychological processes that can become functionally autonomous. The Galatea effect can be fully explicated without recourse to the manager's expectations and leadership. Omitting the manager from the SFP model leaves intact the core motivational processes set into motion by SFP. These processes are intraindividual rather than inter-personal, and are common to both the Pygmalion and the Galatea effects. Since the manager's role in the Pygmalion effect and in other organizational SFP effects is a major topic in itself, the remainder of this chapter will elaborate on the core intrapsychic processes encompassed by the Galatea triangle. Each portion of the Galatea triangle will be discussed later in a separate section. Discussion of the leadership functions of the manager in producing the Pygmalion effect will be deferred to the next chapter.

Subordinate Self-Expectations ⟶ Effort: The Motivation Process

The key motivational process in the SFP model is depicted in figure 3–2. The theoretical basis for postulating that raising subordinate self-expectations leads to intensification of effort is expectancy theory, which was first applied to work motivation by Vroom (1964). It has since been elaborated on and modified (see Galbraith & Cummings 1967; Graen 1969; Lawler 1971; Pinder 1984; Porter & Lawler 1968). The expectancy theory of work motivation and the Pygmalion-at-Work model have much in common, for they share a key variable—performance expectations. The expectation for a level of performance is the variable after which the expectancy theory of motivation is named; it is also starting point of SFP at work. The expectancy theory of work motivation is most useful in understanding SFP at work because it explains parsimoniously how the Pygmalion and Galatea effects work, with no need for additional theoretical concepts. Furthermore, the Pygmalion paradigm suggests a novel way of applying expectancy theory by raising subordinate expectations, which has been conspicuously neglected even by expectancy theorists. Pygmalion and expectancy theory fit together so well that they appear to have been made for each other.

Figure 3–2. The Motivation Process

Often abbreviated VIE theory, expectancy theory can be concisely expressed by the formula

$$\text{Effort} = E \sum I \cdot V$$

where E stands for expectancy, I for instrumentality, and V for valence. According to expectancy theory, expectancy, instrumentality, and valence combine in the manner described below to determine one's level of motivation to exert effort on the job.

Expectancy. The variable designated E in the expectancy equation is often designated "effort-to-performance expectancy," or simply "expectancy." It represents the level of an individual's self-expectations regarding his own competence to perform. Effort-to-performance expectancy is high for workers who are confident that they can succeed in doing a good job, and low for those expecting little of themselves. Its place in the VIE equation reflects its hypothesized primary role in affecting motivation; the higher the level of effort-to-performance expectancy, other things being equal, the greater the effort that the worker exerts on the job. Expectancy is the key intrapsychic variable in both the Pygmalion and Galatea effects. In VIE theory and research, expectancy is almost always defined in terms of a subjective probability. Subjective probability of success (SPS) is a measure, on a scale ranging from 0 to 1, of the individual's belief concerning the likelihood that, if he invests effort in performing the task, he will succeed in doing a good job.

"If he invests effort" is an indispensable element in the definition of expectancy. The expectation of success in the absence of any effort on one's own part is a different construct. Expecting success without effort does not motivate the exertion of effort. If one is certain that the outcomes will be attained anyway, why exert oneself? Believing in success-without-effort, one sits back and enjoys life, waiting for the desired outcomes to present themselves.

Expecting success without effort is different from effort-to-performance expectancy also in the way it is influenced by experiences of success and failure. Successful performance increases effort-to-performance expectancy and failure reduces it. However, when effort is not perceived as influencing outcomes, failure may *increase* expectations for success. The well-known cognitive illusion called "gambler's fallacy" illustrates this. After five consecutive tails, our expectation is much stronger than the objective probability of .5 that the next flip will result in a head. Every additional roll of the wheel in which his number does not come up increases the gambler's belief that on the next roll his number will win. In reality, of course, the likelihood of the outcome on each spin is constant and is not influenced by previous outcomes. The crucial difference between expectancy in the work motivation and performance context and in the gambler's world is the role of ability and effort. Both count on the job, but neither makes a difference in gambling. Therefore, the expectancy relevant to SFP at work is one's belief that if he invests the *effort,* he will be *able* to do the job.

Instrumentality. Also designated "performance-to-outcome expectancy," instrumentality is defined as the individual's subjective probability that successful job performance will result in his obtaining certain outcomes. Instrumentality can range between a value of $+1.00$, indicating subjective certainty that successful performance will result in attaining a particular outcome," and -1.00, reflecting the individual's certainty that successful performance will result in *not* obtaining some outcome. For example, a worker may expect with a high degree of certainty that successful completion of a particular mission will land him a promotion because everyone who has previously accomplished that mission has been promoted and because his boss has guaranteed him of the promotion if he succeeds. The worker in this instance expects successful performance to be highly instrumental for getting a promotion. An example of negative instrumentality would be in relation to the outcome of having more leisure time to spend with family. Successful performance of the mission and getting promoted will require overtime encroachment on evenings and weekends, such that successful performance will increase the likelihood of *not* obtaining more family leisure time. Thus, instrumentality is high, either positive or negative, when the person believes that his chances of obtaining or not obtaining one or more outcomes is largely contingent upon the level of his performance. Instrumentality is low when performance is perceived as having little bearing on outcomes. In the workplace, piece-rate incentive pay usually augments the instrumentality of job performance because workers know that high performance is instrumental in receiving extra money. Instrumentality is low or nil for outcomes seen as having little or no dependency on job performance. Noncontingent rewards, such as fixed wages and seniority-based promotion schemes, have low instrumentalities.

Valence. The valence of an outcome, which for the sake of consistency can be designated "outcome-to-satisfaction expectancy," is the degree of satisfaction or dissatisfaction that the individual expects to derive from obtaining each particular outcome. Vroom (1964) chose the term valence over "value" to emphasize that it denotes *expected* satisfaction rather than the amount of satisfaction actually experienced (Vroom 1964). (Note that all three variables in the VIE equation are expectations, though only one is labeled "E" for expectancy; that is, performance expectations.) The individual worker's own wants, needs, tastes, and aspirations imbue outcomes with valences. Valence has a wide spread of potential numerical values, ranging from very high positive for outcomes from which the worker expects to derive a great deal of satisfaction, to very high negative valence for outcomes expected to be extremely dissatisfying. Outcomes concerning which the individual is indifferent, expecting neither satisfaction nor dissatisfaction to result from their attainment, have zero valence.

$V \cdot I \cdot E.$ According to the expectancy equation, the instrumentality and the valence of each possible outcome which might result from performance must be multiplied. These products are summed across all relevant outcomes. This sum, $\Sigma I \cdot V$, represents the total amount of satisfaction (or dissatisfaction) that the worker expects to obtain as a consequence of successful performance. This sum is multiplied by the effort-to-performance expectancy to calculate the strength of the motivational force impelling the individual to exert effort to perform the job or to abstain from doing so.

A high instrumentality for an outcome with a high positive valence, as in the case of a much-desired bonus whose payment is known to be contingent upon good performance, will yield a high positive $I \cdot V$ product that will contribute to motivation to exert effort. Similarly, high negative instrumentality for an outcome of high negative valence augments motivation to perform well. An example of the latter is the threat of highly undesirable layoff for poor performance, where good performance has a high negative instrumentality for the aversive outcome of job loss. The high positive $I \cdot V$ product that results from multiplying two high, negative values is a force impelling the worker to invest greater energy in job performance.

Outcomes that have instrumentalities and valences of unlike sign—that is, positive instrumentality and negative valence or vice versa—detract from motivation. For example, if a worker has a strong expectation that superior performance will arouse derision on the part of his co-workers (high positive instrumentality), and expects to be deeply hurt or offended by such derision (high negative valence), the strong negative psychological force that results from multiplying these expectancies will weaken his motivation to exert effort to improve his performance. Similarly, negative instrumentality and positive valence, such as in the case of the worker who would have to give up potentially satisfying leisure-time pursuits to perform successfully, result in a demotivating negative force.

The central hypothesis of expectancy theory is that, other things being equal, the more an individual expects that a) effort will culminate in successful performance and that b) successful performance will bring attractive outcomes that promise satisfaction and avoid dissatisfying outcomes, the greater the effort he will choose to invest in performing the job. The model of SFP at work borrows the E from the VIE formulation and uses it as the precursor of its motivational link (arrow 3 in figure 3–1). Thus, the expectancy theory of work motivation and the model of SFP at work are consistent and compatible with each other. VIE theory helps explain how SFP works. Positive SFP at work is productive because high expectations augment the motivation to spur the effort to increase productivity. Negative SFP involves low performance expectations that dampen motivation, eventuating in depressed productivity. Linking VIE and SFP also opens the door to novel ways of applying VIE theory to problems of work motivation by creating SFP.

Virtually all statements of VIE theory cast the motivation issues in terms of choice. The dependent variable predicted by the VIE equation is the magnitude of the psychological force operating on the individual to *choose* to invest a particular level of effort in job performance. This focus on choice, together with the exclusive reliance on the subjective probability of success as *the* measure of expectancy, imposes serious limitations on theories of work motivation and creates unnecessary difficulties in empirical expectancy research. The Pygmalion research overcomes some of these problems. Appendix 3A discusses these issues, proposes an alternative way to think of work motivation without recourse to choice as a mediator between the VIE predictors and effort, and proposes alternatives to SPS for measuring expectancy. Appendex 3B presents an attempt to resolve the long-standing contradictory hypotheses derived from expectancy theory and from the theory of achievement motivation.

Neglect of Expectancy. Effort-to-performance expectancy in VIE theory is special in several respects. A crucial implication of the VIE model is that, no matter how strongly a worker craves certain outcomes and no matter how great his belief that successful performance is the means for obtaining those prized outcomes, he will exert little effort in performance if he lacks confidence in his likelihood of success. Otherwise powerful and appealing incentives lose their work-motivating potential for workers who do not believe they can do a good job. The best designed incentive schemes come to naught with such workers.

Operationally, expectancy is unique in that for any given task there is only one value of expectancy. There may be any number of instrumentality and valence values, depending on the number of outcomes associated with the particular task, which must be multiplied so that their products can be summed. That sum is then multiplied by expectancy to yield the predicted strength of the force impelling the individual to exert effort. Having only one value for expectancy means that a sizable error in measuring it will more seriously distort the prediction than will a comparable error in measuring any one of the several instrumentality and valence values, since there are more of them.

However, despite its prime theoretical and practical importance in the VIE formulation, effort-to-performance expectancy is unique among the three expectancies also in that it has been the least researched experimentally in organizations, and probably the least applied in work settings. For example, in their comprehensive review of VIE research, Campbell and Pritchard (1976) summarized numerous studies of instrumentality and valence. But only two experimental studies of expectancy were cited! Although correlational and cross-sectional studies have shown that expectations and achievement are positively related (e.g., Berlew & Hall 1966; Kopelman & Thompson 1976; Stedrey & Kay 1966), the nonexperimental methods used in such research render it impossible to determine unequivocally whether high expectations caused high performance or vice versa. Direction of causality is crucial in contemplating the application of any relationship.

Considering practical application, a consultant familiar with the body of available VIE research can readily advise managers how to raise instrumentality and valence to improve motivation. Obvious examples are linking pay, promotion, praise, intrinsically interesting assignments, and other rewards to performance to strengthen instrumentality, and individually tailoring the benefits package and other, less tangible, rewards to suit the employee's particular needs and preferences to augment valence. These and similar techniques have been with us for some time as accepted partial solutions of motivational problems at work.

But what of performance expectations, the E in the VIE formulation? Effort-to-performance expectancy is the variable for which "expectancy theory" is named. Nevertheless, expectancy has been blatantly neglected. Current theory and research findings on work motivation offer no practical guidance to the manager or consultant who wants to boost motivation when instrumentality and valence are at satisfactory levels, but expectancy is unacceptably low. The applied organizational research literature has been mute on this issue. Even those who have given performance expectations a central role in their approach to work motivation (e.g., Korman 1970, 1976) provide no practical advice about how to raise expectations. It is left to the practitioner's wits to translate the relationship between expectations and performance into specific actions that will profitably motivate workers. The Pygmalion paradigm breathes content into this vacuum in work motivation theory and practice by addressing the crucial issue of raising performance expectations.

One typical way of neglecting effort-performance expectancy in VIE research has been to fold it into instrumentality, paying it lip service but bypassing it in the actual research. For example, Porter and Lawler (1968) presented an integrative theoretical model of work motivation that includes "Perceived Effort ——▶ Reward Probability" as a major variable. Under the heading "Effort-Reward Probability," they defined it as:

> An individual's expectations concerning the likelihood that given amounts of rewards depend upon given amounts of effort on his part. Such an expectation can in turn be divided into two subsidiary expectations: 1. The probability that *reward* depends upon *performance*. 2. The probability that *performance* depends upon *effort*. Frequently, theoretical presentations that invoke

the concept of probability or expectancy of reward in explaining job performance fail to note the fact that these two distinct components are involved.
We hypothesize that the two subsidiary probabilities are related in an interactive way . . . (p. 19).

However, in their test of their model, these researchers failed even to *measure*
effort-performance expectancy! They reported "particularly high correlations" among three items designed to measure their respondents' perceptions
of the importance of job performance in determining their pay, and inferred
from these correlations that effort-performance expectancy played no role in
their respondents' motivation:

> The model points out that the probability that effort will lead to rewards is
> a product of the probability that effort will lead to performance and the prob-
> ability that performance will lead to reward. This led us to expect a some-
> what lower correlation among these items. Judging from the high corre-
> lations actually found in the present study, it appears that these managers
> did not distinguish between the probability that effort leads to pay and the
> probability that performance leads to pay. This would indicate that for them
> the concern about whether effort was likely to result in performance was
> not a major consideration, and that the major consideration was whether
> performance would result in pay (p. 69).

Thus, Porter and Lawler first paid lip service to effort-performance expectancy
by including it in their model, then neglected to measure it in their empirical
test of the model, and ended up inferring from their data on performance-pay
expectancy and effort-pay expectancy that effort-performance expectancy
"was not a major consideration" for their respondents! Thus, a careful reading of their report reveals that Porter and Lawler eloquently obscured their
neglect of effort-performance expectancy, even while claiming to take it into
account and demonstrate its unimportance. As for many other interpreters of
expectancy theory, for Porter and Lawler expectancy actually appears to have
boiled down to the expectation of obtaining rewards.

Interestingly, expectancy has been slow to get the attention it deserves in
other areas of applied psychology in which the aim is to produce some change
in performance. For example, expectancy plays a central role in Bandura's
(1977, 1986) social learning theory. Two of Bandura's key concepts are self-
efficacy expectations, also called simply self-efficacy, and outcome expectancy, sometimes called response-outcome expectations. These two expectancy concepts highly overlap with the VIE concepts of effort-to-performance
expectancy and instrumentality, respectively. "Perceived self-efficacy is a
judgment of one's capability to accomplish a certain level of performance,
whereas an outcome expectation is a judgment of the likely consequence such
behavior will produce" (Bandura 1986, 391). Bandura pointed to the neglect

of self-efficacy expectations, saying that "virtually all of the theorizing and experimentation has focused on action–outcome expectations" (1977, 204). Nevertheless, "perceived self-efficacy predicts performance much better than expected outcomes" (Bandura 1986, 393).

To redress the neglect by organizational researchers of the concept of self in general, and of self-expectancy in particular, Brief and Aldag (1981) briefly reviewed Bandura's work and proposed incorporating these important concepts in our theories and research on work organizations. Nevertheless, the only approach to work motivation that currently adopts an activist stance toward expectancy is the Pygmalion paradigm. No other management model advocates deliberately raising performance expectations, leaving a rich wellspring of work motivation untapped.

An exception to the rule of neglect of expectations is the use of expectancy-enhancing techniques in psychotherapy and counseling (Coe 1980; Kanfer & Gaelick 1986; Kanfer and Goldstein 1986; Tinsley, Bowman & Ray 1988). The quality of much of the research on the impact of expectancy manipulations in these settings has not been very good (see Tinsley et al. 1988 for a critical review). Nevertheless, some clinical psychologists have applied Bandura's proposals for raising client self-efficacy expectations in psychotherapy (Goldfried & Robins 1982). Bandura's concepts and the clinical applications are relevant for raising expectancy among workers, and can inspire management innovations designed to raise workers' performance expectations. The manager's role in raising expectations will be explored in detail in the next chapter.

To summarize, self-expectancy is the crux of motivation, at least according to VIE theory, which is the most broadly supported cognitive theory of work motivation. Self-expectancy is also pivotal in SFP. To date, most approaches to both SFP and work motivation have regarded expectancy as a variable to be taken as is. The Pygmalion approach is unique in proposing that expectations be deliberately raised. Pygmalion applications seek to harness the analytic power of expectancy theory by devising ways of raising expectations to enhance work motivation and boost productivity. However, before rushing to applications, it is necessary to clarify several additional conceptual issues concerning the nature of expectancy.

State versus Trait Expectancy

State Expectancy. Vroom's (1964) definition of expectancy held it to be a fleeting characteristic of a situation. In Vroom's words, "An expectancy is defined as *a momentary belief* concerning the likelihood that a particular act will be followed by a particular outcome" (1964, 17, italics added). In the case of E in the VIE model, the "particular act" is exerting effort in task performance and the "particular outcome" is successful performance. In the wake of Vroom's influential book, expectancy has typically been treated in the work motivation literature as a situational variable that rises and falls in response to varying situational characteristics, primarily task difficulty. Such labile expectations can be called "state expectancy," implying a temporary belief about future performance in a particular situation. Such beliefs change as circumstances change. Originally, Vroom's expectancy was a cognition about *self in a situation.* However, over the years there has been a subtle shift toward a more situationalist conceptualization.

As an example of how utterly situational expectancy is thought of by motivation scholars, consider Pinder's (1984) recommendation that personnel be assigned to jobs for which they are trained. Otherwise, "their expectancy perceptions will be low, and we will not expect to see them trying to perform" (p. 149). Use of the phrase "expectancy perceptions" alerts us to his view of expectancy as something that the individual perceives in his environment. Pinder goes on to mention the machinery and equipment, staff, and budget as necessary preconditions for positive expectancy, and warns that "countless practical factors can combine to make it very difficult for any supervisor to accurately estimate the expectancy beliefs held by particular employees about specific jobs; accordingly they make it difficult for supervisors to fully implement the implications that follow from the expectancy component of VIE Theory" (p. 150). In other words, for Pinder, as for most work motivation scholars, expectancy is an individual's perception of the situation rather than a belief about himself. Hence expectancy is treated as alterable by targeting the *situation,* rather than the *individual,* for change. Pinder goes on to discuss the manager's role in influencing expectancy strictly in terms of altering task difficulty (p. 276ff).

VIE theory's heavy emphasis on the immediate situation can be traced to the pervasive influence of Lewinian field theory on Vroom's thinking. In particular, overemphasis of Lewin's (1951) principle of contemporaneity, according to which only variables represented in the individual's present consciousness can have any impact on present behavior, has distracted attention from stable expectations formed in the distant past. Citing Lewin (1935), Vroom wrote: "The choices made by a person in a given situation are explained in terms of his motives and cognitions at the time he makes the choice. The process by which these motives or cognitions were acquired is not specified nor is it regarded as crucial to a consideration of their present role in behavior" (1964, 14). Lewin's call for a combination of ahistorical and historical approaches to the study of behavior, also cited by Vroom, has not received adequate attention. Conceiving of expectancy as a situational variable that changes with situational fluctuations does not take into account the fact that individuals in the *same* situation differ in their level of expectancy. One's present level of expectations is undoubtedly influenced by past successes and failures, even at moments when those past events are not specifically recalled. Obviously, a person with low expectations in a particular situation does not harbor these low expectations by conjuring up memories of all the past failures that have contributed to their creation.

Similarly, Bandura (1977, 1986) has conceived of self-efficacy as situation-specific. He has defined it as "people's judgments of their capabilities to organize and execute courses of action required to attain designated types of performances. It is concerned not with the skills one has but with judgments of what one can do with whatever skills one possesses" (1986, 391). Variably called an expectancy, a belief, a percept, and a judgment, Bandura's self-efficacy concept is hardly distinguishable from expectancy in VIE theory. Several authors (for example, Gist 1987; Locke et al. 1984) have pointed out that Bandura's self-efficacy is somewhat broader in scope than effort-performance expectancy in VIE theory. "Efficacy involves a generative capability in which cognitive, social, and behavioral subskills must be organized into integrated courses of action to serve innumerable purposes" (Bandura 1986, 391). Notwithstanding the conceptual differences between expectancy and efficacy, Locke et al. (1984) found that efficacy-performance correlations and expectancy-performance correlations were very similar. Thus, expectancy and self-efficacy may be regarded as practically equivalent.

Nevertheless, it is clear that for Bandura self-efficacy is not a global capacity. He insists that it is specific to a particular situation: "In comparative studies, particularized measures of self-percepts of efficacy surpass global measures in explanatory and predictive power . . ." (p. 397). For this reason, he eschews the concept of generalized self-efficacy and he has not developed a generalized measure of self-efficacy. However, he has not been consistent on this point. He recently described his central construct in terms of "particularized self-percepts of efficacy that may vary across activities and circumstances, rather than in terms of a global disposition assayed by an omnibus test" (Bandura 1986, 396). However, in the same chapter he allowed that "once established, enhanced self-efficacy tends to generalize to other situations" (1986, 399). As Kirsch (1986) concluded in his review, an unresolved issue in the expectancy literature is how much generalization occurs across situations and the dimensions and degree of similarity in circumstances required as preconditions for generalization.

Kirsch has gone so far as to claim that Bandura's term *self-efficacy* "is somewhat misleading. It appears to refer only to people's perception of their abilities, but in fact is codetermined by their perception of the nature and difficulty of the task" (1986, 355). Kirsch proposes the term "expectancy for success in achievement situations."

The situationalist orientation of expectancy-related concepts is so strong that even self-esteem, which also "sounds like" a trait, is defined as a state when theorists distinguish specific self-esteem from global self-esteem (Brockner 1988). Thus, VIE, goal-setting, need-achievement theory, and social learning theory all define expectancy as a momentary state determined by situational factors—that is, state-expectancy.

Trait-Expectancy. Situational theory falls short of explaining the perpetually high motivation of someone who maintains consistently high performance expectations, and the chronically low motivation that results from persistently low expectations. Nor can state-expectancy explain individual differences in initial expectations for performing the *same* task. The relatively stable level of characteristically high or low performance expectations that an individual carries around from situation to situation is the product of previous experiences of success and failure. This can be dubbed "trait expectancy." The classical approach to level of aspiration (Rotter 1943, 1945) eventually gave rise to thinking of generalized expectancies as stable personality traits (Zuroff & Rotter 1985). A person with high trait expectancy has relatively high performance expectations in most any situation. Low trait expectancy is associated with relatively low self-expectations across varied situations. Trait-expectancy is a cognition about self-competence in achievement situations in general; state-expectancy is a cognition about achievement in a specific, ability-related situation. Trait-expectancy is relatively invariant across situations, whereas state-expectancy varies across situations. State-expectancy is influenced by accumulated past successes and failures, even at moments when such events are not recalled. That is, trait-expectancy is one of the factors that influence state-expectancy. A person does not harbor low expectations in a particular situation by conjuring up memories of all the failures that contributed to their creation. Rather, they are the residue of past failures that has assumed an autonomous existence in the landscape of the individual's semi-permanent traits. As such, past experiences *are* part of one's life space and *do* influence one's present behavior.

Trait-expectancy has been ignored by work-motivation theorists even more than state-expectancy. This is an instance of the general neglect of personality by organization scholars (Weiss & Adler 1984). Fortunately, interest in trait-expectancy among management scholars is growing (Gist 1987). Brockner's (1988) comprehensive discussion of the maintenance and enhancement of general self-esteem at work is an example. Outside the realm of management and organizational behavior, personality investigators who conceive of self-efficacy as a stable trait have constructed and validated self-report measures of generalized self-efficacy (Sherer & Adams 1983; Sherer, Maddux, Mercandante, Prentice-Dunn, Jacobs & Rogers 1982; Tipton & Worthington 1984). These scales appear to have high content validity as measures of trait-expectancy in work motivation research. Nevertheless, except for the Pygmalion paradigm, work motivation programs designed to enhance state *or* trait-expectancy have not been proposed.

Trait- and State-Expectancy. Some scholars have been arguing over a trait versus state interpretation of expectancy and self-efficacy without considering the possibility that both interpretations are useful. Neither conceptualization is exhaustive, nor are they mutually exclusive. Debating whether expectancy is a trait *or* a state should give way to granting that it is *both.* Then the relationship between them, and the differential relationships of each with other constructs, could be pursued. Including both trait and state concepts would give both historical and ahistorical determinants, respectively, their due weight in explaining motivated behavior (Lewin 1935). Therefore, we should distinguish between trait-expectancy—relatively stable, generalized beliefs about self-competence in achievement situations—and state-expectancy—momentary beliefs about future performance in specific, ability-related achievement situations—and encompass both expectancies in our models of work motivation.

Simultaneously considering both state- and trait-expectancy is consistent with current social psychological research on self-concept. For example, Markus and Kunda (1986) have argued convincingly that one's self-concept is both stable *and* malleable: "Although the self-concept is in some ways quite stable, this stability can mask significant local variations that arise when the individual responds systematically to events in the social environment" (p. 859). In their laboratory experiment, Markus and Kunda measured subjects' self-concept, exposed them to social situations designed to influence their self-concept, and then remeasured self-concept. They found evidence for both stability and malleability inasmuch as the basic structure of the self-concept remained unchanged, but there were temporary alterations in self-perception as a function of the situational variation. Markus and Kunda concluded that

> the self-concept should not be viewed as a monolithic entity or even as a generalized average sense of the self that is carried around from one situation to another. Instead, the self-concept is more productively viewed as a space . . . or a system . . . of self-conceptions. From this set of self-conceptions, the individual constructs a working self-concept that integrates the core self-conceptions with those elicited by the immediate context (p. 865).

Markus and Kunda call for measures of the self-concept that reflect both stable self-conceptions as well as momentary fluctuations in the self-concept in response to self-relevant changes in the environment. The present call for studying both trait- and state-expectancy in work situations is grounded in the same approach as that of Markus and Kunda.

Somewhat ahead of his time, without dwelling upon the relative virtues of state- versus trait-expectancy, Korman (1970, 1976) incorporated both into his model of work motivation. He defined self-esteem as the extent to which a person sees himself "as a competent, need-satisfying individual."

Differences in self-esteem are said to arise from three sources. First, there is "a relatively persistent level of self-esteem . . . that occurs relatively consistently across various situations." This is trait-expectancy. "Second, one's self-perceived competence concerning a particular task or job may vary as a result of differential learning experiences, or the specific characteristics of the moment" (1976, 51). This is state-expectancy. Korman went on to define others' expectations as a third source of self-esteem. Thus, for Korman, both stable personality traits *and* changing situational factors produce the levels of expectancy that influence work motivation. Rather than engaging in an extended debate over whether self-efficacy is useful only as a particularized concept, it would be more fruitful to build on Korman's work to devise a testable model incorporating both global and particularized self-efficacy— that is, trait- and state-expectancies. More recently, working in the goal-setting tradition, Hollenbeck and Klein (1987) have included self-esteem as a "personal factor" antecedent to "expectancy of goal attainment" (state-expectancy), which in turn is hypothesized to influence goal commitment. Hollenbeck and Klein did not propose purposeful raising of expectations.

The concepts of generalized self-efficacy, global self-esteem, and trait-expectancy all refer to a relatively constant degree of success an individual believes he is capable of attaining in performing across a wide variety of situations, tasks, and occasions. For the sake of simplicity and clarity, in he following discussion these largely synonymous constructs are dubbed "trait-expectancy." Particularized self-efficacy, specific self-esteem, and state-expectancy all refer to a person's belief that he can attain success in performing in a particular situation. These concepts are labeled "state-expectancy."

Trait-expectancy refers to one's belief about one's competency in achievement situations in general, whereas state expectancy refers to what one believes about one's performance in a particular situation in the near future. Trait-expectancy is relatively invariant across different situations, whereas state expectancy varies within the individual across situations. For example, a person high on trait-expectancy will expect to perform both a difficult task and an easy task better than will a person low on trait-expectancy, but both will expect to perform better on the easier task than on the difficult task. What level of performance a person momentarily expects (state-expectancy) is therefore influenced by both internal (trait-expectancy) and situational factors (task difficulty, quality of supervision, adequacy of resources, etc.). Thus, trait-expectancy has some, but not sole, influence on state-expectancy. Persons with high trait-expectancy will not expect to do well in a situation in which circumstances stack the deck against them, and even those with low trait-expectancy will expect to succeed in favorable situations that appear to pose no challenge to their competence. Distinguishing between trait- and state-expectancy in this way can enrich our understanding of motivation in general and can inform Pygmalion applications.

State-expectancy is pliable and therefore a key to short-term, low-cost attempts to boost work motivation. One task for motivation theorists is to discover which manipulable variables raise state-expectancy. Pygmalion research has demonstrated how expectancy can be raised quickly. Conversely, trait-expectancy is a product of a lifetime of experience in many situations, and is unlikely to be amenable to rapid change under short-lived circumstances. Therefore, trait-expectancy should not be targeted for short-term intervention. However, Pygmalion experiments, which manipulate state-expectancy to improve performance, should include a measure of trait-expectancy. This would enable the experimenter to include trait-expectancy in analysis of the results to determine how trait-expectancy interacts with state-expectancy. This analysis would provide an answer to the question of whether raising state-expectancy equally affects individuals with high and low trait-expectancy.

A practical implication of the distinction between trait- and state-expectancy concerns the different means that have to be employed to raise performance expectations. Management can limit itself to dealing with workers as the products of their prior socialization and concentrate its efforts on creating working conditions that are conducive to high state-expectancy. But this would be wasting the additional potential that could be realized by enhancing trait-expectancy. Only short-term, situation-specific gains can be obtained by raising state-expectancy and ignoring trait-expectancy. Easy gains may fade fast. Laboratory experiments, which often are over in a few minutes, cannot influence trait-expectancy. However, expectancy manipulations in Pygmalion experiments and goal setting in field experiments can affect trait-expectancy as well as state-expectancy and performance, since these experiments last for weeks or months.

By raising trait-expectancy, a longer lasting motivational effect can be achieved. Such an effect might generalize to a wider array of circumstances than the limited conditions under which it was originally created. Certainly trait-expectancy is harder to raise than is state-expectancy, as relatively stable personality traits are, by definition, more resistant to change than are characteristics of jobs, roles, and tasks. For example, it is easier to raise state-expectations by making a task perceptibly easier or by providing additional resources than it is to raise trait-expectancy by strengthening an employee's self-esteem. However, once achieved, a change in a stable trait has a more enduring impact on motivation. To increase motivation by raising trait-expectancy, managers must persist in consistently treating subordinates in ways that boost their self-esteem or sense of competence and mastery. This involves a prolonged program of arranging repeated experiences of success and guiding the employee's attributions of success and failure. In short, this calls for the manager to fulfill the role of Pygmalion.

Figure 3–3 shows that subordinate state-expectancy is influenced by the manager's leadership behavior and by the subordinate's level of trait-

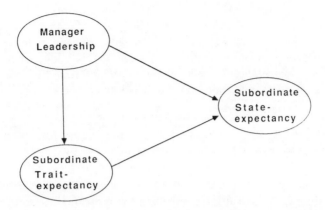

Figure 3–3. **Relationships among Manager Leadership, Subordinate Trait-Expectancy, and Subordinate State-Expectancy**

expectancy. Thus, a worker's current level of expectations in a particular situation is influenced by his generalized trait-expectancy as well as by what level of expectations his supervisor communicates. The broken arrow from leadership to trait-expectancy represents the eventual impact of consistent, Pygmalion-style, esteem-building leadership on trait-expectancy. The broken line is intended to convey that this is a more elusive effect that will result only from persistent, consistent supervisory efforts to guide the subordinate through a graduated program of successive success experiences and assure confidence-enhancing attributions.

The Pygmalion effect can thus be thought of as occurring on two different levels. When managers change subordinates' state-expectancies, a superficial, and possibly only temporary, Pygmalion effect may result. Enhancing subordinates' trait-expectancy can create a more enduring effect. Fairly consistent build-up of small successes by repeatedly having positive expectations fulfilled can spill over to trait-expectancy. The ego-enhancement enjoyed by a worker who experiences a string of successes probably contributes more to self-esteem than direct attempts by management to influence the individual's traits. Managers need not—indeed, *should* not—attempt directly to alter their subordinates' personalities. Managerial talent would be better used by training managers to arrange the conditions on the job to foster sustained, successful performance and to make these successes salient to workers through constructive feedback and attributions, thereby raising low expectations and maintaining high expectations. Martinko and Gardner (1987) have discussed the role of management in raising achievement expectations by fostering productive attributions and inhibiting potentially counterproductive ones. The U.S. Navy's Pygmalion-at-Sea project (Crawford et al. 1980) has been the most ambitious attempt to date to apply this type of approach. The role of management in raising both trait- and state-expectations for future achievement by fostering productive attributions and self-esteem and inhibiting potentially counterproductive ones is discussed further in chapters 4 and 6.

To simplify exposition, in the remainder of this book, when the word *expectancy* or *expectation* is used alone with no modifier, it will denote state-expectancy. When stable trait-expectancy is intended, the word *trait* will be added.

Effort ⟶ Achievement: The Performance Process

The dependent variable predicted by the three expectancy variables in VIE theory is the psychological force impelling the individual to exert effort, not actual performance. Numerous studies that have attempted to predict job performance from motivation have yielded only modest results. The proportion of variance in performance explained by the VIE model has typically been small (see review of research by Campbell and Pritchard 1976). Consequently, most researchers have come to expect a theory of motivation to predict effort rather than performance. Predicting effort rather than performance makes theoretical sense, as strong motivation should make a person try harder. However, the extent to which intensification of effort culminates in higher performance depends on additional variables that are not necessarily related to motivation, such as ability, quality of supervision, clarity and difficulty of goals, adequacy of tools, scheduling of work, and organization. Lack of experimental control over these other determinants of performance can explain our inability to predict performance accurately on the basis of motivation alone.

The performance process modeled in figure 3–4 distinguishes between effort, performance, and achievement. Performance is the individual's productive *behavior* on the job. Achievement is *output*, in the form of either products or services, that results from an individual's job performance. When performance is effective, other things being equal, the level of output achieved is high. For example, operating a computer is performance, and the output is what is achieved by means of this performance. Printed reports, listings, addressed envelopes, bills, production schedules, and weighted students' grades are all examples of output. Other things being equal, proper computer operation results in high computer output. Effort is a quality of behavior. An individual may exert a great deal of effort in the attempt to maximize performance, for example, trying hard by concentrating mentally and flexing muscles to get a machine to run right, or only minimal effort. Because of individual differences in ability, one person may have to exert much more effort than another to achieve the same level of output. Other things being equal, investing greater effort improves performance and yields higher achievement (figure 3–4). However, in some jobs, a very able individual can perform well effort-

Figure 3–4. The Performance Process

lessly and achieve extraordinary levels of output despite low motivation, and a very highly motivated person who exerts extraordinary effort can perform well enough in some cases to achieve impressive output despite limited ability.

The reason for emphasizing the relationships among the variables that comprise the performance process is that we often confuse motivation, effort, performance, and achievement at the expense of understanding the motivational determinants of high output. The model in figure 3–1 specifies that the casual chain is motivation $\longrightarrow$ effort $\longrightarrow$ performance $\longrightarrow$ achievement. The difference between motivation and effort is that motivation is an *internal psychological state* that is not subject to direct empirical observation, whereas effort is an *observable characteristic of behavior*. Effort implies that the individual is striving to use his ability in performing his job, and can be measured by comparing the amount of ability a person is using to the amount of ability he has. The difference between effort and performance is that performance is the productive *behavior* in which the individual engages on his job and effort is *how hard he is trying* to perform well. Finally, performance is productive activity, and achievement is the *product* of that activity. To assess performance one must observe behavior, whereas measurement of achievement requires the quantification of output.

It is high levels of achievement among subordinates that management strives to obtain. This is managers' major dependent variable. When they can, they measure output. When they cannot, they make do with the next best thing, which is performance ratings. Performance ratings are often (but not always) considered proxies for the real thing—the level of output achieved.

Omitting ability from further discussion of SFP at work by saying "other things being equal" is not intended to discount its *direct* contribution to performance and output and its *indirect* contribution via its influence on trait-expectancy. It rather implies that ability is not influenced by the motivational process in SFP. The SFP process involves raising subordinates' effort-to-performance expectations. This motivates them better to mobilize their own resources, including whatever actual abilities and other resources they have, and to apply them toward performing as best they can to maximize achievement. *Perceived* ability to perform a job, as distinct from *actual* ability, is very close in meaning to Bandura's self-efficacy concept. Asking someone to rate the likelihood that he will succeed in performing a task provided he exerts the necessary effort calls for an implicit ability estimate. Therefore, perceived ability is included in the model.

Invoking the familiar caveat "other things being equal" deserves the retort, "but they never are." Particularly in the SFP process, the manager's influence over the subordinate's level of achievement can augment or weaken the motivational effects described above. If self-expectations strongly motivate a subordinate to exert a great deal of effort and improve performance, while at the same time the manager is facilitating the subordinate's performance by direct managerial action that contributes to the efficiency of the subordinate's efforts, the resulting positive SFP will be greatly augmented. Conversely, if in addition to demotivating the subordinate by conveying low performance expectations, the manager also withholds requisite resources and information and provides inadequate direction, instruction, and feedback, the resulting negative SFP will be magnified. Arrow 7 in figure 3–1 represents these direct effects of the manager's behavior on the outcomes of the SFP process. These direct effects operate independently of the subordinate's internal motivational processes, though there are certainly differential motivational repercussions among workers treated to good and poor supervision. To summarize, actual ability is not altered in the SFP process. Rather, one's subjective assessment of one's task-relevant ability and one's motivation to use one's ability are altered.

Achievement ⟶ Self-Expectancy: The Attribution Process

As depicted in figure 3–5, the SFP model treats the subordinate's achievement as a cue that is perceived by both the manager and the subordinate. The

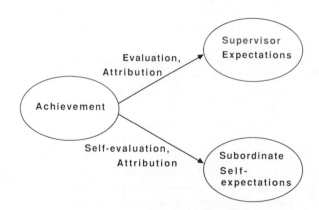

Figure 3–5. The Attribution Process

manager's response to subordinate achievement will be discussed in depth in chapter 4. The present section deals with the impact of the level of the subordinate's achievements—successes and failure—on his own self-expectations. This impact is mediated by the attribution process.

The link between achievement and self-expectancy in the SFP model represents the closure that the subordinate-as-prophet gets in the SFP process. It parallels the reinforcement link in the general SFP process. Experimental findings from studies of achievement motivation show that a person's initial high expectations are reinforced when he receives information evidencing success. These expectations are then maintained, or even raised to a still higher level. In the event of low achievement, or failure, the subordinate's most likely response is to reduce his level of expectations.

The impact of achievement on performance expectations is conditioned by attribution. Attribution is a cognitive process by which we infer what causes behavior, either our own or someone else's. In the present context, we are interested in the causal inferences managers and workers make about the causes of subordinates' successes and failures in job performance. This is important in the SFP process at work because whether a person responds to his own success and failure with higher or lower expectations for future performance depends on the factors to which he attributes success and failure (Weiner, 1974; Weiner, Frieze, Kukla, Reed, Rest & Rosenbaum 1971). Table 3–1 displays Weiner's (1979) classification of the different sources to which a worker may attribute success and failure in job performance according to two dimensions: stability and internality. A person may attribute success or failure to relatively stable, unchanging factors such as ability and task difficulty, or to unstable factors such as effort and luck. Ability and effort are internal (to the individual) causes of performance; task difficulty and luck are external factors. Effort is under the individual's control, since it results from his level of motivation, whereas ability, task difficulty, and luck are not.

Weiner has hypothesized that if a person attributes success to stable causes, such as ability, expectation for future success is increased more than if he attributes it to unstable factors, such as luck, which might change for the worse. Attributing success to ability also arouses positive, reinforcing feelings of accomplishment, pride, and self-confidence. "I was able to do it once, so I'm pretty good, and I'll be able to do it again." Conversely, attributing

Table 3–1
Sources to Which Individuals Attribute Success and Failure

Stability	Internal	External
Stable	ability	task difficulty
Unstable	effort	luck

failure to stable factors (lack of ability or task difficulty) decreases self-expectations ("I won't get any abler and the task won't get any easier"), and attributing failure to internal causes (lack of ability or effort) arouses negative affective responses, such as diminished self-esteem ("I'm not so good"). Since lack of ability is both internal and uncontrollable ("It's my fault and I can't help it"), attributing failure to lack of ability is particularly devastating.

Therefore, the attributions that are most conducive to maintaining a high level of expectations are internal attributions (ability and effort) for success and unstable attributions (lack of effort or bad luck) for failure. If a person thinks he has succeeded because of ability and effort, he has reason to feel good about himself and to expect future success; if he thinks he has failed because of lack of effort or bad luck, he can still reasonably expect to succeed in the future if he tries harder or if his luck changes. Thus, the impact of achievement on self-expectation is tempered by the individual's attributions. Making the "right" attributions (ability and effort for success and effort and luck for failure) promotes high expectations for future achievements and promotes positive SFP. Making the "wrong" attributions results in low expectations, impeding positive SFP and facilitating the Golem effect. It is noteworthy that effort attributions foster high expectations in the aftermath of both success and failure.

The attribution process is further complicated by certain types of errors, distortions, and biases that have been found in attribution research. These are cognitive illusions (Tversky & Kahneman 1974) that lead people to make wrong attributions, or misattributions. One type of misattribution is self-serving bias, which is the tendency to attribute success internally, to oneself, and to attribute failure to external causes (Bradley 1978; Miller & Ross 1975). While perhaps undesirable in some ways, this self-serving bias may serve to promote positive expectancy effects, inasmuch as it preserves positive self-expectations for future performance. Provided employees do not exaggerate in the use of external attributions as a cover-up for their failures and as an excuse not to take corrective action to prevent similar failure in the future, the self-serving attribution bias may be a blessing in disguise, at least from the point of view of SFP at work.

Another type of distortion is the tendency of "actors," such as employees, and "observers," such as managers, to make different attributions for the same behavior (Jones & Nisbett 1972). In particular, subordinates are apt to attribute the cause of their performance to situational conditions, whereas managers are more likely to attribute the same performance to factors internal to the subordinates. Gioia and Sims (1985) found evidence for both of these types of attribution distortion in a well-controlled experimental simulation.

The tendency for managers to distort their cognitions in a way that leads them to attribute subordinate failure to internal sources in the subordinates can be highly dysfunctional and can trigger negative SFP. By blaming subordinates for failure, managers not only exonerate themselves from any responsibility, but they also impose upon their subordinates the added burden of an internal attribution and its concomitant low expectations. If the manager so dominates the subordinates psychologically that his attributions overpower theirs, and his internal-to-the-subordinate attribution over-shadows or supplants their external attributions, they are likely to lower their expectations concerning their future performance. This has the makings of a Golem effect. Thus, the self-serving bias helps immunize subordinates against the Golem effect, whereas the supervisor's tendency to misattribute failure to internal causes in the subordinates constitutes a risk factor in the Golem effect.

To summarize, high self-expectations motivate exertion of great effort, which improves performance and boosts achievement. Experiencing success reinforces expectations for continued success, particularly if the individual attributes success to his own ability and effort. Attribution is an intrapsychic process that is mostly a result of the individual's previous history of success and failure experiences. Individuals arrive at the workplace with previously established levels of self-expectations and with previously acquired tendencies to make certain kinds of attributions and misattributions. The role of the manager as Pygmalion in guiding the subordinate's attributions is discussed in the next chapter.

Summary

This concludes our discussion of the Galatea triangle. The Galatea triangle encompasses the intrapsychic motivational processes that underlie both the Galatea and the Pygmalion effects. The manager-as-Pygmalion motivates his subordinates by getting them to raise their self-expectations. By so doing, he sets into motion a motivational process that culminates in the subordinates' investing great effort in performance and achieving high output. Subordinate self-expectancy is the key to motivation, and motivation is the key to the Pygmalion effect. Pygmalion achieves impressive results by increasing his subordinates' motivation. He takes full advantage of the opportunities that arise to guide subordinates' attributions of success and failure. He does not take credit for his subordinates' successes, which would deprive them of their hard-earned right to some self-satisfaction and of the opportunity to raise their expectations by making an ability attribution. Nor does he ignore or white-wash failure, which would only make him an ally in escapism. Rather, he helps his subordinates to attribute their successes to their own ability and effort and to attribute their failures to insufficient effort, to bad luck, or to task difficulty, always encouraging them to view their prospects for future success optimistically. Pygmalion is ever alert to the dangers of triggering a

Golem effect that is liable to result from attributing failure to ability. While some persons have been graced by their upbringing or prior work history with high trait-expectancy, a manager should never take high expectations for granted. High trait-expectations should be treated as a precious human asset whose value can erode if ignored, neglected, or mismanaged. Managerial actions should be designed to support existing high expectations, as well as to raise low ones. For Golems who are products of a long history of failure, forbearance on the part of the manager is required. A well-planned string of successes, reinforced by ability attributions, may build self-confidence and elevate expectations, weaken the Golem effect, and perhaps even "turn it around." We need to document cases of subordinate turnarounds, parallel to the popular business turnarounds that currently abound.

To come to grips with the motivational processes that underlie SFP in management it has been most useful to invoke VIE theory. The Pygmalion model relates to VIE theory by addressing the practical question of how one might go about raising motivation beyond the conventional approaches to strengthening instrumentality and valence. Pygmalion illuminates the way to raising effort-performance expectancy deliberately to augment motivation and boost output. Performance expectations lie at the heart of both VIE theory and SFP at work. So great is the affinity between the two approaches that the idea of creating SFP by raising performance expectations might seem to have been purposely designed with the aim of applying VIE theory. The integration of SFP and VIE theory can redress the imbalance in the work-motivation literature created by treating instrumentality and valence, but largely ignoring expectancy, in applying the VIE model in actual work situations. The Pygmalion and Galatea research shows that performance expectations *can* be raised experimentally. The present chapter highlights the pivotal role of raising workers' expectations in improving their performance. The next chapter describes in detail the manager's role in raising workers' expectations.

Appendix 3A

Choice and Subjective Probability of Success: Unnecessary Complications in Work Motivation Theory and Research

Vroom's (1964) conceptualization of expectancy as SPS was heavily influenced by Atkinson's theory of achievement motivation (Atkinson 1957; Atkinson & Feather 1966; Atkinson & Raynor 1974; McClelland, Atkinson, Clark & Lowell 1953). Interpreted in the achievement-motivation context as how risky the task is, SPS is associated with one's motivation for choosing to undertake or to avoid a task. Vroom's definition has been so influential that the evolution of the expectancy construct entered a quarter-century freeze. Following Vroom, "Almost without exception, (expectancy) has been measured as a subjective probability" (Ilgen, Nebeker & Pritchard 1981, 191). For reviews of the development of the expectancy concept, see Zuroff and Rotter (1985) and Kirsch (1985).

The variable predicted in research on achievement motivation is *choice.* Typically, a subject is offered a range of goals (or tasks) of different levels of difficulty and is asked to state SPS for each and to choose one. Vroom maintained this focus on choice and adopted the SPS conceptualization of expectancy as a determinant of choice: "To sum up, we view the central problem of motivation as the explanation of choices made by organisms among different voluntary responses" (1964, 9). Workers were viewed as making rational choices among available alternatives. Thus, Vroom's theory posits choice as a mediator between the predictors in the VIE equation and the amount of effort actually exerted.

Insistence upon choice as a mediator has retarded progress in work motivation theory. It imposes a restricted view of motivation. Choosing to work at a task is not the same as working hard to perform it well. If the motivation issue is recast in terms of how hard the individual will work, bypassing choice, alternatives to SPS can prove fruitful in conceptualizing and measuring expectancy. Predicting choice dictates certain operations, such as defining different levels of performance and establishing preference among them. When people are *told* to choose, as in achievement-motivation experiments, they do so. However, in many situations workers choose neither how much they produce nor how much effort they exert; instead, they "groove in" to a level of effort and maintain it without choosing over and over again. Nevertheless, their work behavior appears to be motivated. Furthermore, excepting occupational psychologists, predicting choice is seldom on the practitioner's agenda. Our practical aim is more often to maximize output than to place workers in maximally motivating jobs.

Moreover, imposing difficult goals boosts performance (Locke et al. 1981). Although Erez and Zidon (1984) have shown that goal acceptance makes a difference (see also Erez and Kanfer 1983), the nature and scope of choice in the process is ambiguous. Subjects assigned a difficult goal are *prima facie* given less "choice among voluntary responses" than those asked to do their best or to set their own goals. A theory of motivation must explain why those who are assigned difficult goals, and are thereby given little or no choice, outperform those asked to choose a goal; simply concluding that the former *choose* to work harder is circular. Thus, choice needlessly complicates our view of the motivational process. Without it we may be able to explain some long-standing contradictions, and to build a useful model of work motivation. The SPS-Performance Paradox and its resolution illustrates the complications caused by viewing motivation as a choice and by measuring expectancy only in terms of SPS.

The SPS-Performance Paradox. The integration of goal setting and VIE had been blocked for years because of a contradiction that was resolved by Garland (1984). A VIE hypothesis is that, other things being equal, the higher the level of expectancy, the greater the force to exert effort, and the better the performance. Goal setting experimenters have consistently found that goal difficulty is related positively to performance (Locke et al. 1981). However, goal difficulty is also related negatively to SPS (Garland 1982, 1983; Matsui, Okado & Mizuguchi 1981; Mento, Cartledge & Locke 1980). The resulting inference, supported by goal-setting findings (Locke 1968), is that SPS is negatively related to performance. This contradicts VIE theory, according to which SPS, as a measure of expectancy, should be *positively* related to performance.

Garland (1984) has shown that this SPS-performance paradox is an artifact of the way expectancy is measured in the goal-setting experimental paradigm, which assigns subjects to different goal conditions. Naturally, those assigned hard goals rate their SPS lower than those assigned easy goals. However, despite their low SPS, they obviously *expect* to produce more output than those assigned easy goals. *But SPS does not measure how much subjects expect to produce!* The paradox stems from the fact that subjects rate the probability of achieving hard goals lower than that of achieving easy goals, even though they *expect* to produce more output when assigned hard goals. Consequently, hard goals are associated *positively* with performance expectations and with performance but *negatively* with SPS. Reanalyzing two of his own experiments, Garland correlated SPS and performance separately for subjects *within* each goal-difficulty level, and found the hypothesized positive relationship within each. But the correlation between the same variables on the entire sample was *negative*. What is true *within* levels is not true *across* levels. This is an instance of ecological masking (Alker 1969). Garland unmasked the underlying positive association between SPS and performance by holding goal difficulty constant. The key to unraveling the enigma is that SPS, intended to measure expectancy, is a negative correlate of expectancy in certain circumstances, such as goal-setting (and achievement-motivation) experiments. Expecting to succeed in attaining a goal is not the same as expecting to perform well or to produce a great deal of output, nor is expecting to fail to attain a goal the same as expecting to perform poorly or to produce little output.

Further work by Locke et al. (1986) replicated Garland's findings and completed the resolution of the SPS-performance paradox. However, no one has proposed replacing SPS-based measures of expectancy with measures that would be consistently positively correlated with the amount of output workers expected to produce. In the level-of-aspiration and achievement-motivation traditions, expectancy has sometimes been measured in terms of *level*—that is, by asking subjects what level of performance they expect to attain—and sometimes in terms of *strength*—that is, by asking subjects to state the degree of confidence that they will perform at a particular level, or SPS (Kirsch 1986). VIE research has been needlessly restricted to measuring strength and has neglected level. Earlier use of a level measure may have spared us the SPS-Performance Paradox in the first place. A quarter century ago, Feather (1963) already had found a negative relationship between a strength measure of expectancy and goal difficulty. Operationalizing expectancy solely in terms of SPS artifactually created the vexing negative relationship between goal difficulty and expectancy because SPS is so profoundly influenced by goal difficulty, a situational variable. However, the validity of expectancy theory in tying the constructs together never was seriously jeopardized. It must have been apparent all along to goal-setting researchers that subjects with difficult goals *expected to produce more* despite their low SPS. Post-Garland, it is clear that the real problem was the way expectancy was operationalized.

Although resolution of the SPS-Performance Paradox has relieved us of a disconfirming finding, operationalizing expectancy in terms of SPS remains susceptible to distortion. How, then, should we operationalize expectancy?

Operationalization of Expectancy

There have been proposals for revising SPS-based measures of expectancy. However, these are all faulty. Garland proposed measuring expectancy by having subjects state SPS for each of several levels of goal difficulty. This method has been endorsed by mainstream goal-setting researchers (Locke et al. 1986). However, it is a very cumbersome measure. It burdens the subject with the job of providing a probability estimate for each of several levels of output, the more the levels the better. We would be better served by measures of expectancy that correlate positively with performance *both within and across* goal-difficulty levels and that are invulnerable to ecological masking. Moreover, the SPS measure requires subjects to express expectancy in probabilistic terms. However, laymen do not commonly think about their productivity this way. When required to do so, their estimates are often distorted because they misunderstand the most elementary probability concepts (Tversky & Kahneman 1974).

Another drawback in using SPS is the necessity to invoke additional concepts to explain why people perform at all when SPS = 0. According to the SPS conceptualization, when people believe they have no chance of attaining the goal, they should invest no effort, because a null product results from multiplying valence by an expectancy value of zero. Performance obtained when SPS = 0 must be explained away unparsimoniously in terms of intrinsic motivation, forced minimal compliance, or demand characteristics. However, expecting failure to achieve a goal does not imply expecting no output. When people do not expect to attain the goal, many busy themselves in the activity anyway. They do so because they think of output in terms of a gradient, not as an all-or-none entity with a probability scale attached to it. There is a parallel gradient of expectancy. We should measure expectancy in terms of this gradient. The output expected from efforts to reach an unreachable goal may have high valence. Multiplying this valence by expectancy yields a non-zero level of force to exert effort, even when SPS = 0. Thus, cumbersome operations and surplus theoretical explanations can be avoided by measuring expectancy in terms of a continuous variable that is consistently positively correlated with performance. SPS does not fit the bill.

To illustrate the motivational effects of expecting worthwhile outcomes to result from performance despite the expectation of failure to achieve a goal, consider the following statement made by a resident of Chatanooga in an interview broadcast over National Public Radio on March 31, 1986. The interviewee had been instrumental in bringing Mr. James Rouse to the city with the goal of making all the housing for the city's poor, estimated at ten thousand units, fit and livable within a decade. "If we only improve three thousand, or five thousand, or eight thousand homes for the poor, well then we'll just go on into the next decade," he said. "But what a wonderful failure, to have fallen a little bit short on an extremely ambitious goal!" While not expecting to achieve the goal, people in Chatanooga are evidently very highly motivated and are expending tremendous energy to renovate dilapidated housing. Operationalizing expectancy as SPS, VIE theory would not predict this.

Exceptions to the preferability of a continuous expectancy scale are all-or-none tasks in which partial performance has no value, such as solving a riddle or meeting a deadline. For pass-fail tasks, SPS may be the best measure of expectancy. Such is the nature of the tasks typically used in achievement motivation experiments, such as looping the target in a ring-toss game. The tasks were not selected to simulate everyday work. Experimenters' use of these tasks was dictated by the SPS conceptualization of expectancy within the framework of a choice theory. SPS was carried over to workplace research, where it is often inappropriate.

Two alternatives to SPS are proposed:

Comparative Quantiles. Quantiles (for example, quartiles, deciles, percentiles) can be used to operationalize expectancy without the deficiencies that plague SPS. In the adjutancy experiment in the IDF, we (Eden & Ravid 1982) measured expectancy in terms of the trainee's expected quintile (that is, "better than 20 percent, 40 percent, etc. of the other trainees"). Though based on only a single item, the quantile measure had high test-retest reliability and yielded highly significant results. This measure can be improved by using deciles or percentiles, since reliability increases with the number of points on a scale (Nunnally 1978). The quantile measure assesses expectancy in terms of a subjective, social comparison; the frame of reference is the individual's achievements relative to those of his peers, not to his own past success. Therefore, the quantile measure should be relatively impervious to task difficulty and fairly constant across goal-difficulty levels. Another advantage is that the quantile scale in not an inverse of goal difficulty.

Amount of Output Expected. Expectancy can be operationalized in terms of the amount of output expected—that is, level—by asking workers how many units they expect to produce if they try hard. For example, loggers could be asked to state the quantity of logs they expect to load per time period and university faculty members can be asked how many articles they expect to publish in the coming academic year. Amount of output expected is simple to measure. It is scaled in familiar units of output, simulating the way workers think about their productivity. Moreover, since performance is usually a continuous variable, and most people think of it as such, we should measure it on a continuous scale. SPS is a probability statement about a level of difficulty that treats performance in discrete, all-or-none terms. Having the subject state SPS for several levels of output still renders subjective probability continuous and performance discrete. Both quantiles and amount of output expected treat performance appropriately as a continuous variable.

Quantiles and amount of output expected complement each other's shortcomings. The quantile measure lacks specification of an absolute level of expected attainment, and amount of output expected lacks relativity; any particular absolute amount of output expected may seem a lot to some and a little to others. Taken together, these two proposed expectancy measures may provide a reliable alternative, or supplement, to SPS that is worthy of testing in future expectancy and goal-setting research.

Appendix 3B

A Resolution of the Contradiction between VIE Theory and the Theory of Achievement Motivation

A long-standing anomaly in work motivation theory is the rival hypotheses derived from the theory of achievement motivation and from VIE theory concerning expectancy, measured as SPS, and motivation. A VIE hypothesis is that the higher the expectancy, the stronger the motivation. In contrast, need-achievement theory postulates that people are most strongly motivated to work on tasks that have an SPS of .5—that is, tasks on which the individual believes he has even chances of success and failure (Atkinson 1964). Asked to choose, persons high in achievement motivation opt for tasks of intermediate SPS over tasks of very high or very low SPS. Persons low in need for achievement prefer tasks on which success or failure is assured in advance. Presumably, individuals high in need for achievement prefer the risk of tasks with uncertain outcomes, which test their ability; those low in need for achievement prefer to avoid such challenges. The hypothesized curvilinear relationship between SPS and motivation has been found in achievement motivation research (Atkinson 1964; Atkinson & Feather 1966; Mahone 1960; McClelland 1958; Morris 1967). Thus, VIE hypothesizes that maximal expectancy is most motivating, whereas achievement motivation findings confirm that an intermediate level of SPS is maximally motivating. This contradiction has never been resolved, though both theories have strong support (Pinder 1984).

This contradiction may be resolved by comparing the dependent variables and how they are measured. Again, choice and SPS complicate matters. In most (but not all) need-for-achievement experiments the dependent variable is *choice*. Typically, subjects are asked to express preference for a level of difficulty by choosing how far from the target to stand. In contrast, what VIE theory most often (but not always) predicts is the amount of *effort* the individual is willing to exert, or actual *performance*. Although motivation scholars often treat these two dependent variables similarly, choosing a level

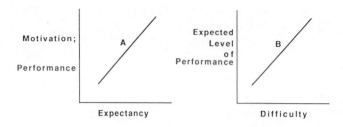

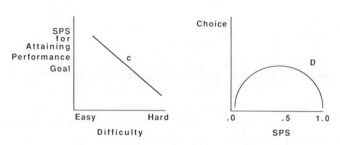

Figure 3–6. Relationships among Expectancy, Subjective Probability of Success (SFP), Performance, Task Difficulty, and Choice to Undertake Performance of a Task

of difficulty is not the same as expending effort. There is no a priori reason to assume that motivation to undertake a task and motivation to exert effort in performing it operate by the same process. Yet, expectancy theorists apply the same prediction formula indiscriminantly to choosing a task, a vocation, and a level of effort. Using SPS to measure expectancy in all such studies masks the difference between choosing a level of difficulty and expecting to produce much or little.

The graphs in figure 3–6 show the relationships involving expectancy and SPS in the VIE, goal setting, and achievement-motivation approaches. Curve A embodies the VIE hypothesis that, other things being equal, high expectancy enhances motivation and performance. Curve B shows that persons striving for hard goals expect to produce more than those who accept easy goals; raising goal difficulty boosts expectancy. Curve C is the negative relationship between goal difficulty and SPS for attaining a goal, which contradicts VIE theory when SPS is used to operationalize expectancy in goal-setting studies. The harder the goal, the less the likelihood of achieving it (curve C) even though more output is expected (curve B) and the resulting high expectancy motivates better performance (curve A). Operationalizing expectancy in terms of a variable that correlates positively with expected performance yields curve B rather than curve C and eliminates the contradiction between goal-setting and VIE theory. Curve D shows the curvilinear relationship between goal difficulty and choice found in achievement-motivation research. Since curve D involves a different dependent variable, it does not contradict any of the other curves. Thus, although when goals are very difficult subjects *expect* to produce more (curve B) and *do* produce more (curve A), their SPS is low (curve C) and they would *prefer* to work at somewhat easier goal levels (curve D). The preferred difficulty level is not that which motivates maximal effort. Indeed, goal-setting research has found that subjects instructed to choose their own goals do not opt for very difficult goals (Locke et al. 1981).

Knowing that SPS is the inverse of expectancy and distinguishing between choosing a level of difficulty and exerting a level of effort, the VIE and achievement-motivation formulations no longer conflict. This proposition could be tested by including both choice of a level of effort and the amount of effort actually expended as dependent variables in the same experiment. The present proposition would be confirmed if achievement motivation theory better predicted choice and VIE better predicted level of effort exerted.

4
The Pygmalion Leadership Style: How Managers Get Workers to Fulfill Their Expectations

I n this chapter the manager's part in the SFP model is described. The aim is to understand the origin of manager expectations and how they influence subordinate performance both directly and via the processes encompassed by the Galatea triangle. This is accomplished by superimposing the Pygmalion triangle upon the Galatea triangle to show how those intrapsychic, motivational phenomena are embedded in the broader Pygmalion effect.

The direct impact of the manager's leadership on subordinate performance needs no special exposition here. The contribution of good leadership to performance, represented by arrow 7 in figure 3–1, implies nothing more than what countless management theorists have already said in countless ways: leadership makes a difference. In particular, work facilitation behaviors on the part of the manager promote subordinate effectiveness whether or not an SFP is occurring. Arrows 1 and 2 are unique to Pygmalion in management, for they concern how expectations influence manager leadership and how manager leadership in turn influences subordinate expectations. Therefore, nothing much will be said about arrow 7.

For workers, the manager is a source of information that raises and lowers their self-expectations. Viewed from the perspective of the Galatea triangle, the manager's performance expectations and leadership behaviors are antecedents of employee work motivation. What the manager expects influences how he treats his subordinates, and how he treats them affects their motivation and performance. The Pygmalion research has demonstrated that one important ingredient in effective managerial leadership is the communication of positive information that fosters high subordinate self-expectations. Many workers are frequently exposed to positive or negative information concerning their ability and the likelihood of their future success. Many workers are receptive to such information and are affected by it. These effects occur whether or not the manager is aware of them. It is worthwhile for managers to become cognizant of this interpersonal expectancy process, as it is a key to unlocking the mystery of work motivation, and to harnessing motivational forces for productive ends. Understanding the origin of manager expectations is indispensable for attempting to raise them, and raising expectations is the central focus of this book. This chapter focuses on the ways in which managers form expectations, and act on them, in leading their subordinates to perform in a manner that conforms to the managers' expectations.

Understanding the relationship between the expectations of the manager-as-prophet and the performance of the employee who fulfills the prophecy requires answers to three questions. First, how do manager expectations originate? In controlled Pygmalion experiments, the answer is clear: the experimenter imparts the expectations to the manager by design. But such experiments are rare. Managers in everyday situations form performance expectations on the basis of information from a variety of sources. The origin of naturally formed manager expectations is dealt with in the next section.

The second question concerns the translation of the manager's expectations into overt behavior. Expectations are cognitive constructs that exist in the mind, but not in the material world of tangibles. Since subordinates cannot read managers' minds, something in managers' concrete behavior must signal what those expectations are. Understanding how manager expectations inform manager behavior leads to an examination of the differential behaviors that managers emit in leading subordinates of whom much or little is expected.

The final objective of this chapter is to shed light on how the cues that emanate from the manager's overt behavior toward the subordinate are perceived and interpreted by the subordinate. This focus casts the subordinate as the object of supervisory behaviors and explains how his productive behavior is influenced by the manager's leadership. This is the point at which the managerial leadership included in the Pygmalion triangle links up with the motivational processes that comprise the Galatea triangle.

The Origin of Manager Expectations

Manager expectations regarding subordinate performance originate from many different sources. Both the sources and the expectations themselves can and do change from time to time, although they tend to become relatively fixed, or rigidified, with the passage of time (Jussim 1986). There has been little research on manager expectations as a dependent variable. However, there has been quite a bit of research on the origins of teacher expectations (Dusek & Joseph 1985; Baron, Tom & Cooper 1985; Good & Findley 1985). For the most part, the origins of teacher expectations seem highly plausible as sources of manager expectations as well. Therefore, much of the following discussion is based on observation, common sense, and research on teacher expectations. For a discussion of some of the methodological

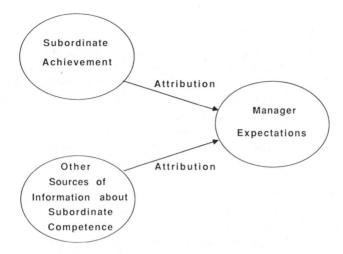

Figure 4–1. The Attribution Process That Informs Manager Expectations

problems involved in generalizing from research on teacher expectations to managers, see appendix 4A.

Figure 4–1 displays the portion of the SFP-at-work model that involves the sources of information that determine manager expectations and the process by which this occurs. It shows that manager expectations are based on knowledge of past subordinate achievement, mediated by attribution. The manager either observes workers' current performance and evaluates their achievements, or evaluates information about workers' competence obtained from other sources. On the basis of this information, the manager assesses how competent each employee is. The arrows in figure 4–1 show that this assessment informs the manager's expectations for future achievement. Ordinarily, expectations are for "more of the same." Knowing either firsthand or from secondary sources that an employee has performed well in the past leads to high expectations for that employee's performance in the future, whereas evaluating past performance as poor produces low expectations. However, the manager's assessment of the employee's potential for future success also involves an attribution process similar to that described for workers themselves in the previous chapter. If the manager attributes the subordinate's success or failure to lasting, internal causes such as ability, he is most likely to expect more of the same. If he attributes success or failure to worker effort, task difficulty, luck, or other external or unstable cause, he may expect different performance in the future.

This attribution process is compounded by the additional tendency of many managers to take credit for their subordinates' achievements and to disavow failure on their own part by attributing it to others, often their subordinates. Such managerial self-aggrandizement and dumping of blame onto subordinates depress subordinates' expectations. This is a special case of the actor–observer bias in attribution discussed in the previous chapter. It can have dire expectancy consequences in the aftermath of poor subordinate performance, particularly unjustly so when the cause of the failure is *mis*attributed to the subordinates. The manager may be entirely unaware of what is happening, but the motivational damage is done. The effective manager makes it a point to give credit to subordinates for their successes. He fortifies their expectations by making sure that they attribute their successes to their own ability and effort. Whenever appropriate, he discourages workers from attributing their failures to their own incompetence.

Moreover, it may be worthwhile for managers to give subordinates credit even when it is *not* entirely due. It is of prime importance that performance expectations be high, even if high expectations are "inaccurate," or not in line with accurate assessment of past performance. This of course runs counter to the thrust of the enormous efforts being made by organizational psychologists and psychometricians to improve employee rating forms by eliminating bias (e.g., Feldman 1981). However, our present purpose is to motivate workers, not to assess them. As we shall see below, manager expectations are based on information about subordinate competence which can be accurate or inaccurate. These expectations can therefore be higher or lower than the level "justified" by the subordinate's actual competence. As Snyder (1984) has pointed out, "The initial accuracy or inaccuracy of beliefs and attributions may be a moot point. For, over time, even errors may create their own reality" (p. 296). However, it is important to distinguish between different kinds of errors, for they create different realities. Depending on the direction and degree of inaccuracy of manager expectations, different types of expectancy effects are produced. The following discussion is based on the implications of the accuracy of expectations and attributions involved in the cognitive process depicted in figure 4–1.

Accurate versus Inaccurate Expectations

The sources of manager expectations can be classified according to the likelihood that they will yield accurate expectations. Actual competence is the yardstick against which the accuracy of performance expectations can be evaluated. The accuracy of expectations is defined as the degree of fidelity of the *expected* level of performance to the worker's *actual* level of competency for doing the job. Accurate expectations are for a level of performance that is commensurate with what the worker actually *can* do, regardless of his past performance record; inaccurate expectations are for levels of performance that are appreciably higher or lower than what the employee is truly capable of achieving. Expectations are inaccurate to the extent that they deviate from the level of performance that the employee is competent to achieve. The greater the discrepancy between expectations and competence, the greater the inaccuracy.

In general, accurate and inaccurate expectations are derived from different sources of information. A valid source of information about subordinate competence is one whose predictions of future success have been found objectively to be related to achievement. Valid sources of expectations include past achievement, aptitude test scores, and performance ratings by previous supervisors. These are the kinds of predictors typically used in personnel selection programs that have passed the acid test of validation. This does not mean that these predictors are flawless, error-free indicators of potential. No test is perfectly reliable or accurate. All numbers are fallible. Every measure has some degree of error and bias. What makes the valid predictors likely to yield relatively accurate expectations is that each test score, performance rating, or datum so classified has repeatedly demonstrated its ability to predict some measure(s) of performance or productivity. If managers based their expectations only on entirely valid predictors, they would be accurate. In reality, it never happens this way.

Sources of Accurate Performance Expectations. Table 4–1 classifies the sources of manager expectations according to the likelihood of their accuracy. The first column of the table shows the sources of expectations that are most likely to be accurate. Accurate performance expectations can be formed on the basis of such valid sources of information about employee competence as psychometrically sound tests of aptitude and ability, well-executed ratings of past performance, and honest recommendations by previous employers or supervisors. These sources of information are to be found in employee records. Managers sometimes have access to the information contained in personnel files. Tests of competency, performance ratings, and grades are evaluations of employees' job-relevant skills, abilities, and knowledge that are accumulated to aid managers in making objective, accurate assessments of employee potential for success. A manager basing his expectations on these and similar sources of information about the subordinate is likely (but not certain) to form expectations commensurate with the subordinate's actual ability to do the job. In such cases, the manager's predictions concerning the likelihood of the subordinate's success or failure on the job are apt to be borne out because of the relationship between competence as measured by these sources and job performance, even in the absence of any expectancy effects.

Such objective assessments are the best available sources of unbiased information on which managers can base their expectations, short of first-

Table 4–1
Sources of Manager Expectations Classified According to
Accuracy of Information They Usually Provide

Accuracy of Manager Expectations	
Accurate	*Inaccurate*
Records, files	Stereotypes
Competency tests	race
Performance ratings	gender
	social class
Grades	age
Recommendations	national origin
Firsthand knowledge	Physical traits
	height and weight
	physique
	attractiveness
	Personal habits
	cleanliness
	neatness
	orderliness
	discipline
	mannerisms

hand experience in working with the particular employee. However, expectations based on a candidate's test scores can still be inaccurate because of measurement error. The reliability and validity of a test are determined on the basis of large samples of testees. But even high reliability and validity are no guarantee of accuracy in the assessment of every individual or in the prediction of future performance. Error is a statistical feature inherent in every measuring instrument. Even a highly reliable and valid test or rating form can yield an inaccurate score for a particular individual because of measurement error.

Besides statistical *error*, accuracy in valid measures is lost to simple *mistakes*. Laudon (1986) has shown that dossiers and personnel files are notoriously misinformative. Faulty tallying of responses, careless computation of summary scores, misfiling (Murray Smith's score is entered into Mary Smith's record), illegible entries, omission of some data, retention of outdated information in personnel files, and countless other snafus produce flawed information that leads to inaccurate expectations despite the validity of the original source. Moreover, untutored in psychometrics and testology, managers often misinterpret test results. Therefore, even the best sources of information often lead to inaccurate expectations.

Recommendations by previous supervisors and employers are sources of narrative, rather than quantitative, information about workers' competencies. Recommendations are sometimes very convincing. Their importance increases when the other sources of information are not available. Although well-intended as sources of relevant information, recommendations are often so ridden with generalities and exaggerations that they are not taken very seriously. Since they are not quantitative, there is no way to compute their reliability and validity. Moreover, they are sometimes purposely slanted or falsified. For example, a manager who wants to foist off an incompetent subordinate onto someone else may write a glowing letter of recommendation to accompany a superlative rating. Thus, deliberate misuse of valid tools can degrade the accuracy of the information that they yield. Therefore, managers may either discount them in forming their expectations or base inaccurate expectations on them.

The firsthand knowledge that comes from experience in working with a subordinate for a period of time is arguably the best basis for forming accurate expectations. Indeed, all the other sources listed in the first column of table 4–1 are useful only to the extent that they can accurately predict subsequent job performance. Firsthand knowledge of current performance on the job ought to be a better basis for predicting future performance than any previous test, rating, or recommendation. Furthermore, in forming expectations on the basis of present performance, managers are relying on their own powers of judgment rather than on someone else's. They may give their own perceptions greater weight than the contents of the worker's file. Therefore, manager evaluation of subordinate achievement on the present job is displayed in figure 4–1, together with other sources of information about subordinate competence as a determinant of manager expectations. It is likely that evaluation of current achievements dominates the formation of manager expectations in ongoing work settings. Firsthand knowledge of the subordinate's performance makes manager expectations resistant to change. The impact of information in the files is greater in the absence of face-to-face acquaintance, particularly regarding new employees.

However, even the manager's evaluation of the subordinate's current job performance is not always an accurate basis for forming expectations. Accuracy is defined in terms of competence. Actual achievement and competence are not to be confused. Achievement does not necessarily reflect competence. An underachiever has the potential to use competencies that are not being tapped in the current job. In the case of an underachiever, the manager's firsthand knowledge of the current level of performance will lead him to form inaccurate expectations that fall short of what the subordinate actually *can* do. These low expectations will be highly resistant to change, for the manager has the evidence in hand to justify them.

Another force that militates against raising expectations toward known low performers to realistic levels is the tendency to attribute unexpected behavior to temporary situational factors and to forget it rapidly (Johnson & Judd 1983). Unexpected high performance by a chronic low performer is less likely to be perceived, and if perceived, it is likely to be soon forgotten, and the manager's low expectations remain unaltered. Inevitably, and unintentionally, the low expectations will continue to depress the underachiever's future performance.

To summarize, the best sources of accurate information that can influence a manager's performance expectations are objective evaluations of ability and past achievements that are often in personnel files. Although such information is often of known reliability and validity, it is still quite fallible. It is in files that may be inaccessible or only partially accessible, it may contain errors and mistakes, sometimes intentionally, and some of the information may be "stale." Files may contain an accumulation of the results of assessments made many years ago. Such information may misrepresent the individual's current level of competence.

Sources of Inaccurate Performance Expectations. The sources of information listed in the second column of table 4–1 most frequently produce inaccurate expectations. These sources of biased performance expectations are stereotypes based on workers' demographic characteristics, such as social class, race, age, national origin, and gender; physical traits such as height, weight, physique, and bodily attractiveness; personal habits such as cleanliness, neatness, orderliness, punctuality, and behavioral and speech mannerisms. These are workers' personal traits that are often thought by managers (and others) to be correlated with competence in the absence of any clear-cut evidence. In reality, these characteristics bear no inherent relationship to the performance of most jobs.

Implicit Worker Theory. The way these characteristics influence manager performance expectations parallels "implicit leadership theory" (Eden & Leviatan 1975). An implicit theory is a preconceived set of associations among various personality traits or behavioral dispositions which people carry around with them in their heads and use in making sense of their world. Simple everyday examples include the commonplace presumption that redheads are ill-tempered or that fat people are jolly, and that a neat worker is efficient. The original evidence for the existence of implicit leadership theory was based on data we (Eden & Leviatan 1975) collected by having respondents complete questionnaires in which they described the leadership behavior of anonymous managers. Factor analysis of these responses yielded the leadership factors obtained when workers use the same items to describe their actual managers. Under anonymous conditions, the relationships among the items that yielded the leadership factors must have been preexisting in the respondents' minds. Hence the term "implicit theory." More recently, we have found that people rate a manager as relatively ineffective if he is described as operating under objectively stressful conditions. These low ratings obtain even in the face of contrary objective, quantitative information that evidences the manager's excellent performance. We have dubbed this phenomenon "implicit stress theory" (Westman & Eden 1989a).

There is a parallel "implicit worker theory" that influences managers' expectations of workers. Their implicit worker theories lead them to believe that certain traits are associated with competence, and they form their performance expectations accordingly. This leads to inaccurate expectations. When a manager bases his performance expectations on a worker's class background, race, national origin, gender, age, or outward appearance, he is allowing prejudice to displace objective assessment of qualifications. These "predictors" bear no inherent relationship to a person's competence or job performance. The resulting performance expectations are biased and are likely to be inaccurate as well. These sources of expectations are usually obscured or denied by those who entertain them.

Sound personnel selection and placement procedures and equal-opportunity legislation have attempted to reduce the most blatant manifestations of stereotypes and prejudices in democratic societies. For sure, some forms of unfair discrimination in hiring and promotion have been reduced. However, the more elusive, unconscious, and unintentional manager expectancy effects cannot be legislated away. These effects are most insidious when they are based on *low* inaccurate expectations, as in the case of competent women who are expected to fail because of a gender stereotype adhered to by many managers, or qualified minority workers who are expected to perform poorly because of racial stereotypes.

Intentionally Favored But Unintentionally Harmed. Even well-intended palliative measures aimed at fighting discrimination can backfire by unintentionally strengthening existing negative SFP. In a laboratory experiment, Heilman, Simon, and Repper (1987) manipulated subjects' perceptions of having been assigned to a leadership role on the basis of merit by having proven leadership competence in a paper-and-pencil self-report inventory, or on the basis of sex preference ("there just haven't been enough female subjects so far, so regardless how you did on the inventory, *you*, since you're a woman, will get to be leader for this task"). The women who were preferentially selected for the leadership role, compared to women ostensibly selected on the basis of their merit, took less credit for their success and rated their leadership competence and their leadership performance lower. They also reported less desire to persist in the leadership position. Similar effects were not evident among male subjects who were led to believe that they had been assigned to the leadership role because of sex preference.

These findings have implications for any organization that hires minorities under a mandated quota system, such as "affirmative action" plans that are currently widespread in the United States. Minority individuals and managers in such companies could assume that *all* members of the minority group hired by the company got their jobs because of the quota system, including highly qualified individuals who would have been hired *without* the quota. These competent workers may be unfairly stigmatized by a "hired-under-quota" image. It could be assumed both by the workers themselves and by their managers that they are unqualified for their jobs. Under such circumstances, a Golem effect is inevitable. Intentionally favored by preferential selection, such workers may be unintentionally harmed. Thus, due to SFP, a program undertaken to ameliorate a social ill imposes that same ill on new victims. Well-intended interventions can arouse unintended negative expectations and disastrous consequences. Alertness to SFP processes in organizations can aid in the detection and elimination of such phenomena.

The personal traits and habits of workers listed in table 4–1 influence the impressions that managers form of workers, including workers' competence. Reddin (1970) has dubbed this "apparent effectiveness." Some people simply *look* competent, and enact the role of a competent worker well. This may or may not be a sign of *actual* competence. Workers who are always on time, maintain a tidy work station or neat desk, are punctual, conduct themselves in a courteous and businesslike manner, and are well-prepared by doing their "homework" create an image of effectiveness. The impression of ineffectiveness is created by the opposite traits and behaviors. These impressions may be misleading, especially in the absence of good measures of actual output. Nevertheless, such impressions do influence the formation of manager expectations, many of which are inaccurate because they are not based on valid information.

Thus, many of the sources of information from which managers draw in forming their performance expectations are often error-prone, mistake-ridden, or biased, and therefore often yield inaccurate expectations. However, not all the inaccuracies in expectations are alike in their effects. Therefore, not all inaccuracies should be treated alike. The central thesis of this book is that high expectations are productive and low expectations have debilitating effects on workers. Therefore, *inaccurate high expectations may be beneficial, whereas inaccurate low expectations can be devastating.* In a later chapter we will focus on the prevention and correction of inaccurate low expectations.

The right expectations for the wrong reasons. Just as the sources classified in table 4–1 as accurate can yield inaccurate information, so the generally invalid, inaccurate sources sometimes yield accurate expectations. A biased expectation can be accurate by chance. Not every person subjected to negative prejudice is competent, and not every subject of a positive prejudice is incompetent. Stereotypes might lead to inaccurate expectations about some or most individual targets, but not all of them. There are some incompetent blacks, women, unattractive people, very young people, and elderly people. Their lack of competence for the particular job may be unrelated to the reason that the manager expects them to perform poorly. Similarly, some tall, athletic, and attractive men are competent for their jobs for reasons that have nothing to do with their gender and physique. These are instances in which managers form the right expectations for the wrong reasons. For example, a manager might expect an incompetent woman to perform poorly because of a gender stereotype he holds. His expectation may be accurate by chance; her lack of competence for the particular job may be utterly unrelated to her gender, and he "hit" on an accurate expectation by chance rather than on the basis of a valid predictor.

The only real measures of the accuracy of expectations are sound competency testing and actual performance on the job. Manager expectations are more likely to be biased and inaccurate to the extent that these measures are unavailable. In the absence of objective information, managers' stereotypes may dominate the formation of their performance expectations. Because of the powerful effects of partial reinforcement, the fact that these biased expectations are sometimes confirmed strengthens the stereotypes, stiffens their resistance to extinction, and can be cited to justify managers' reliance on them. It is generally lost on managers (and other people) that both chance and SFP may play a crucial role in producing the performance that confirms the expectations derived from stereotypes. One aim of this book is to propose ways of preventing, or at least vitiating, the formation of inaccurate low performance expectations based on stereotypic thinking.

Self-Fulfilling versus Self-Sustaining Prophecy

The distinction between self-fulfilling and self-sustaining prophecy (Salomon 1981) hinges on the source and accuracy of the manager's expectations, shown in figure 4–1. A worker who has been performing far below his potential may be expected by his new supervisor to continue performing poorly. The effects of this supervisor's low expectations would be negative. However, this would not be an example of SFP. The present supervisor's low expectations did not *instigate* this employee's low performance. Rather, his low expectations perpetuate the low level of performance that had been initiated long before he even knew the employee. This kind of manager expectancy effect is the result of a self-sustaining prophecy. Self-*fulfilling* prophecy implies the operation of an expectation that *changes* the subordinate's performance, molding it to conform to the manager's expectations. Expectations for *maintaining a past level of performance* irrespective of the subordinate's actual level of ability create an expectancy effect that is more appropriately dubbed "self-*sustaining* prophecy." Managers often have access to knowledge of employees' past performance, which informs their expectations regarding these employees' future performance. This knowledge makes self-sustaining prophecies much more prevalent in nature than self-fulfilling prophecies. Furthermore, ability places a ceiling on performance, limiting positive expectancy effects. There is no parallel "floor" that limits poor performance. Therefore, self-sustaining Golem effects are more likely to occur than are self-sustaining Pygmalion effects.

Strong versus Weak Expectancy Effects

Table 4–2 shows the combinations of high and low manager expectations and employee ability and classifies the resulting expectancy effects accordingly. Even if manager expectations were absolutely accurate and based solely on valid predictors of performance, manager expectancy effects would still occur. Such effects would be self-sustaining, rather than self-fulfilling, prophecies. The most widely used of the valid predictors of job performance probably are ability tests. Since the direct impact of manager expectations is on motivation rather than on ability, expecting a high-ability subordinate to do well and expecting a low-ability worker to do poorly are accurate expectations that foster the outcomes expected because of their impact on employee motivation. By the process described in the previous chapter, high manager expectations augment the motivation of highly able subordinates and thereby facilitate their excellence. The result is a Pygmalion effect. Low manager expectations detract from the motivation of the less able workers and impede their performance, producing a Golem effect. These effects are like the Matthew effect in science (Merton 1968), inasmuch as success breeds success and failure results in further failure. As the rich get richer, so too the able appear to get abler; as the poor get poorer, so too the incompetent become

Table 4–2
Type of Expectancy Effects Produced by Commensurate and Discrepant Manager Expectations and Subordinate Ability

	Manager Expectations	
Subordinate Ability	*Low*	*High*
High	Strong Golem effects SFP	Weak Pygmalion effects SSP
Low	Weak Golem effects SSP	Strong Pygmalion effects SFP

SFP = Self-fulfilling prophecy
SSP = Self-sustaining prophecy

even less competent. Thus, accurate manager expectations increase inequality among subordinates. In the absence of manager expectancy effects, workers with different levels of ability perform at different levels of achievement. The incremental effect of accurate manager expectations is to raise still further the achievement of the able and to impair still further the performance of the less able, thus magnifying the performance differences between the more and less able. However, both of these incremental effects are relatively weak. Since the manager's expectations are consistent with the subordinate's ability, they add only marginally beyond ability's predominant influence on performance.

Like accurate expectations, inaccurate expectations can produce either a positive Pygmalion effect (a manager expects more from a subordinate because he is well-groomed, or more from a middle-class worker than from an equally qualified lower-class employee), or a negative Golem effect (expecting less from a homely worker despite his abundant qualifications). Since the expectations aroused by variables related only remotely, if at all, to actual ability are likely to influence performance in a direction different from that of ability, the resulting effect is more likely to be a self-fulfilling than a self-sustaining prophecy. Such effects will be stronger than in the case of expectations that are consistent with ability. When a manager harbors low expectations toward a highly able subordinate, or high expectations toward a low-ability worker, these expectations are highly discrepant from the employee's actual ability. The resulting discrepancy effects are different, depending on the validity of the source of the expectations.

Taking job-related ability as the most valid predictor of job performance and as the criterion for the accuracy of expectations, a manager might accurately expect a highly able worker to excel. This accurate combination of high manager expectations and high worker ability appears in the upper right cell of table 4–2. Expecting a worker with a fine record of past achievement to do well in the future contributes to his continued success. If that worker has been overachieving—that is, outperforming peers with similar ability because of highly motivated effort that boosts his performance—then high manager expectations can sustain such overachievement. If the worker confirms the manager's expectations by excelling, it would most likely be the result of his high ability, marginally augmented by a Pygmalion effect. Conversely, if an unable worker is expected to fail and does so, the failure could be the result of his low ability and the added Golem effect produced by low manager expectations (lower left cell in table 4–2). When manager expectations are accurate, that is, when they are in the direction that would be predicted by valid indicators of job-relevant ability, as in these two cells, the type of expectancy effect that occurs is a self-sustaining prophecy. When manager expectations are commensurate with worker ability, the influence of manager expectations is in the direction of ability effects, and is consistent with the subordinate's past performance.

While more frequently found in nature, these self-sustaining manager-expectation effects are not very dramatic. They do not constitute a drastic break with the employee's past work experience, and the marginal effect of expectations in these instances is relatively small. They are therefore labeled "weak" expectancy effects. The ubiquity of weak expectancy effects makes their detection difficult.

Less frequent, but more potent, are the manager-expectation effects that result from inaccurate manager expectations that are not commensurate with subordinates' actual ability. When a manager harbors low expectations toward a highly able subordinate, or high expectations toward a low-ability worker, the manager's expectations are highly inaccurate and contrary to the employee's actual ability. Strong discrepancy effects can result. The instances of discrepant manager expectations are shown in the High-Low and Low-High cells of table 4–2. The impact of manager expectations in these discrepant cases is stronger than in the commensurate cells because the gap between manager expectations and subordinate ability is wider. Highly discrepant manager expectations are more likely to produce a break with the subordinate's recent past. Highly inaccurate manager expectations, whether positive or negative, are likely to be more salient to the worker than mildly discrepant manager expectations or expectations for "more of the same." Therefore, the effects of inaccurate manager expectations are likely to be stronger than the effects of accurate manager expectations.

When manager expectations contradict actual employee qualifications, the resulting expectancy effect is a self-*fulfilling* prophecy. Treating a low-qualified worker as one likely to succeed can produce a positive Pygmalion effect, as the positive treatment may stimulate such an employee to apply himself to the limits of his ability and perform better than he would have otherwise. Such an effect would stand out as remarkable, as it would be surprising good news against a backdrop of much bad news. This would be regarded as a credit to both the worker and the manager. Conversely, treating a highly qualified employee as one likely to perform poorly is likely to impair that worker's performance and result in a strong Golem effect. George Allen's treatment of Curt Knight in the scenario in the introduction exemplifies this. Expecting failure from an able employee can create needless, and therefore especially tragic, failure on his part. Since manager expectations are usually informed by past employee accomplishments, this type of SFP is relatively uncommon. However, it is a strong effect that undoubtedly does occur.

Obviously, there is a limit to how discrepant high expectations can be from proven competence and still have any effect at all. Expecting out of the blue that the local dummy will suddenly rise to stardom will arouse derision. Extremely discrepant low expectations may not share the same limitation. Again, George Allen and Curt Knight are a case in point. In this sense, it is easier to create negative SFP than to create positive SFP.

Tragically, there are workers whose ability has never been tapped fully because of past SFP resulting from the treatment they got at the hands of teachers and supervisors who underestimated their true potential. Their record does not reflect their ability. A fair-minded manager who reads the record and expects such workers to continue to be low performers will unintentionally create a self-sustaining prophecy and perpetuate a Golem effect. In such a case the manager does not originate the underachievement, but his expectations lead him to treat the worker in a manner that sustains the underachievement.

Pygmalion experiments do not directly examine self-sustaining prophecy. Since experimenters randomize the assignment of subordinates to manager-expectancy conditions, as a group the high- and low-expectancy subjects do not differ in past achievement or ability. However, practicing managers in everyday situations do not form their performance expectations at random. Employee records, recommendations, firsthand observation, and other sources of competency evaluation inform manager expectations. Therefore, natural expectations *are* correlated with past performance. Naturally, managers expect workers with good records to perform well, and expect those with poor records to fail. Treating workers in accordance with their past record paves the way for sustaining past expectancy effects. Self-*fulfilling* prophecy, which by definition entails treating workers in a manner that is discrepant from the record that naturally informs expectations, is therefore less frequent.

The foregoing discussion assumes that employee ability is reflected in the record and that the record informs manager expectations. This is not always the case. An employee may have been a long-term underachiever before being assigned to his current supervisor. In such a case, the record would under-report his ability, and he would be expected to perform in accordance with his performance as reflected in the record. The manager would be sustaining a past Golem effect. After all, managers do not administer psychological tests to their workers, and the record of past performance is a very compelling guide to expectations! Even when the record does contain valid and accurate information about ability, there is no guarantee that it will inform the manager's expectations. Sometimes managers, for whatever reason, form expectations that contradict the record, such as George Allen's inexplicably low expectations of Curt Knight's ability to kick a field goal despite his outstanding kicking record. This brought on a needless Golem effect. Furthermore, prejudice may overshadow objective data. Thus, availability of valid information about ability neither guarantees its use nor precludes strong SFP effects.

Selecting Low-scoring But Competent Candidates:
A Colossal But Benign Mistake

The National Commission on Testing and Public Policy reported that, between 1976 and 1980, the United States armed forces enlisted two hundred thousand candidates who should have been rejected according to the rules governing selection at the time. These enlistees comprised one-third of all the men enlisted into the army during those years. The mistake derived from erroneous inflation of their scores on selection tests.

However, despite their under-par true test scores, the performance of these enlistees was no worse than that of their peers whose true scores were high enough to be enlisted.

This is a fascinating case that illustrates many of the points discussed above. When large bureaucracies make mistakes, they are on a grand scale. However, in terms of SFP, this appears to have been a mistake with benign, perhaps even beneficial, consequences for the hundreds of thousands of individuals involved, as well as for the U.S. armed forces. Assuming that the tests were valid predictors of performance, the two hundred thousand-man "mistake" gave candidates who were actually underqualified a chance to prove themselves under ideal conditions of both high self-expectations and high expectations on the part of others who "knew" that the men tested favorably. Their subsequent up-to-par performance can be interpreted as SFP at work, in part a Pygmalion effect produced by military administrators, instructors, and commanders who were swayed by the faulty high test scores to expect good performance from them, and a Galatea effect on the part of the men themselves, who were led by their very induction into the armed forces to believe that they were qualified for service. For those whose true scores were just shy of the cutoff score for induction, this was a weak Pygmalion effect. The inductees whose true scores were considerably below the cutoff score experienced a strong Pygmalion effect. The entire incident may exemplify the benefits of inaccurate high expectations that were derived from a generally valid source of information about competence. Apparently, all parties gained from these inaccurate high expectations. Had this "mistake" not occurred, countless thousands of low-scoring but otherwise evidently competent individuals would have undergone another cycle of self-sustaining prophecy. The "mistake" averted a massive Golem effect. The inflation of their scores disrupted the negative SFP which would have kept them once again from actualizing their potential.

It is tempting to propose deliberate inflation of test scores to facilitate productive SFP!

Summary. Leadership is a key to understanding the Pygmalion effect and other SFP processes in management. The leadership a manager enacts toward subordinates is determined in part by his expectations. The discussion above portrays the sources of manager expectations as myriad. They may be accurate or inaccurate, valid or biased, and objective or prejudiced. The less accurate the expectations relative to an objective yardstick of subordinate competence, the stronger the potential expectancy effect. When manager expectations are largely in accord with actual subordinate competence, "self-sustaining prophecy" is likely to occur. If the psychometricians had their way, manager expectations would be accurate, because they would be formed on the basis of valid information derived from objective instruments. Even then, "weak" manager expectancy effects, some of them detrimental to productivity, would occur. Such skin-deep surface traits as physical appearance exacerbate the problem, since they are most often implicated in the formation of unwarranted, Golem-producing, low expectations. This state of affairs implies a twofold agenda for using expectancy effects for productive purposes. First, inaccurate low expectations that are derived from biased sources such as stereotypes, prejudice, and faulty records must be uprooted and replaced with higher expectations. Providing managers with better information and getting them to use it as a basis for forming their performance expectations would be steps in the right direction. Second, even *accurate* low expectations should be raised with the aim of motivating individuals of lower ability to try harder, and to minimize the prevalence of Golem effects. Practical proposals for achieving this agenda are provided in chapter 6.

It should be noted that making inaccurate high expectations more accurate is *not* on the agenda, for this would require reducing expectations, and that would be detrimental to performance. Management's aim is to increase productivity, and that requires high expectations. In this context, it is more important that expectations be high than that they be accurate. Sacrificing accuracy to raise expectations can be productive, whereas lowering expectations to gain accuracy would be counterproductive. If productivity is the desired end, then increasing the *level*, not the accuracy, of performance expectations is the means.

This point is not obvious, and has been missed by some. For example, after researching the issue (Green & Mitchell 1979; Mitchell, Green & Wood 1981; Mitchell & Wood 1980), Mitchell and his colleagues have developed a two-stage model of how to manage poor performers. The two stages are *diagnosing* the poor-performance problem and *deciding* what corrective action to take. These authors have thoroughly explored the manner in which managers' attributions influence the diagnoses they make and, consequently, the actions they deem it appropriate to take. Unfortunately, in Mitchell and Larson's (1987) textbook presentation of the issue, they stress the importance of establishing *clear* expectations (p. 534). The authors specify what they mean by clarifying expectations in terms of setting very specific performance goals and providing specific guidelines for how subordinates should behave. All their advice is worthy of endorsement, except that it is not enough that managers specify *clear* performance goals for poor performers. If managers make it very clear that very little is expected, the poor performance problem will persist. The thrust of the present argument is that it needs to be stressed that low performing workers should be told that *more* is expected of them.

Manager Expectations ———▶ Leadership:
The Allocation of Leadership to Subordinates

"Leadership" in the SFP model refers to a broad spectrum of behaviors on the part of managers that communicate their performance expectations to their subordinates and influence their subordinates' performance. Effective leadership involves holding subordinates in high regard and treating them accordingly. Leadership includes clusters of managerial behaviors that we conventionally call "leadership styles." Managers allocate leadership selectively. They enact a more effective leadership style toward subordinates who are expected to do well, and that leadership style contributes to the subordinates' success. This cluster of expectancy-arousing leadership behaviors is called the Pygmalion Leadership Style. The Pygmalion Leadership Style is discussed at length later.

Figure 4–2 shows that the manager allocates leadership to subordinates according to the level of performance he expects of them. This allocation is not always the result of a conscious decision. In postexperimental debriefing, Eden and Shani's instructors denied treating any of their trainees differently. King (1971) also reported unawareness on the part of the vocational instructors he studied. Teacher-expectancy experimenters have reported similar lack of awareness on the part of their subjects. It is unlikely that these supervisors were dissimulating. Rather, they probably were simply unaware of the fact that they were providing their subordinates with differential treatment in accordance with their expectations. Raising their expectations induces managers to enact a more effective leadership style without their even knowing it! One purpose of this book is to help make managers aware of the largely subconscious allocation of these leadership resources so that they can assert rational, goal-oriented control over it.

Whether on the basis of a conscious decision or not, managers *do* distinguish among their subordinates, treating as high achievers those expected to do well, and treating as low performers those expected to do poorly. Managers make this discrimination on their own, without being trained or cajoled to do so. Managers allocate their leadership to subordinates according to their expectations. This allocation promotes achievement on the part of those expected to do well. However, it also contributes to the failure of those expected to perform poorly. Graen's work on leader-member exchange, cited in chapter 2, has demonstrated the differentiation of treatment. Individual subordinates perceived by managers to be highly able are treated more favorably. They comprise an "in group" whom the manager takes into his confidence and with whom he consults. He especially relies on them to come through in a pinch. Subordinates of whom less is expected are ignored as members of an "out group." The Pygmalion research converges with Graen's in showing that when the manager has a basis for expecting effective perfor-

Figure 4–2. The Impact of Managers' Expectations on Their Leadership

mance from a subordinate, that subordinate is treated to a more effective leadership style. Hersey and Blanchard's (1977) normative model of leadership similarly calls for the use of more participative and delegative leadership styles in managing "mature" subordinates—subordinates of high ability and motivation, who can be relied upon to be productive in the absence of directive control.

Thus, managers treat some subordinates "better" than others. Proponents of situational leadership would argue that better or worse cannot be judged apart from the particular circumstances in which the leadership is being exercised. However, the effectiveness of high-expectancy leadership is not dependent upon particular characteristics of the situation. Situational conditioning effects do not limit the universal applicability of high-expectancy leadership. Furthermore, high-expectancy leadership can be used in combination with, or as a supplement to, any other leadership style. For example, a manager can use the Pygmalion Leadership Style to a very great extent and still engage in a great deal of telling, selling, participating, or delegating. This is because managers of all styles can communicate high expectations.

Leadership Expansion

In the IDF combat experiment, supervisory behavior improved even though it was not directly targeted by the intervention, no consulting or training resources were invested in it, and the supervisors were unaware that it was occurring (Eden & Shani 1982). Managers induced by King to expect higher output also led their plants to achieve better productivity with no additional training or other resources. By their own wits, they mobilized their leadership resources in the service of their expectations. A similar expansion of leadership resources must have occurred in the IDF squad leaders experiment in which commanders led whole platoons to better performance without being instructed, trained, or coached in how to do it. The repeated replication of the leadership expansion phenomenon means that high expectations induce managers to mobilize more of their leadership resources. Managers already *possess* the requisite leadership skills for getting subordinates to increase their productivity; raising their expectations gets them to *use* these skills more than they do when their expectations are lower. Hence, some of the costly investment in leadership skill training can be saved by raising managers' performance expectations.

It can be argued that managers instinctively allocate this scarce organizational resource—good leadership—in a suboptimal manner. They should invest their best leadership talent where it is needed most—in those suspected of being less capable than the others. These are the workers who have the greatest need for good leadership. By not treating them to the best leadership he or she can muster, the manager "wastes" it on others who need it less. Furthermore, being ignored, or underloaded, deprives those expected to fail of the opportunities to try, learn, and show what they *can* do, and is likely to produce a Golem effect. The resulting underutilization of their capability constitutes a loss to them personally and to the organization.

It can also be argued that the allocation is optimal. Managers lavish their best leadership upon those who appear to have the best prospects of excelling and they refrain from squandering it on those deemed unlikely to succeed regardless what is invested in them. This kind of thinking is evident in the common wisdom among managers that "when you have something really important that has to be done well and in a hurry, give it to your busiest subordinate." The implicit assumption is that the busy subordinate has proven competence, has been called upon to undertake a heavy load of important tasks, and can therefore be expected to succeed in the next mission as well. The very act of assigning important tasks to a subordinate communicates confidence in that subordinate's ability to succeed. This is Rosenthal's (1973) "opportunities for output" factor. Moreover, both overload and underload are sources of role stress (Kahn, Wolfe, Quinn, Snoek & Rosenthal 1964), and acute role stress can impair performance (Westman & Eden 1989b.) Mere overloading is only one means, and surely not the best means, of providing special treatment to subordinates expected to succeed. There is much more to SFP-generating leadership than that. Having decided that a subordinate is likely to succeed, the manager supervises him using the Pygmalion Leadership Style.

The Pygmalion Leadership Style

The only supervisory behaviors we assessed in the IDF combat-course experiment were the four factors of leadership measured by the questionnaire devised by Bowers and Seashore (1966). These factors are support, work facilitation, goal emphasis, and interaction facilitation. Although Bowers and Seashore culled these items from a rich diversity of valid leadership research instruments, and although the items have proven applicability to a great variety of management situations, they capture only the types of behaviors typically conceived of as characterizing overt supervisory style. Much significant managerial behavior that comprises the Pygmalion Leadership Style eludes such scales. For example, the subconscious, nonverbal communication of warmth and positive regard, detected by King (1971) using photos of the supervisor with dilated pupils, could not be assessed by means of conventional self-report questionnaires. Similarly, intonation is a dimension of verbal behavior with profound SFP implications that goes undetected by written questionnaire measures. To illustrate, depending on vocal inflection, the simple words "you can do it" can convey very high or very low performance expectations. Body language is an often undetected medium for the unconscious communication of expectations. There are countless other ways in which managers discriminate in their treatment of subordinates in accordance with their expectations. Thus, the use of conventional leadership concepts and questionnaires in the attempt to capture the behaviors that mediate the effects of manager expectations on subordinate performance perforce underestimates the role of the mediators. As the sources of manager expectations are myriad, so are the styles, channels, and contents of their expression. In this section, the diverse ways in which managers' expectations influence their behavior are enumerated.

The central feature of the Pygmalion Leadership Style is the explicit and implicit communication of high performance expectations. Communicating performance expectations is part of every leader's behavior. Many managerial acts can be interpreted as an expression of manager expectations and influence subordinate self-expectations. What is unique to the Pygmalion Leadership Style is the consistent encouraging, supporting, and reinforcing of high expectations resulting in the adoption, acceptance, or internalization of high expectations on the part of the subordinates. In the simplest and most straightforward instance, it is a manager reassuringly telling a subordinate, "I know you can do this well." This message can be transmitted in an endless variety of ways. The hallmark of an effective leader is his ability to get this message across convincingly and to inspire high self-confidence among the other persons around him. This is attested to by the recently renewed interest among management scholars in charismatic leadership (Conger & Kanungo 1987).

The wide range of behaviors that comprise the Pygmalion Leadership Style includes all of Rosenthal's (1973) four factors of socioemotional climate, feedback, input, and opportunities for output, described in chapter 1. Rosenthal's factors are couched in classroom terminology. Below is a rendition of Rosenthal's factors in language more familiar to the management reader. This is a classroom-to-workplace translation that enumerates some of the managerial behaviors included in the Pygmalion Leadership Style and foreshadows some of the practical applications proposed in the next chapter.

Socioemotional Climate

This factor includes all the nonverbal behaviors of the manager during interaction with the subordinate that subconciously convey an emotional message and create a supportive interpersonal climate, or "chemistry," between manager and subordinate. The manager behaviors that contribute to this climate include looking the subordinate in the eye, nodding affirmatively and approvingly, smiling, drawing near to the subordinate physically, voicing warm, supportive intonation, and holding one's body in an erect, attentive posture during conversation with the subordinate. These are the manager behaviors that naturally accompany high expectations. Through these nonverbal behaviors the manager maintains Likert's (1961) "principle of supportive relations." Such behaviors result in a high score on support, one of the Bowers-and-Seashore four factors of leadership. These are the behaviors that led the welding trainees in King's (1971) experiment to choose the wide-eyed version of their supervisor's photo as being most like him. Other things being equal, enacting these leadership behaviors is likely to improve performance.

Feedback

The high-expectancy manager provides more feedback to his subordinates than does the manager who expects little. Providing feedback promotes learning. Withholding feedback is not a neutral behavior; it is an expression of neglect. Evaluating subordinates' performance and letting them know where they stand are management acts that make subordinates aware that someone is watching and keeping accounts. Komaki (1986) sought to reveal the behaviors that distinguish effective from ineffective managers. She found two supervisory behaviors in which the effective managers engaged significantly more than ineffective managers. The effective managers did more *performance monitoring* by collecting information about subordinates' performance through work sampling, direct observation of work behavior, asking subordinates for self-reports about their performance, or consulting secondary sources about subordinates' performance. The second type of supervisory behavior characteristic of effective managers is what Komaki has dubbed *performance consequences*. Through "consequences" behaviors the manager indicates to the subordinates that he has knowledge of their performance. The behaviors include recognizing work well done, noting corrections, and providing feedback. Pygmalion does not wait for the annual performance review to let people know where they stand. He finds many opportunities in day-to-day intercourse to comment on subordinates' performance, sometimes to compliment them for a job well done, sometimes to correct an error and to teach the proper method, but frequently letting the subordinate know that he is watching and that he cares how the subordinate is performing. These interactions are opportunities for expectancy-raising. Giving positive feedback affords the manager a good opportunity for communicating confidence that the good work will go on, and negative feedback can be supplemented with encouragement based on the manager's confidence that the subordinate is capable of improving his performance and that he will do so.

Input

The Pygmalion Leadership Style entails increased investment in subordinates. Pygmalion never views training as a waste of time, nor does he regard training his subordinates as someone else's job. Many of the Pygmalion management behaviors have a training flavor. The specific behaviors include such acts as staying with the subordinates the extra hour, giving the additional explanation, providing know-how, demonstrating again how to do it right, challenging subordinates to stretch their current abilities by getting involved in more demanding work, and taking advantage of every opportunity to elevate subordinates to higher levels of competence. These are managerial behaviors that foster workers' growth and propel them to ever higher levels of achievement.

Output

Pygmalion provides subordinates with ample opportunity to "show their stuff." By giving people the chance to tackle tough assignments and to work for the achievement of challenging goals, the manager makes a concrete expression of his confidence in the subordinate's competence. This is especially powerful when there is some risk to the manager if the subordinate fails. In such cases, the subordinate realizes that the boss must believe in him. Managers unwilling to take such risks forever pay the price of never revealing what their unchallenged subordinates might be capable of achieving. Giving workers opportunities to show what they can do thus fosters high performance both by expressing high expectations and by allowing for excellence to occur. One can only speculate how many Golems have been needlessly created by managers who never challenged their subordinates with difficult tasks or goals.

Pygmalion and Charisma: Transformational Leadership Inspires High Expectations

The impact of managerial behavior upon subordinate self-expectations can profitably be viewed on a much grander scale than in the preceding section. Traditional leadership research has been based on the behavioral theories developed by scholars at Ohio State University and at the University of Michigan. It has been focused on the specific task-oriented and employee-centered microbehaviors that distinguish managers from one another. These behaviors comprise "transactional" leadership; they are part of an exchange relationship between the manager and the subordinate in which they transact a workable deal: production in return for decent treatment.

A new conceptualization of leadership has recently begun to emerge. Organizational scholars are renewing their interest in Weber's (1947) concept of charisma. Some are attempting to articulate charisma in concrete terms to demystify the concept and to make it more readily amenable to research and application (for example, Conger & Kanungo 1987; House 1977).

As part of this "new look" at charisma, leadership theorists have developed the concept of transformational leadership. The transformation concept addresses a leadership phenomenon broader than transactional leadership that extends far beyond the confines of conventional conceptualizations of "managerial style." Charismatic and inspirational leadership are dubbed "transformational" because they alter workers' beliefs in their capacity to achieve outstanding levels of performance, levels that exceed their previous achievements and expectations. Such leadership transforms subordinates by changing their values, ideals, motives, and concepts of what levels of achievement are possible. Hence Bass (1985) titled his book on transactional leadership *Leadership and Performance beyond Expectations*. Borrowing heavily from political science and psychohistory, and acknowledging a particular debt to Burns (1978), Bass (1985) described transformational leadership as a broad phenomenon that encompasses both charisma and Pygmalion. Characterizing transformational leaders, Bass wrote: "Charismatics take advantage of the Pygmalion effect . . . and reciprocate in their confidence in their followers and in their optimistic expectations about their followers' performance. Follower self-esteem and enthusiasm are raised as a consequence, and the effort is increased among followers to fulfill the leaders' expressed expectations" (p. 47). Expanding House's conceptualization of charisma to include inspirational leadership, Bass includes "making use of the Pygmalion effect" as an inspirational behavior: "In its most general form, the Pygmalion effort (*sic*) is a performance-stimulating effect. People who are led to expect that they will do well, will be better than those who expect to do poorly or who do not have any expectations about how well or poorly they will do. . . . The leader who arouses in subordinates confidence in their own capabilities and confidence in those with whom they work, all things being equal, by raising expectations about the success of their efforts, will increase such efforts to succeed" (p. 71). Bass has thus incorporated the Pygmalion effect into his model of transformational leadership.

In a similar vein, Bennis and Nanus (1985) described the "transformative" leaders whom they interviewed as "visionary." "The visions these various leaders conveyed seemed to bring about a confidence on the part of the employees, a confidence that instilled in them a belief that they were capable of performing the necessary acts" (p. 30). Believing one is capable of performing the necessary acts is precisely Bandura's (1977) definition of self-efficacy. "Positive self-regard seems to exert its force by creating in others a sense of confidence and high expectations, not very different from the fabled Pygmalion effect" (Bennis & Nanus 1985, 65).

Emphasizing leadership style in the traditional sense focuses attention on one-on-one relationships between the manager and each subordinate individually. This focus makes it possible to consider different styles for different subordinates on the part of the same manager. On the other hand, transformational leadership is an all-encompassing, generalized style that the manager directs to *all* subordinates without distinction. The object of the transformational leader's high expectations is the entire organization, rather than individual subordinates. This kind of leadership behavior suits Pygmalion. Such leadership is most likely to result in productive SFP, as each individual worker touched by the transformational leader's confidence is likely to become a party to a positive expectancy effect. The more visible the inspirational manager and the greater the number of individuals affected by his positive expectations, the larger the number of individual Pygmalion effects that combine in producing the dramatic boost in collective effectiveness.

Beyond the additive combination of numerous individual Pygmalion effects, there can also be an emergent effect at the group or organizational level that results from the synergistic impact of many individuals' maintaining mutual high expectations. This makes organizationwide SFP possible. Indeed, inspirational leadership, Pygmalion, and SFP may be behind many successful business turnarounds (Iacocca 1984). Similarly, low expectations regarding the outcomes of a merger are part of the "merger syndrome" and result from a failure of leadership. Marks and Schriber (1988) found that top level leadership in handling corporate mergers was related to employee expectations that the merger would lead to improved organization and enhanced business results. Thus, success and failure in mergers appear to be in part caused by SFP produced by top management.

Describing the ideal school principal in terms of "visionary leadership," Sashkin (1988) wrote:

> Only if there exists the belief that the organization can control its destiny is it likely to even try. Moreover, such trials may well change the "reality," so that the organization *becomes* more capable of controlling its environment and its ultimate destiny. Thus, while it is foolish and perhaps even destructive to hold to values that are in obvious conflict with reality, there is much to be said for taking "optimistic" positions, even when one realizes that there may be some question about whether the value is, in fact, consistent with objective reality (p. 242).

Sashkin thus described the visionary leader's impact in terms of getting people in the organization to share in an optimistic vision—that is, high expectations—of the organization's future. Adopting a rosy vision sparks an organizationwide SFP that contributes to the ultimate realization of the vision. Through the collective action of the individuals affected, the vision ultimately transforms reality.

To summarize, a transformational interpretation of the process depicted in figure 4–3 is appropriate. A manager can inspire his subordinates to believe in their individual and collective ability to excel—that is, to have very high self-expectations—by himself believing in them and consistently demonstrating this belief in myriad ways. Such a manager can dramatically improve a unit's performance. This is an omnibus approach, as it implies a contagious exuberance that radiates from the manager to those surrounding him, creating general expectations for a revolutionary departure from entrenched routine that will drastically raise the effectiveness of the organization. This kind of leadership is exemplified by the Chrysler television commercials showing the wink, reassuring smile, and thumbs-up optimism of bouncy Lee Iacocca, accompanied by the rock jingle "The Pride is Back—Born in America." The ad may be directed as much to the hundreds of thousands of Chrysler employees as to the millions of potential automobile customers among the viewers.

Leadership ⟶ Subordinate Self–Expectancy: The Influence Process

The crux of the Pygmalion effect is the manager's influence on the subordinate's self-expectations. It is by raising or lowering the subordinate's self-expectations that the manager energizes or de-energizes the motivational process conceptualized by the expectancy theory of work motivation, embodied by the Galatea triangle. The subordinate's self-expectations are the key to greater productivity, and this key is turned by managerial leadership that provides the basis upon which the subordinate can build high expectations. It is the manager's job to provide subordinates with the greatest possible array of supports for high-performance expectations. The influence of the manager's leadership on the subordinate's expectations links the Pygmalion triangle to the Galatea triangle. This is the link between managerial behavior and subordinate motivation. This is probably the single most important aspect of manager-subordinate relations, at least insofar as productivity is concerned. This link is displayed in figure 4–3. The influnce of the Pygmalion Leadership Style on the subordinate's internal psychological state results in a high level of expectations and eagerness to exert effort in task performance. The Pygmalion Leadership Style builds subordinate confidence regarding what can be accomplished. In terms of Bandura's (1986) social learning theory, the Pygmalion Leadership Style is effective because it boosts the subordinates' own sense of their efficacy for achieving outstanding performance. We have demonstrated experimentally that raising supervisors' expectations boosts self-expectations among their subordinates (Eden & Ravid 1982). In this section we shall spell out some mechanisms via which manager leadership influences subordinate expectations.

Figure 4–3. The Influence of Manager Leadership on Subordinate Self-Expectations

Bandura's (1986) theory of self-efficacy is a fruitful source of ideas about *how* subordinate self-expectations are influenced by manager behavior. Self-efficacy theory can also serve as a source of practical ideas for training managers to raise subordinate self-expectations. Bandura (1986) has delineated four sources of information that influence an individual to raise or lower his self-efficacy. They are enactive attainment, vicarious experience, verbal persuasion, and physiological state. These sources of self-efficacy information are partially under managers' control. Therefore, they are relevant to the leadership ⟶ subordinate self-expectancy link in the SFP-at-work model. They are means by which a manager can enact the Pygmalion Leadership Style toward subordinates by enhancing their sense of self-efficacy.

Enactive Attainment

Achieving success at some activity or task that requires the use of a particular skill or set of skills strengthens one's sense of self-efficacy. Failure has the opposite effect. Successful performance is the most potent source of positive self-efficacy information, since one's own personal experience of success in executing a course of action is incontrovertible evidence of one's ability to effect the required performance. Hearing encouragement from others or seeing one's colleagues succeed is just not the same. Indeed, "nothing succeeds like success." An enlightened manager seeking to use the Pygmalion Leadership Style can readily make enactive attainment part of the experience of his subordinates through thoughtful planning of assignments.

Some unenlightened managers brag about their policy of throwing young management trainees or interns into the "deep water" to find out whether they will sink or swim. Those who swim will certainly emerge with greatly enhanced self-efficacy, and the resulting self-confidence, optimism, and eagerness to undertake challenging assignments in the future will generalize to activities similar to that which led to the success experience. But the water is deep, and these youngsters are just getting started. For the many who sink, the premature experience of failure will inflict lasting—if not permanent—damage to their self-efficacy. Their career development will be slowed down, as they will shun challenging assignments until their depressed self-efficacy can recover. How foolish and wasteful of valuable human resources!

Early enactive attainment determines how influential the remaining three sources of self-efficacy information will be. Having experienced success, positive vicarious experience and verbal persuasion will be readily absorbed, and negative examples and messages will be rejected. Conversely, early failure experiences will render other sources of positive self-efficacy information unacceptable, as the frustrated individual finds it easier to accept information compatible with his fresh experience of failure.

The managerial imperative is clear and obvious: Prevent avoidable failure! Lead subordinates through experiences of success by structuring tasks and assignments in ascending order of difficulty. Don't impose unattainable goals, and don't let overly ambitious subordinates qualitatively overload themselves. Pygmalion builds self-efficacy gradually over time by assuring a long string of successes in gradually more challenging tasks.

Nobody is perfect. Everyone fails at something from time to time. The manager cannot stave off his subordinates' experiences of failure forever. What he can—and should—do is to delay serious failure until after subordinates have accumulated sufficient successes to serve as a buffer against damage of failure to their self-efficacy. Knowing that the same degree of failure is more damaging earlier than later, and that past success constitutes a protective mechanism for people's self-efficacy, Pygmalion exposes his protégés to risk gradually, when he knows they can absorb failure with their self-efficacy intact. Moreover, in the wake of every significant outcome experience, whether success or failure, Pygmalion is on the scene making sure that the subordinate attributes success to his own competence and attributes failure to insufficient effort or to bad luck. If the attribution process is mismanaged, successful performance may be lost to cognitive misinterpretation instead of being experienced as efficacy-enhancing mastery.

Vicarious Experience

We learn some things by observing others. Witnessing, or sometimes merely imagining, the success or failure of someone deemed to be similar to us, we draw conclusions about our own self-efficacy for performing the same or similar activity. While not as powerful as enactive attainment in determining self-efficacy, vicarious experience is widespread in our lives, including our working lives. We are frequently in a position to see others attempting to perform tasks and assignments similar to our own. Sensitive managers purposely expose younger, less experienced employees to successful seniors in the anticipation that some of the seniors' prowess will "rub off" onto the juniors. Because of the depressing effects of vicarious failure experiences on self-efficacy, certain failures are wisely concealed to protect the self-efficacy of the impressionable.

Behavior role-modeling is a successful personnel training method developed on the basis of Bandura's social learning theory (Goldstein 1986). Behavior modeling is successful (Goldstein & Sorcher 1974; Latham & Saari 1979) because it takes advantage of the fact that we learn many things quite well through imitation. Watching someone else, a model, demonstrate how to perform a job well not only facilitates our mastery of the requisite skills, but also strengthens our confidence that we, too, can master it. The model's success becomes our success, vicariously, and our self-efficacy is enhanced. Thus, behavior modeling is an effective training method for its positive effect on self-efficacy owing to the trainee's vicarious experience while observing the model as much as for its facilitation of actual skill acquisition.

It is not only specific behavioral skills that workers learn through vicarious experience. They may also acquire the manager's work orientation, philosophy, and commitment to work, to their roles, and to the company. Managers are always in the limelight, forever being watched by dependent subordinates. Whether aware of it or not, the manager is always having an influence. Sometimes, merely being in the presence of a manager who exudes optimism can increase one's self-confidence, even when the optimism is not specifically directed toward oneself. Confidence can be catchy. However, this, too, is a double-edged sword. A cynical, defeatest, or otherwise discouraging attitude on the part of a manager can be a contagious malady that spreads and afflicts vulnerable others, peers and subordinates alike.

Both behavior modeling and vicarious experience have their strongest effects on one's sense of mastery when the model is similar to the observer and when the behavior observed is similar to the behavior to be executed. Potential managerial applications of vicarious experience are thus based on planning for employees' exposure to positive models and avoiding negative examples. When both actual and vicarious success experiences are unavailable or impractical, the manager can still raise employee self-efficacy by using the third source of the employee's self-efficacy information as defined by Bandura.

Verbal Persuasion

The best parents, teachers, and managers invest enormous effort trying to convince children, pupils, and employees that they are capable of achieving success in their endeavors. This type of mentoring effort is well spent. Instead of, or in addition to, actual, imagined, modeled, or otherwise perceived successful performance, a respected person considered to be a credible source of information can talk someone into higher self-efficacy. This is especially appropriate for those workers who tend to underestimate their abilities, such as underachievers who are unaccustomed to exerting effort and using their capacity. However, mismanagement can undermine the self-confidence even of outstanding performers. Redskins coach George Allen's expressions of doubt concerning Curt Knight's ability to kick field goals is an example of negative verbal persuasion.

Verbal persuasion is not limited to superiors vis-à-vis their subordinates; it is also a way we can help our colleagues. An encouraging conversation with an able peer experiencing temporary self-doubt can convince him he is exaggerating his difficulties, underestimating his true competence, and thus contribute to uplifting his self-efficacy sufficiently that he may at least try harder.

Physiological State

The last source of self-efficacy information that Bandura defined is the individual's sensations of his own physiological reactions. People respond physiologically as they experience events in their daily lives, and they sometimes interpret their bodily reactions as evidence of high or low self-efficacy. A simple example is feeling aches and pains, racing heartbeat and strong heart palpitations, breathlessness, and in general feeling "beat" during and after the performance of a physically strenuous activity. People may read these physiological reactions as signifying a lack of capacity for performing adequately in the situation in which the reactions occur, particularly if they are in poor physical condition. This interpretation reduces their expectations for successful performance.

On the positive side, one of the rewards of maintaining physical fitness by regular exercise is the sense of self-efficacy that it provides. From personal experience over the years, I can attest to the exhilarating feeling of well-being, potency, and confidence derived from jogging three miles or swimming a thousand meters when in condition. The resulting sense of mastery generalizes to apparently unrelated spheres of endeavor. This boost to self-efficacy resulting from an improved physiological state is undoubtedly fueling the current physical fitness craze.

We also sense our physiological state in response to intense emotional experiences. One such experience is the feeling of exhilaration that accompanies success and achievement. Noticing reports of such feelings on the part of subordinates, Pygmalion speaks up to facilitate their attribution to the knowledge that a job has been done well.

Stress as a Self-Fulfilling Prophecy

Stress is another type of emotional response reflected in one's state of physiological arousal, even in the absence of taxing physical activity. We experience job stress when we perceive the threat of being overwhelmed by too big a job whose demands outstrip our capacity. Such job stress can arise as a result of SFP.

Workers react emotionally and physiologically to difficult job demands that threaten to overwhelm their coping capacity. When demands appear to outstrip ability in situations where failure will be costly to the individual, he will experience stress (McGrath 1976). Experiencing this kind of acute job stress has been shown to arouse stress-responses, or strain, including elevated blood pressure, quickened heart rate, and psychosomatic symptoms such as headaches, lower-back pain, and strong heart palpitations among nurses (Eden 1982) and among computer users (Caplan & Jones 1975; Eden 1990). Such experiences of physiological strain constitute a source of negative self-efficacy information. For the worker threatened with impending failure, strain reinforces the feelings of inadequacy that gave rise to the sense of being overwhelmed in the first place, and self-efficacy wanes.

Job stress and subsequent performance decrements can come about as a result of SFP. If an individual who is fully competent to perform an assignment gets the wrong idea, for whatever reason, that he lacks the wherewithal to succeed, the resulting experience of stress will impair performance. This is because the anticipation of failure arouses anxiety and causes people to ruminate about their lack of self-efficacy for meeting the demands and to worry about how they will endure the shame of failure. Thus, they fret away the capacity that they should be using to meet the challenge. Recall Redskins place kicker Curt Knight's words when asked why his performance had slipped so badly, as quoted in scenario B in the introduction: "Every time I get out there and miss I feel like I committed a federal offense, so all I ever do is think about missing." Thus, lack of confidence arouses stress, which breeds failure, which in turn reduces confidence still further, which in turn fuels more failure, and so on. This vicious cycle can be dubbed "stress as a self-fulfilling prophecy." It is undoubtedly widespread, as many workers are confronted from time to time by assignments, goals, or constraints that tax the limits of their performance capacity.

Stress-as-SFP is preventable. Managers can contribute to prevention in several ways. First, they should refrain from exaggerating in the level of demands that they impose on their subordinates. Demands, goals, and expectations should be difficult but realistic. If the manager is reasonable in his high expectations, one potential source of sky-high expectations is kept in check. Second, managers should keep in touch with their subordinates' levels of anticipation. When managers perceive that subordinates are exaggerating their estimates of the demands being made upon them, for whatever reason, the manager should bring the subordinate back to reality. This is especially important in managing overly ambitious subordinates, who lack a sense of realistic bounds. Third, managers should be sure to provide the necessary support when subordinates *are* overwhelmed. This involves both emotional support in the form of treating subordinates with empathy as well as instrumental support in the form of extra doses of work-facilitation leadership.

To summarize, Bandura's four sources of self-efficacy information are helpful in defining concrete ways in which the manager can fulfill his leadership role in SFP by communicating high expectations to his subordinates. A manager who is masterful at influencing the self-efficacy information which reaches his subordinates can almost guarantee that they will have a high level of expectations. Bandura's concepts have thus proven useful as a way of spelling out how to implement Likert's (1961) call for managers to communicate high-performance expectations to their subordinates. Keeping expectations within reasonable bounds can also prevent costly stress.

Summary

The Pygmalion effect is the result of a leadership process in which a manager who expects outstanding performance treats subordinates in ways that stimulate their productivity. Performance expectations can arise from many sources. Some of these sources usually yield accurate information, whereas some most often misinform managers' expectations. Records of past performance are particularly notorious sources of erroneous information. Physical appearance and various stereotypes also frequently lead managers to mistaken expectations. Whereas high expectations trigger productive Pygmalion effects, low, inaccurate expectations precipitate unfortunate Golem effects. Unquestioning acceptance of previous performance levels as indicative of the upper limits of a subordinate's ability can lead to a self-sustaining prophecy, in which previous underachievement is perpetuated. Therefore, low expectations should always be checked for accuracy.

Managers treat different subordinates differently depending on what level of performance they expect from each subordinate. When expectations are high, the manager enacts the Pygmalion Leadership Style. The manager can enact the Pygmalion Leadership Style by engaging in the following behaviors:

a. Communicate high but realistic performance expectations;

b. Encourage subordinates to accept difficult but realistic goals and objectives;

c. Persuade subordinates that they are capable of achieving success when the subordinates appear to harbor self-doubt;

d. Create supportive relationships and a warm socioemotional climate;

e. Provide feedback about performance;

f. Invest considerable task-oriented supervisory input in informing, instructing, directing, and otherwise facilitating subordinates' performance;

g. Provide subordinates ample opportunities to test their abilities, to improve their skills, and to prove what they are capable of accomplishing;

h. Provide successful role models;

i. Prevent avoidable failure;

j. Arrange for graduated successes by assigning subordinates to easy tasks at first, followed by more demanding work until the upper limits of the subordinate's ability are approached (but not exceeded);

k. Help subordinates to attribute their successes to their own abilities and to attribute their failures to insufficient effort, task or goal difficulty, or bad luck.

The common thread running through all these leadership behaviors is the facilitation of strong confidence among subordinates regarding their competence and high expectations that they will perform successfully.

Some managers naturally use the Pygmalion Leadership Style, for they believe in their subordinates' capacity for excellence, and are confident in their own ability to bring out the best in people. Their naturally high expectations spark the Pygmalion leadership behaviors in their treatment of their subordinates. Natural Pygmalions do not wait for subordinates to prove themselves. Instead, they give employees the benefit of the doubt, presume that they are capable of achieving good performance, and then treat them to leadership that facilitates the fulfillment of their high expectations. The final chapter of this book discusses how managers who are not natural Pygmalions can be trained to use the Pygmalion Leadership Style.

Aroused by the prophecy of good performance, the Pygmalion Leadership Style is the behavioral key by which managers get their subordinates to fulfill their high expectations, and the subordinates' self-efficacy is the latch that that key turns. Subordinates who are fortunate enough to have a Pygmalion for a boss respond favorably because of his impact on their sense of self-efficacy. Experiencing enactive mastery by succeeding in successive tasks assigned by the manager, observing the positive models made available by the manager, and listening to the manager's persuasive words telling them that they have what it takes to excel, subordinates develop an enhanced sense of their own capability to effect the performances required to succeed on the job. Managers' use of the Pygmalion Leadership Style transforms workers' concept of what they can accomplish, and the result is performance "beyond (previous) expectations."

This summarizes what we know about SFP at work at the individual level. We have by now completely demystified the Pygmalion effect in management. The interpersonal influence processes involved in SFP have been explicated in terms of directly or indirectly observable psychological variables at the individual level, including expectations, motives, and behavior. The theoretical model is stated parsimoniously, it is backed by empirical evidence, and it can be tested further.

However, there is more. Managers influence workers not only through direct, one-on-one contact, but also via the medium of the organization that envelopes them all. In the next chapter we shall examine the role of the organization and its culture on SFP processes at work.

Appendix 4A

Deficiencies in Teacher Expectancy Research

There are some serious methodological shortcomings in the teacher expectancy research. Most of these studies have been based on laboratory experimentation in which subjects, often students rather than professional teachers, are given descriptions of objectively equally qualified pupils in which only race, gender, or social class is varied. When "teachers" rate the likely future academic performance of these stimulus pupils differentially on the basis of race, gender, or class, the results are interpreted as evidence for demographic biasing of teacher expectations. These data-collection circumstances are a far cry from natural classroom settings. Such studies may convincingly demonstrate causal effects of demographic variables on expectations, but they may not be generalizable to the actual field conditions where the findings would be applicable. In other words, these laboratory experiments may have a high degree of internal validity, but are seriously wanting in external validity.

Some of the teacher expectation research has been conducted in the field. Professional teachers have been asked to state their expectations for their actual pupils who differ in demographic background. However, the interpretability of such field studies is even more problematic than in the laboratory experiments. This is because any relationship found between demographic background and teacher expectations regarding pupil achievement could result from teachers' knowledge of actual differences in achievement between the demographic groups studied. Such studies have a high degree of generalizability, since practicing teachers are rating their own actual pupils. But their cross-sectional design precludes unequivocal causal interpretation. Finding a relationship between demographic variables and teacher expectations without experimental manipulation of the demographic variables, it is impossible to determine whether the demographic characteristics caused the teacher's expectations or whether the teachers' expectations were caused by their pupils' past achievements, which are known to the teachers. These studies are externally valid but seriously deficient in internal validity. Confronted with confirmatory findings from numerous studies with the strengths and weaknesses described above, some analysts would say that the combined strengths of the laboratory experiments and the field studies make the findings acceptable, with some studies compensating for the shortcomings in others. Other analysts would be more skeptical. Therefore, the reader is advised to take these findings as suggestive.

5

Organizationwide
Self-Fulfilling Prophecy

Frogs to Princes: A Desperate Experiment

The IDF runs a program of special training for inductees who do not meet normal standards for service. These people have either borderline IQ or mild psychological problems that make their adjustment to the rigors of military life very difficult. While not actually disabled, they are regarded as needing special attention to get through basic training and go on to complete their service obligations. Most armies routinely exempt such individuals from service. However, the IDF's manpower needs are so great that it cannot afford the luxury of simply rejecting marginally qualified draftees. Rather, initially under-qualified candidates are carefully classified and many of them get trained in basic skills so they can be of some service to the military. Those who make it through the program serve in low-level logistical, clerical, or other non-combat roles. The special program is one that many of its graduates are grateful for because it reclaims them from an unsavory future by giving them a significant success experience in life, by teaching them how to adjust to a formal organizational setting and to authority, and by training them in basic skills that are of value in the civilian job market. The officers who run the special program revel in their success. They have a sense of mission and frequently quote the sages of ancient Israel: "He who saves one soul . . . is likened to him who has saved the entire world." They are proud of their role in taking in society's rejects and rehabilitating them for a more fulfilling life.

The program has evolved over the years and has gone through several revisions. Its key elements are a separate training facility, a specially selected, trained, and dedicated volunteer staff, an extended period of basic training, classroom literacy training to supplement military training, and initial relaxation of military discipline, followed by gradual tightening as the trainees learn to handle the rigors of army life. Through it all, an extraordinary amount of individual attention and genuine caring are lavished upon each trainee. These elements are regarded as essential for the program's success, being dictated by the special needs of this population. Nobody would have thought of sending these vulnerable youths to the large, impersonal boot camp where the bulk of IDF inductees undergo basic training. "Everybody knew" they couldn't make it there, with no one to cater to their special needs.

Then, a number of years ago, the special training facility was overwhelmed by a backlog of too many inductees for it to handle at one time. Some of these men had had their induction date postponed, at great inconvenience to their personal lives. The alternatives were to postpone their induction again and severely disrupt their lives, to exempt them from conscription and thereby lose their service and stigmatize them in civilian life as unsuitable misfits, or to send them to regular basic training at the boot camp without the cushioning provided by the special program. In desperation, the command opted for the latter.

It was a bold, natural experiment. A number of companies of inductees initially slated for the special program went through basic training at the boot camp. The training staff at boot camp was not told of the original plan for these trainees. They did have access to the types of information that instructors routinely retrieve from trainees' personnel files. But they were not told that these men had special problems and had been initially slated for basic training at the special facility to avoid alarming the instructors and to preclude stigmatization of the trainees through unnecessary labeling.

The experiment succeeded far beyond everyone's expectations. The dropout rate, disciplinary infractions, and proficiency levels achieved by the soldiers in these companies were not different from those of the other companies at boot camp. When treated as "regular" trainees, borderline inductees responded as ordinary soldiers despite their potentially debilitating problems.

This frogs-to-princes experiment is an instance of SFP at the macroorganizational level. Rather than one expecter and one or several expectees, organizationwide SFP is a more diffuse process that involves a much larger number of people. At its extreme, *everybody* in the organization shares in exceptionally high (or low) expectations regarding what the organization is capable of achieving. When the object of the expectations is the organization as an entity, rather than individual members, such widely shared expectations give rise to processes that are emergent at the macroorganizational level. These types of diffuse expectations, the organizational processes they spark, and the results they effect are the topic of this chapter.

The special IDF training facility for marginal inductees is reminiscent of the forward treatment centers for psychiatric combat casualties described by Noy and his colleagues (1983). Each of these facilities is an organization that has an easily identifiable culture that expresses clear assumptions and expectations about what its individual members are capable—and incapable—of doing. Deal and Kennedy (1982) call such pervasive and influential cultures "strong cultures." Individuals take on roles dictated by the culture of the organization that engulfs, and in some sense overpowers, them. The organization's culture is a rich repository of expectations, and most people tend to act as they are expected to act. The assumptions, manifest and latent, that comprise the organization's culture impinge upon individual members. The organization's assumptions become its members' assumptions, and its expectations become their expectations. When everything about the organization conveys to its members that they are abnormal, marginal, symptomatic, slow, and in need of remediation, individuals enact the role of fragile, dependent helpee. When they are treated as normal, they respond as normal individuals under the same circumstances.

The culture of the special facility, designed as a solution to a problem, actually may have contributed to the perpetuation of that problem. Whether all men classified as special could have succeeded in boot camp is not crucial to the argument; that some of these men could succeed if treated routinely as in the frogs-to-princes "experiment" makes the point for organizational SFP. These borderline individuals could have become "special" (frogs) or "normal" (princes). Organizationwide SFP determined which they became.

Frogs and Princes: An Epilogue.

This lesson was lost in the treatment of subsequent waves of similarly underqualified inductees. The special training facility was maintained, and later expanded, despite the fact that it is more costly because of the diseconomies of scale and the protracted length of the training programs it runs. Why didn't the successful "experiment" result in the closing down of the special facility? Perhaps the administrators who chanced exposing these inductees to the rigors of regular training were so relieved by the results that they attributed the success to luck and dared not risk it again unless similar dire circumstances force such a decision upon them. After all, this was not a randomized experiment, and it appears that in selecting underqualified candidates for regular boot camp, the commanders wisely "creamed" from among all the backlogged inductees those who had the mildest problems. Or, like bureaucrats everywhere, perhaps those in charge of the special program had a stake in its perpetuation and didn't *want* to learn a lesson that would render their pet project superfluous. Moreover, the program enjoyed very strong, public support of commanders at the highest levels of the general staff. Informing them that the program was not making a worthwhile contribution could involve career risks. At any rate, the special facility continued training men classified as needing it as before the "experiment," its many powerful supporters remaining convinced that the facility was essential for assuring the service of the inductees assigned to it. For the most competent minority of these men, the program was probably perpetuating their underachievement. One can only wonder how many similarly well-intended remedial programs unwittingly sustain preventable Golem effects the world over.

A Model of Organizationwide SFP

Figure 5–1 portrays a model of organizationwide SFP. It retains as its core the triangular-shaped SFP model depicted in figure 1–1. The fundamental notion behind organizationwide SFP is Merton's three-step expectancy ─────► new-behavior ─────► prophecy-fulfilled model. In the case of organizationwide SFP, expectations for some domain of organizational performance are widely shared among the members. For example, most people expect their organization to attain its profit goals or to succeed in finishing an important project on schedule. Acting on their expectations (arrow 1), the members enact both individual and collective behaviors that influence organizational processes such as leadership and collaboration. These processes have an impact on the organization's performance (arrow 2). The project is completed on time and the profit goals are reached. In such cases, when the subsequent increase in organizational productivity confirms members' initial collective expectations (arrow 3), those expectations are reinforced and sustain the SFP process. The same SFP process is at work when expectations for a decline in productivity are followed by poor performance.

Belief in the effectiveness of the organization itself, or in a program being run by the organization, can trigger an organizationwide SFP. In the frogs-to-princes experiment, the problematic inductees who were expected to be typical by the commanders and instructors running the basic training program at boot camp were led, trained, disciplined, motivated, and treated in every other way as normal trainees; they ended up performing on par with their nonproblematic peers. Acting on a collective expectation of normalcy, the boot camp staff used standard operating procedures, training and command techniques, and all the other organizational tools at their disposal to bring out the effective performances expected of their trainees. Not knowing of their trainees' "special limitations," the instructors' expectations and behavior toward the trainees were not influenced by these limitations. Similarly, in the forward treatment centers studied by Noy and his colleagues, expecting that after a short period of relief and treatment the combat-stress casualties would return to the front rather than being evacuated to a rear-echelon recuperation unit, both the staff and the soldiers performed the requisite behaviors that culminated in the evacuees' speedy recovery and return to their fighting units. Acting together on the basis of shared expectations, individuals joined efforts to fulfill their prophecies. Finally, in King's innovation-and-expectancy experiment, acting on the expectation that job enlargement or rotation would improve productivity, the managers and workers in the high-expectancy plants enacted the requisite behaviors that culminated in effecting the expected productivity gains. In all three examples, the basis for the organizationwide SFP was a program that was expected to work.

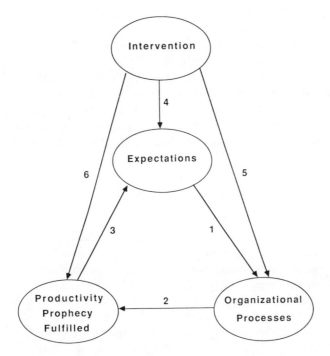

Figure 5-1. A Model of Organizationwide SFP

The Origin of Organizationwide Expectations

Past Performance

Where do organizationwide expectations originate? In some organizations, no one need do anything out of the ordinary to create high expectations. The organization's record of achievement, its reputation, and its public image are sufficient to sustain long-term, collective, positive expectations. Bell Labs, Harvard University, IBM, 3-M, NASA (prior to the Challenger explosion), and the Israeli Air Force are examples. Each of these organizations has an outstanding public record of sustained, extraordinary achievement, consistently "beating the competition" in its particular field of endeavor. Knowing of the outstanding past performance fuels positive expectations concerning the future accomplishments of such organizations, and nurtures members' willingness to exert the effort required to maintain the effective organizational processes that fulfill their collective prophecy of success. Thus, the organization's past successes are the source of high expectations, and the resulting organizationwide SFP.

The truism that success begets success is widely known. The business world recognizes that past success is an asset. The value of past success for future accomplishment is manifest in the accounting practice of assigning a dollar value, sometimes a very high one, to a successful going concern far in excess of the market value of its current assets. Furthermore, it is undoubtedly a valuable asset, and source of organizationwide high expectations and positive SFP, for Merck & Co. to have been rated by Fortune Magazine as the "most admired" corporation in the United States for two consecutive years. Phenomenally successful enterprises have a lot going for them. Competing with them is an uphill struggle, for it means overcoming their reputation for success and all of its implications. Indeed, Number 2 *must* try harder.

Unique Events that Unfreeze Expectations

Besides such long-standing and long-lasting effects, the ongoing ebb and flow of organizational events present many causes for spontaneous rise and fall of collective expectations. An extraordinary event can dramatically alter how people assess the organization's prospects. The 1986 explosion of NASA's Challenger space shuttle is an example of an event that influenced the expectations of the organization's entire membership. In the wake of such a tragedy, it is nearly impossible to prevent sagging expectations. Postdisaster low expectations may have been behind the string of failures that plagued NASA after the Challenger disaster. It required the nearly flawless Discovery One mission to reverse NASA's performance curve. In general, any clearcut success or failure in achieving an important organizational goal has repercussions on collective expectations.

Chief-executive succession is another powerful, naturally occurring trigger for changing organizationwide expectations, depending on the new chief's reputation and record of past achievement (Iacocca 1984). Such events unfreeze expectations as people grope for some picture of what is to occur in the future. It is this unfreezing that gives executives a period of grace, or honeymoon, during which an "expectation window" opens for them. How they handle this opportunity to implant positive expectations, and thereby sow the seeds of future productive SFP, is crucial. Once the window closes, and expectations crystallize, change will be difficult.

Planned Organizational Change

Sometimes the source of change in expectations is a planned intervention designed to bring about some improvement in the structure or functioning of the organization. An organizational development (OD) program (Huse & Cummings 1985) would be an example. In such cases, a new fountainhead of expectations is introduced into the organization. The intervention program can create an organizationwide SFP (such as King's innovation-expectancy experiment) even though no one in particular had SFP, or even expectations, in mind. In King's experiment, belief in the program's efficacy was sufficient to produce the SFP effect. To represent this type of source of organization-wide expectations, a fourth class of variables, labeled intervention, has been added to the basic SFP triangle in figure 5–1. It represents a novel force that disturbs the organization's equilibrium and triggers a process of change by altering the level of collective expectations of the members (arrow 4). As open social systems that respond to changes in their environment, organizations are immanently influenceable by such changes (Katz & Kahn 1966). The inter-vention may originate from outside the organization, as when an outside consultant is brought in. It may be a new productivity program, as in King's job-enrichment experiment. The intervention may be imposed on the organi-zation by "nature," as in the Challenger disaster. Finally, the "intervention" may originate from within the organization, as when a new machine layout is developed by the production department and implemented locally with the enthusiasm characteristic of people who are bringing their own ideas to fruition.

The intervention may have direct effects, positive or negative, on orga-nizational processes (arrow 5) and on productivity (arrow 6). These effects are represented by broken arrows in figure 5–1. The new CEO may have far-reaching outside connections that facilitate access to investment capital or to markets, job redesign may make work more efficient, accidents like the Challenger explosion cause long delays because of prolonged clean-up, investigation, redesign, and retraining, and a new machine layout can result in savings in time and labor. Such direct, tangible results of a change are of obvious importance for productivity and profitability, and will leave their mark on the balance sheet. However, these direct effects of the intervention on organizational processes and effectiveness are not of interest in the context of SFP.

Rather, it is the impact of the intervention on *expectations* (arrow 4) that is of special interest in the present context. The effect of the intervention on members' perceptions of the situation and on their expectations for future suc-cess or failure is what makes the intervention part of the SFP process. A change in performance expectations among a significant number of members can trigger organizationwide SFP. It is only when expectations have a unique effect of their own, beyond the direct effects of whatever gave rise to the expectations, that SFP occurs. Although King created productive SFP in his innovation-and-expectation experiment, he himself interpreted his findings methodologically. He called for expectancy control groups in organizational-development experiments to tease out the effects of the intervention being tested from the effects expectations which confound the OD experiment. He viewed expectancy effects in OD as a nuisance variable that ought to be controlled. He did *not* call for the deliberate creation of expectancy effects as a productive intervention in its own right. It remained for others to see this practical implication.

French and Bell (1978) reviewed King's experiment and stated that, for the OD practitioner, expectation effects have "definite positive implications: tell the clients to expect positive gains from the program (any program) and 'expectation effects' will help positive gains to be realized" (p. 248). Note the parallel to the deliberate creation of the placebo effect by physicians. However, French and Bell did not elaborate on *how* to create expectation effects. Woodman and Tolchinsky (1985) more recently discussed expectation effects in OD. They invoked several psychological theories to explain how expectations influence the OD process and addressed the problem of handling the discrepancy effects that result when the outcomes of an OD program are appreciably higher or lower than the level initially expected.

With these few exceptions, OD has not cashed in on the potential of expectation effects. OD innovators should be designing ways of maximizing positive expectation effects and eliminating Golem effects in the practice of OD. Some of the proposals offered in the next chapter for SFP applications are relevant to OD practice and partially redress past neglect of these important effects.

Organization as Culture

Even when no particular watershed event can be identified as the source of collective expectations, organizationwide SFP still occurs. This is because there are shared expectations among the members of every organization. Such expectations are anchored in the organization's culture. Culture is intimately involved in organizational SFP because it is such a rich source of performance expectations.

Definition of Organizational Culture

Morgan (1986, chapter 5) has defined the organization-as-culture metaphor in a most useful way for understanding culturally generated SFP in organizations. "Culture (is) an ongoing, proactive process of reality construction . . . through which people create and recreate the worlds in which they live" (p.131). For Morgan, each organization is a minisociety that has its own distinctive culture. Culture implies a pattern of shared beliefs or meaning which, when supported by compatible norms and rituals, "can exert a decisive influence on the overall ability of the organization to deal with the challenges that it faces" (p.121). According also to Schein (1985), organizational culture exerts a dominating influence over organizational effectiveness: "Productivity is a cultural phenomenon par excellence, both at the small-work-group level and at the level of the total organization" (p. 43–44).

According to Morgan, people enact the reality implied by the organization's culture through imagery. Social process, symbols, and rituals sustain the image. Culture is so pervasive that "organizations end up being what they think and say, as their ideas and visions realize themselves" (p. 133). For example, an organization may be permeated with the idea, "We're the best in the industry and intend to stay that way." Believing and declaring that they can be more productive will help make the members of an organization more productive. What Morgan described as organizational culture is actually SFP at the organizational level.

There is little agreement among organizational scholars on the definition of culture. Schein (1985) has pointed out that most uses of the term "culture" in the organizational literature bear little fidelity to its original, anthropological meaning. Culture is a slippery concept that concerns phenomena that are hard to pin down. Being close to these phenomena may not help one to grasp them. To appreciate culture, one must observe the organization anthropologically, "*as if one were an outsider*" (Morgan 1986, 121).

Moreover, the question of whether management can purposely alter culture is being hotly debated. For Schein (1985), organizational culture involves complex, underlying beliefs and assumptions about the organization's capabilities and frailties. These assumptions, which were derived initially from primal events that transpired early in the organization's history, have slipped out of the awareness of the individuals originally involved, and may never have been known to members who subsequently joined the organization. These assumptions, and the organizational culture they embody, therefore become highly resistant to change: "Do not assume that culture can be manipulated like other matters under the control of managers. Culture controls the manager more than the manager controls culture. . ." (Schein 1985, 314). Morgan also has expressed caution about rushing head-on to change culture. "There may be much more to corporate culture than is evident in the popular idea that it is possible to 'manage culture.' Culture, like organization, may not be what it seems to be" (Morgan 1986, 220). Nevertheless, Morgan's book is rich in proposals for changing organizational culture.

Bennis and Nanus (1985) unreservedly view culture as pliable. They prefer using the term "social architecture," which for them is virtually synonymous with the trendier buzzword 'culture,'" to refer to "the norms and values that shape behavior in any organized setting. . . . 'Social architecture' implies change and tractability and that leaders can do something about it, whereas 'culture,' as ordinarily used, implies an unbridled rigidity or intractability" (p. 111). The present discussion adopts the approach of Morgan and of Bennis and Nanus and of others in assuming that culture can be altered by management for productive ends.

Changing Culture

Smircich and Morgan (1982) have called leadership "the management of meaning." Morgan has described how managers can shape an organization's culture through the use of imagery, theater, and gamesmanship. Symbolic management is one of the ways in which managers can exercise leadership in creating productive SFP that goes beyond the management of everyday supervisor–subordinate relations. Molding the organization's culture is a prime means for exercising transformational leadership. Thus, transformational leadership and organizational culture are intimately related. By changing culture, the transformational leader influences many members with whom he never even comes into direct personal contact. As Sashkin and Burke (1987) pointed out in their review of OD in the 1980s, "The real key to changing culture . . . is not the sort of micro-OD intervention approach, like team building, that we are familiar with. As has now been recognized more appropriately, the key is in leadership, specifically the leadership of the chief executive officer" (p. 224).

This is the crossroads at which SFP, transformational leadership, the management of culture, and OD all meet. By creating a high-expectancy culture, the transformational leader produces productive SFP at multiple levels in the organization. Changing organizational culture is an act of transformational leadership, and transformational leadership is implemented most effectively by means of culture change. In Morgan's words, "Leadership ultimately involves an ability to define the reality of others. . . . In managing the meanings assigned to a situation, the leader in effect wields a form of symbolic power that exerts a decisive influence on how people perceive their realities and hence how they act. Charismatic leaders seem to have a natural ability to shape meaning in this way" (Morgan 1986, 176). Morgan discussed images, language, symbols, stories, ceremonies, rituals, and various forms of theatricals as tools that managers use to manage meaning and hence to shape power relations in organizations. The same tools can be used to raise expectations—and productivity—organizationwide as well as in one-on-one relations.

Discussing the role of leadership in organizational change and development, Beer and Walton (1987) have made essentially the same point. Leadership begins with the articulation and propagation of a vision, an agenda, or a prophecy. Next, the leader structures for himself and for others in the organization a cognitive world by assigning significance to events and interpreting their meaning. He essentially translates the vision into specific expectations. "The leader achieves results . . . by creating an understanding of reality that then motivates behavior. . . . *The manager creates a set of expectations that powerfully influence behavior in the organization*" (p. 348, italics added). Summarizing Peters and Waterman's (1982) bestseller *In Search of Excellence,* Beer and Walton wrote, simply but right on target, "Performance is achieved via expectations and peer review rather than management direction and sophisticated control systems" (p. 346).

It is apparent that expectations are common to all these approaches. Creating productive SFP is centered at the confluence of much current thinking in the fields of leadership, OD, and organizational culture. Conceptualizing these processes in terms of SFP links them all together and gives the manager a tool that can be used at many levels, with varying time perspectives, and under highly varied circumstances. That tool is expectancy raising. The next chapter provides practical ideas for raising expectations.

SFP Embedded in Organizational Culture: A Personal Example

I would like to take advantage of my author's license to engage in what Van Maanen and Kunda (1985) have dubbed "emotional recall." This is a subjective description of one's own past personal experience to share it with others. Van Maanen (1985) has described this ethnographic method as an interpretive exercise that is not based on objective data. Thus, it is more art than science. Using Van Maanen's method, I shall describe retrospectively a period of my own life when my performance was drastically changed by an institutionalized SFP. I make no claim to neutrality. However, the experience as recalled conveys what I mean by culturally embedded SFP better than any objective data available.

It was during my four-and-a-half years of graduate study at the psychology department at the University of Michigan in the late 1960s. That department was, and still is, widely regarded as one of the best in the world, and according to many, *the* best. Before going to Michigan, I was completing my master's requirements at a less prestigious university, to which I had come with an undistinguished undergraduate record. I knew I wanted to go on to doctoral studies, and was considering applying to Michigan. However, every time I looked at the application form I put it aside with despair, particularly when I eyed the item requesting a list of my scientific publications! They also prepared applicants for the worst by letting them know that out of more than six hundred applicants each year, only sixty were admitted. In my case, self-selection was surely at work weeding out one more hopelessly unqualified candidate.

As the deadline for applying drew near, ambivalence gave way to the fateful decision to gamble an hour of typing time and postage. I applied. I had procrastinated down to the wire, and had to mail the application special delivery. Meantime, I applied also to a mediocre university where I was more likely to be accepted. I didn't put all my eggs in the Michigan basket, sensing that my chances of being admitted there ranged between slim and nil.

When Michigan's letter of acceptance arrived several months later, I was certain that someone had made a mistake. I delayed notifying them whether I would be coming until the latest allowable date. All the while I was expecting to receive an apologetic letter from the admissions committee informing me that a grievous error had been made, that I had not been admitted after all, and that they regretted having to rescind the previous letter of acceptance. As the deadline approached, I marshaled all the chutzpah at my disposal and decided to go to Michigan.

My discomfort was only beginning. Upon arrival I felt threatened by a course load that was overwhelming, both qualitatively and quantitatively, and by having to compete with fellow students who had outstanding records from schools like Harvard, Yale, Princeton, Stanford, and Berkeley, in comparison to whom my record of past academic achievement paled. Again, I felt distressed by the nagging thought that they had made a mistake in admitting me. I was living with the persistent premonition that, having bitten off more than I could chew, I would eventually have to endure the embarrassment and shame of failure.

It was the special culture of Michigan's psychology department that prevented me from inflicting upon myself a tragic Golem effect. That kind of organizational culture is the topic of this chapter. The chairman of the doctoral committee and other mentors in the department made it clear to me that they believed in the validity of their selection procedures, that they don't make errors in selection, and that if someone fails it's the department's fault because an undoubtedly qualified student had not been handled properly. "If we accepted you, you can succeed in the program. If you didn't, it would be our failure. We don't fail." For me, the timely message was that they had good reason to expect me to succeed. I don't think they were faking it; they actually believed what they were telling me. They believed in their own capacity to select and train good students, and they believed in the ability of the students so selected.

The same high-expectancy message was conveyed in another way. Virtually every graduate student in the psychology department was guaranteed financial support in the form of either a teaching fellowship, a research assistantship, or a stipend. The department placed most students as either teaching fellows or research assistants, and granted a stipend only as a last resort. Economically, the times were good and funds were abundant; still, such support was not guaranteed every student in every department! The message to me was, "The best psychology department in the world thinks you qualify for financial support."

Looking back, the very act of universal support reinforced their expressions of confidence in their selection procedures and was as important for its impact on my self-expectations as for the money itself. I have no doubt that these departmental expressions of confidence in my ability to succeed contributed to boosting my self-confidence sufficiently to motivate my efforts to get through the first semester. After that, the process became self-sustaining.

I own my career to that departmental culture. Had the culture been different, I would have persisted in expecting much less of myself, and consequently would not have tried so hard nor performed as well. There are undoubtedly countless other individuals whose achievements and lack thereof have been profoundly influenced by the cultures of the organizations of which they have been members. The next chapter provides some practical suggestions about how to create high-expectancy organizational culture.

The Impact of National Culture

"If you will it, it is no mere legend."
—Theodor Herzl, 1902

The culture of any particular organization is influenced by the more pervasive culture of the larger society in which the organization is embedded. To understand culture as a source of SFP-producing expectations, it helps to know something about the culture of the larger society. Morgan discussed the impact of cross-national differences in culture on industrial organizations using Japan as his prime example. He cited Sayle's (1982) analysis of Japanese industrial prowess as deriving from the cultural values that dominate life in the rice fields and from the spirit of service of the samurai. Cross-national differences in culture also play an important role in productive SFP at the collective level. My example is the national culture of Israel, which is the one I have experienced firsthand throughout my professional career.

Industrialization as SFP

There are enormous differences between countries in their rate of economic development. These differences cannot be explained solely in terms of economic factors. Industrialization as SFP is a special case of expectancy effect in which people in a developing country expect industrialization to proceed rapidly and successfully (Eden 1988, November). Such expectations induce the productive individual and collective behaviors that promote rapid industrialization. An SFP hypothesis is that countries in which people in many walks of life expect rapid development industrialize faster than countries in which slow development is expected. High expectations undoubtedly have contributed to rapid industrialization in many newly industrialized countries. Conversely, low expectations are the bane of multitudes worldwide who are underusing their productive potential. This national Golem effect is exorbitantly costly in terms of wasted human potential in the least developed countries. The widely shared expectation that economic development will be slow, painful, and unachievable "in our lifetime" can produce a collective Golem effect and impede industrialization. Negative labeling exacts its toll here, too. Imagine the destructive effect of calling a country "a basket case." The larger the number of people blighted by the Golem effect, the greater the potential for productivity gains in the national economy through raising expectations.

SFP and Economic Development in Israel

During its formative years, modern Israel had an optimistic culture that generated productive SFP. The messianic prophecy of ultimate national and spiritual redemption, envisioned by the prophets of ancient Israel, had sustained the Jewish people throughout its long, tragic exile from its own land. Modern political Zionism evolved as a pragmatic, secularized version of that messianic promise. The anticipation of a better future was a cornerstone of the Zionist ideology that emerged in nineteenth-century Europe. The ensuing processes of the ingathering of exiles and nation-building can be seen as a case of SFP. Human resources were the only wealth available to achieve the goal. The prophetic tone of the ideology was instrumental in mustering these human resources to solve seemingly intractable problems of economic development encountered by Jews returning to the barren, resource-depleted homeland. The foregoing quote is the motto on the title page of Herzl's prophetic novel, *Old-New Land,* about life in the state-to-be. In these few words he voiced his confidence in his follower's ability to create an independent Jewish state, and expressed as well *their* high hopes and optimistic expectations that they could overcome the odds and bring it off. He concluded his book thus:

> But if you do not will it, then it remains a legend which I have recited. Dream and action are not as widely separated as many believe. All the acts of men were dreams at first and become dreams again.

Realistic and even sympathetic contemporaries looked on with derision, considering the handful of Zionists to be naive dreamers.

History ultimately proved Herzl uncannily right. Fifty years after he had prophesied that within fifty years the National Home would be recreated, the State of Israel was established. The confidence of the national leadership that, after centuries in disuse, Jews could regain the skills to drain swamps, irrigate the desert, till the land, and industrialize and defend the country, was shared by a populace that was sure of its ultimate success. The prophecy of yore was partially fulfilled in the reestablishment of national sovereignty. That culture of confidence continues to nurture the mobilization of the tremendous human effort required to advance on the path to a better future. The rise of Israel is an ongoing prophecy fulfilled.

Israel has exported a version of that same SFP to scores of developing and newly industrializing countries in Asia, Africa, and Latin America, to whom Israeli advisers have carried the message that if *we* could do it, so can *you*. Thousands of Israeli Pygmalions have generated much Third World development with very little budget.

Unfortunately, with time some problems have not been solved, and some new ones have arisen. An example is the legacy of British colonial rule. During the nearly thirty years of the British Mandate, the British adversarial system of labor relations took root in the country. Britain's history of class distinctions gave rise to a culture of management-labor conflict (Morgan 1986, 117). This foreign culture came to dominate Israeli industrial relations and has since been developed locally into a national sport. Industrial strife exacts an enormous toll in terms of strikes, walkouts, lockouts, and legal action. Another example is in the life-and-death sphere of international relations. The elusiveness of the goal of achieving peaceful relations with her neighbors has had a sobering effect on many of the country's unrelenting optimists. The intractability of this hostility has tempered many people's prophetic vision of peace and prosperity. Moreover, modernization appears to have weakened some of Israel's cultural moorings to the messianism of the past. It remains to be seen whether the messianic prophecy will continue to inspire positive SFP into the next generation of Israeli endeavor, and how this may be expressed in terms of organizational effectiveness.

6

Managing Self-Fulfilling Prophecy in Organizations

MEDKIT Ltd.

MEDKIT is a pseudonym for a firm in Israel that produces disposable sterile medical kits for use in blood dialysis and transfusions. The plant manager at MEDKIT was having a problem with the low productivity of consecutive waves of new employees. Production workers in the plant, who assembled and packed the kits, were either native or immigrant women from Eastern Europe. In this plant, "everyone knew" that, in comparison to immigrants, natives were poor workers, adjusted slower, were undisciplined, took longer to achieve standard levels of production, and had difficulty maintaining these levels. In particular, the head production supervisor, who for years had been responsible for putting new hires to work, "knew" that the native women would give her trouble and not reach standard production soon, if ever.

The plant manager, who had heard a lecture about SFP and expectation effects in management, believed the native workers were every bit as capable as the immigrants. Suspecting the operation of a Golem effect, he summoned the head production supervisor and told her that a) he had personally hand-picked the group of native new hires slated to come on board the following week and they were excellent people, b) they should be expected to give her no problem and to attain standard production rapidly, and c) as always, she, the head supervisor, was to assume personal responsibility for their integration into the plant and to report any problems to him. What followed was the smoothest intake of native new hires that anyone in the plant could remember. They achieved standard production in record time and soon appreciably exceeded it. The supervisor complimented the plant manager for having improved his hiring decisions.

This chapter enumerates and describes some of the many ways in which productive SFP can be deliberately created. Many of the expectation-raising acts are readily available in every manager's behavioral repertoire. These are existing skills that only require activation to actualize their potential for increasing productivity. Others require more investment, preparation, fore-thought, and sustained managerial effort. All the proposed techniques are derived from the research and principles discussed in previous chapters.

Managers are not the only professionals who stand to gain from adoption of a utilitarian approach to SFP. Expectations can have a significant impact on the course and outcomes of organizational development programs (Huse & Cummings 1985), as well as on other types of management consulting interventions. King's (1974) experiment on the introduction of an organizational innovation showed that client expectations can make the crucial difference in the success of an intervention. The implications of expectation effects for OD theory and practice are no less profound than for management. Many OD scholars and consultants intuitively "know" that expectations are important in OD. However, with only rare exceptions (e.g., Woodman & Tolchinsky 1985), the role of expectations in OD has not been taken seriously. OD practitioners, like managers, should grab the expectation bull by its horns and intentionally raise expectations to reap the benefits of positive SFP. OD affords abundant opportunities to imbue clients with high performance expectations and to help rid organizations and their managers of the crippling effects of low expectations. Some familiar OD interventions have expectation-raising as a naturally built-in component, such as management-by-objectives and goal setting. In addition, consultants can use expectation-boosting add-on microinterventions to buttress interventions that chiefly target other variables. Thus, many of the practical proposals in the present chapter can be implemented by OD professionals and other consultants to improve the effectiveness of their consulting practice.

Expectancy-raising is not feasible as a stand-alone program. Merely *telling* managers to raise their expectations won't work. This book is not an endorsement of *The Power of Positive Thinking* advocated by Norman Vincent Peale. Expectation-raising has to be embedded in a credible program that can serve as a basis for convincing clients that performance will improve. Recall that King did not have a "high-expectations only" condition in his innovation and expectation experiment. In his 2 × 2 design, he piggybacked his high-expectation manipulation onto job rotation as the "low innovation" condition. Expectation effects are powerful enough to boost output even when combined with so diluted an "innovation" as job rotation, which ordinarily is considered a very weak treatment by job redesign specialists. But expectation-raising cannot stand alone. This add-on nature of expectation-raising does not detract from its applicability to the task of unleashing now-dormant human potential in organizations. On the contrary, expectations are *always* there, and raising them can conveniently supplement virtually any other change, planned or unplanned, with little effort or cost. Such easy applicability should make expectation-raising particularly appealing to practitioners.

To illustrate, consider assessment centers and management training. Many participants interpret the mere fact of being invited to participate in an assessment center or prestigious training program as a signal that a lot is expected of them (Maister 1985; Turnage & Muchinsky 1984). The managers in charge of these operations are ordinarily unaware of such implied expectations and their effects. Proposing that posh assessment programs or training junkets be lavished upon employees merely to raise their expectations would be absurd. No one would embark on a costly program of assessment or training with the sole intention of tricking individuals in the program into raising their expectations. But every assessment or training center that does not have expectation-raising on its agenda is squandering golden opportunities for the organization to gain the additional benefits of expectation effects. The marginal cost of adding expectation-raising is negligible, and, as we have seen, the payoff can be substantial.

Creating Productive SFP

The following proposals are intended to provide managers and consultants with applicable suggestions for expectation raising in their practice and to stimulate further thinking about expectation effects on the part of management scholars. These proposals differ along several dimensions. Some are directed toward individual clients, some toward whole groups or organizations; some aim at implanting positive expectations while others are geared toward the reduction of negative expectations; some get managers to play the role of Pygmalion unwittingly and others encourage him to do so knowingly; some have been proven to be effective in empirical testing and some await research evaluation.

Create the Pygmalion Effect

> "I have the best soldiers in the world."
> —Captain Levi, commander of an infantry company in the Israel Defense Forces in response to a request in a radio interview to divulge the secret behind his successful leadership on the battlefield after his unit, outmanned and outgunned, performed brilliantly under fire in a rescue mission across enemy lines.

The huge and growing data base demonstrating the Pygmalion effect in educational settings, as well as among adult members of work organizations, leaves little doubt that expectation effects are a common part of everyday behavior in organizations. The practical implication of this research is that managers should deliberately play the role of Pygmalion in their interactions with their subordinates. There are some leaders, like Captain Levi, who are natural Pygmalions. They expect the best of their subordinates. They do not need to be convinced, trained, cajoled, or reminded to express their belief in their subordinates' capacity to excel and to treat them accordingly. They do so spontaneously as appropriate occasions arise. Managers who are not predisposed to behaving in accord with this approach would be more successful in their managerial roles if they would acquire the awareness and skills of Pygmalion. One aim of writing this book is to aid managers in transforming themselves into more effective Pygmalions.

However, reading a book is unlikely to change behavior. Writing about the use of expectancy effects in education, Hall and Merkel (1985) recommended that teacher educators "should make students familiar with the more prevalent positions, current research findings and . . . provide them with the basic skills necessary to read and evaluate new research" (p. 89). This recommendation is incredibly naive. It is unrealistic to expect that practicing teachers or managers are going to master research methods that require advanced academic training and begin investing the hours needed to read the current research literature! Even if they did master the literature, that would bring them no closer to mastery of the requisite behavioral skills without which academic knowledge remains inoperative. Surely we can offer something more useful to the practitioner. It will take more than knowledge of research findings to get managers to adopt Pygmalion behaviors. Especially to the extent that SFP operates subconsciously, book knowledge cannot suffice.

Therefore, consultants should create the Pygmalion effect by raising the expectations of their manager–clients toward their subordinates. In the course of myriad interactions with managers at different levels in the client organization during any consulting project, the consultant who would convert his client into a more positive Pygmalion should repeatedly point out to the client untapped potential among members of the organization, and especially among the client's subordinates, to get the client to expect more. If successful, raising the client's expectations toward his subordinates' performance will trigger a Pygmalion effect and improve performance beyond any gains that may result from whatever other consulting program may be undertaken simultaneously. Relevant information about subordinates' underused talents can be recovered from personnel files, conversations with people in the training department, and interviews with managers and with the employees themselves.

The role of "consultant" as used here is not limited to officially labeled outsiders. A manager can be helped into a positive Pygmalion role by a superior or by peers, and even by savvy subordinates, who can raise his awareness of underused capacity and get him to expect more. Furthermore, expectations of managers regarding their subordinates can profitably be raised *without* specific evidence of untapped subordinate potential. In the typical Pygmalion experiment, subjects are assigned to high- and control-expectation conditions at random; therefore, those whose performance is enhanced by the Pygmalion treatment comprise a mix of relatively high- and low-ability individuals. It follows that being treated as a high-potential subordinate is productive for subordinates of quite varied ability levels. In Pygmalion experiments, the SFP effect has been found among personnel assigned at random. Eden and Ravid (1982) tested the interaction between manipulated expectations and trainee aptitude, and found that it was not significant. This means that trainees of all levels of aptitude benefited equivalently from having their supervisors' expectations toward them raised indiscriminately. The practical implication is that consultants can raise managers' expectations across the board, knowing that no harm will come to any subordinate and that many will likely gain. Our successful whole-group Pygmalion treatment in the squad leaders course also demonstrated this.

Eradicate the Golem Effect

> Another illustration that people can often do more than their IQ limits suggest: After the Second World War the GI Bill financed a college education for 2.3 million men, including half a million whose backgrounds suggested that they were not "college material" and who said they would not otherwise have gone to school. James B. Conant, the president of Harvard, called the bill "distressing," because it did not "distinguish between those who can profit most by advanced education and those who cannot." In the same spirit Robert Hutchins, of the University of Chicago, warned that when the GIs came home, "colleges and universities will find themselves converted into educational hobo-jungles." In other words, this was a scheme to push people beyond what their intelligence would permit. Of course, when the returning GIs enrolled, they confounded all predictions and proved to be famously mature and successful in class. Researchers found that those who would not have gone to college without help from the GI Bill did slightly better in course work than other equally able veterans (Fallows, 1985).

The postwar passage of the GI Bill thus saved millions of capable American veterans from their future status as Golems. This is a marvelous example of the constructive disruption of an insidious SFP. Low expectations are the bane of multitudes of people who are not using their potential. Many underachievers have grown accustomed to just getting by with minimally acceptable performance simply because nothing more is expected of them. The debilitating Golem effect is undoubtedly widespread and costly in terms of wasted human potential. Raising the currently low expectations harbored toward underachieving Golems should yield appreciable productivity gains because underachievers, by definition, have great potential for improvement before reaching the limits imposed on performance by their ability. If, as one might suspect, the number of underachieving members in organizations who are blighted by Golem effects is large, then eradicating these effects could potentially make a lot more people a lot more productive. Major stumbling blocks to eradicating Golem effects are a) managers' overlearned low expectations toward chronically underachieving subordinates and tendency to attribute poor performance to enduring traits of the subordinates, b) subordinates' own tenacity in clinging to their low self-expectations, and c) prejudice that depresses expectations without regard to actual ability. These stumbling blocks are treated later.

The narrative about the MEDKIT plant at the beginning of this chapter exemplifies the shrewd demise of a costly Golem effect. The MEDKIT case illustrates how easy it can be to apply SFP within a particular organization. Surely opportunities for such inexpensive, quick, and effective applications of SFP abound in the practitioner's world.

Create the Galatea Effect

Whether one produces a Pygmalion effect or a Galatea effect depends on whose subordinates' expectations one is raising. Managers have daily opportunities to convey positive expectations to their own subordinates. When they do so, they are in the Pygmalion role. Managers also have frequent opportunities to raise the expectations of *other* managers' subordinates—that is, to create the Galatea effect. We (Eden & Ravid 1982) found similar effect sizes for the Pygmalion and Galatea treatments in the adjutant experiment. Therefore, an additional intervention, distinct from the Pygmalion treatment, is to trigger the Galatea effect by conveying directly to personnel at different levels in the organization that they have high potential. The Galatea treatment can complement the Pygmalion treatment, as when a consultant raises both the manager's expectations of his subordinates and the subordinates' self-expectations. Alternatively, the Galatea treatment can be applied in lieu of Pygmalion, as when the manager's expectations appear to be intractable. Consultants should take advantage of the numerous opportunities available to them during an extended intervention to comment favorably about the level of human resources to a variety of persons in the organization, for example, formal and informal interviewing, training, feedback sessions, and widely circulated written reports.

Another example of attempting to apply SFP by creating a Galatea effect is writing this book. I hope I have succeeded in convincing you, the reader, that you can succeed in accomplishing much more than you have to date by raising your level of self-expectations. This puts me in the role of Pygmalion, and makes you, the reader, my Galatea. Make the best of it. I *know* you can do it!

Pygmalion Leadership Training

A large public service organization in Israel conducts an in-house executive training program that emphasizes transformational leadership. In the opening session, before any theoretical presentations or normative exhortations, the trainees are asked to form small groups. In each group one participant is chosen to play the role of group leader. The participants are told that in the next segment of the workshop they will be asked to do jump-ups.[1] Each participant is asked to jot down on a piece of paper how many jump-ups he knows he can do. Those chosen as leaders are taken to another room, separated into two groups, and briefed about the exercise. One group is told to use the numbers written down in leading their subordinates in performing as many jump-ups as they can.

Leaders in the other group are told that the numbers written down are not to be taken very seriously because people commonly underestimate their ability when asked to write down a forecast of future performance. The facilitator explains in a few sentences why people underestimate their capacity in this way. He concludes the briefing by telling the group leaders that they should be able to get their subordinates to perform appreciably more jump-ups than the numbers that they had written down.

It works every time. Those told to expect more get more—a lot more. They become instant Pygmalions. The exercise demonstrates SFP in action and makes it easier to explain transformational leadership.

Pygmalion Leadership Training refers to any training program emphasizing expectancy effects, specifically designed with the Pygmalion concept in mind, with the aim of facilitating managerial applications that will create productive SFP at work. This is the SFP application that most directly grabs the expectation bull by its horns. Rather than seeking a variety of channels to convey high expectations to managers and/or workers, the program enlightens them about SFP, expectation effects, and Pygmalion, and teaches them how conscious use of this knowledge can improve motivation and boost productivity. Pygmalion Leadership Training involves fully informing managers about the SFP process. In short, Pygmalion Leadership Training is a program designed to teach managers how to enact the Pygmalion Leadership Style.

The Pygmalion-at-Sea project (Crawford, Thomas & Fink 1980) exemplifies Pygmalion Leadership Training. Although the Pygmalion-at-Sea program was aimed at raising expectations, the high expectations had to be supported by other means. Crawford et al. reported that the supervisors' "initial reluctance gave way to guarded optimism and later to enthusiasm . . . due in part to the training segment that consisted of teaching the principles of behavior modification and then brainstorming actions that would constitute positive reinforcers in the eyes of the low performers. The supervisors were thus given some *specific tools to back up their newly acquired positive expectations"* (p. 489, italics added). This is probably as close as a program can get to being a stand-alone expectation-raising intervention. Without providing the behavioral tools, it is doubtful that positive effects would emerge; providing tools *without* raising expectations is what many other types of leadership training programs do.

The range of skills imparted to managers in Pygmalion Leadership Training should be considerably broadened beyond what was included in the Pygmalion-at-Sea program to encompass the major components of the Pygmalion Leadership Style described in chapter 4. One important addition is workshop training designed to help managers to become skillful in applying Rosenthal's four factors that mediate the Pygmalion effect: socioemotional climate, feedback, input, and output. This should be interwoven with training in the use of Bandura's sources of self-efficacy expectations, in particular enactive mastery, vicarious experience, and verbal persuasion, to develop managers' capacity to raise their subordinates' self-expectations.

Another important component of Pygmalion Leadership Training is attribution training. Managers should be trained in the skills needed to give good performers credit for their accomplishments and to relieve chronically poor performers of their learned helplessness. Training in attribution management should teach managers how to conduct performance reviews with their subordinates in a manner that promotes "the right" attributions of success and failure. That is, managers should be taught to get their subordinates to attribute successes to their own (the subordinates') stable, internal, and global traits, ability in particular, and to attribute their failures to external, unstable, or specific, nongeneralizable causes. Workers whose attributions are guided in this manner by their manager are likely to have higher expectations of themselves in the wake of success, and to abstain from drastically lowering their expectations in the aftermath of failure. Consequently, according to the predictions of both VIE theory and self-efficacy theory, they will be more motivated to exert the effort required to face future job challenges. Managers who are made aware of the importance of these attributions for subordinates' future success, and who are armed with the behavioral skills for shaping subordinates' attributions, are more likely to succeed in the Pygmalion role. Their expectations *will* be higher, and their behavior toward subordinates will foster greater subordinate motivation and productivity. In short, the manager is to be taught that it is part of his managerial responsibility in taking the role of Pygmalion to see to it that his subordinates make the right attributions.

We can learn an important lesson from clinical psychology regarding attribution training, particularly regarding chronic low performers who persist in maintaining low levels of self-esteem and self-efficacy. Beck (1976) proposed a cognitive approach to therapy based on requiring clients to undertake a series of graded tasks, beginning easy and progressing to ever harder tasks, so that they can accumulate success experiences. Similarly, Kanfer and Gaelick (1986) have discussed the importance of the therapist's actively fostering a sense of self-efficacy in clients by guiding their attributions. Citing Bandura's (1977) four sources of information that influence an individual's self-efficacy, Kanfer and Gaelick agree that past performance is more important than vicarious learning through observation of others, being exposed to verbal persuasion, or emotional arousal accompanying performance. Therefore, they recommend that the therapist establish a program of therapeutic tasks that progress from the easy to the difficult so that the client will succeed each time, and gradually achieve more difficult performances. At no stage should the task exceed the client's capacity, because the resulting failure would jeopardize whatever fragile level of self-efficacy had been built up to that point. Repeated successful performance boosts self-efficacy. The therapist's role is in structuring the tasks, preparing the client for performance by using role-playing and behavioral rehearsal, and developing contingency plans in case the task does not go as planned. The therapist must make sure that the client attributes the successes to his own stable, internal traits. One way to foster the "right" attributions is to encourage clients to compare their performance with their own past performance rather than to high goal levels or to levels achieved by successful others.

Goldfried and Robins (1982) prescribed a number of specific steps that therapists can take in facilitating self-efficacy among their clients. Some of these therapist interventions can be translated into managerial behavior toward subordinates in work settings. One such intervention is to aid subordinates who are locked into chronic low self-expectations to distinguish between past and present performances. Then they can get these subordinates to realize that they are improving by anchoring their evaluations of their present performance in comparisons with their own past performance. Many people have a tendency to downplay their improvements and to cling to their low self-efficacy perceptions. By comparing their present performance to a difficult, distant goal, they remain discouraged and pessimistic that they will ever be able to improve enough. By looking back at their own past performance, the present can show encouraging gains which are missed when people compare present performance to a tough goal or to outstanding colleagues.

Goldfried and Robins (1982) also proposed adding an objective vantage point to the person's subjective viewpoint. We know that people typically attribute the causes of their own behavior to situational factors, whereas observers of those same people tend to locate the causes within the observees. Goldfried and Robins speculate that people have this built-in tendency to attribute novel success experiences to external factors because their eyes are located in their heads, making them more likely to attend to their environment than to internal variables. At any rate, the practical proposal is to aid subordinates plagued by chronic low self-efficacy to achieve a more objective (higher) assessment of their abilities and accomplishments by providing objective feedback, and by getting these subordinates to monitor their own performance objectively. Quantitative data would help in their self-monitoring process.

Thus, the therapist's role in attribution treatment has much in common with the manager's role in motivating workers. It is interesting that the clinicians call this approach to therapy "self-management." Though many of the recommendations for therapists are appropriate for managers as well, one important difference is that most workers are not as susceptible as clinical patients to minor failures. Therefore, their development can be paced faster, and failure can be handled routinely by fostering the right attributions and encouraging the worker to try again.

In addition to the Rosenthal factors, the Bandura sources of expectations, and attribution training, Pygmalion Leadership Training should sharpen managers' awareness of the special vulnerability of new employees and young workers to expectancy effects. Opportunities for employees to prove that they are capable of producing outstanding levels of output should not be left to chance. Managers should be encouraged to rotate their new employees through a variety of different jobs and tasks to give them the opportunity to accumulate a variety of success experiences on the job and to find out what they do well. Workers need to be given the chance to prove themselves. Not all workers get such a chance, but Pygmalion makes sure that his subordinates do.

The Role of Awareness. Pygmalion Leadership Training differs in a basic way from both the field experiments on the Pygmalion effect and the previously discussed proposals for raising expectations. The experiments and the previous SFP proposals do not target manager *self*-expectations for change, nor do they prescribe any role for the manager. They get the manager to play the role of Pygmalion unwittingly. Raising expectations leads to unintended changes in supervisory behavior, which in turn cause improvements in subordinates' productivity. In the previous SFP techniques, supervisory behavior improves even though it is not directly targeted by the intervention, no consulting or training resources are invested in it, and the manager is unaware that it is occurring. In this respect these techniques are reminiscent of King's expectancy-and-innovation experiment in which the managers were not aware that their expectations were the independent variable in the experiment; whatever changes were brought about in managerial behavior were indirect consequences, rather than direct objects, of the experimental manipulation. The direct object of the manager productivity expectations that King raised was the potential of the *innovation* (job enlargement and job rotation), not the potential of the manager, to effect productivity gains. No manager *self*-expectations were targeted for change. This was also true of King's earlier

Pygmalion experiment with disadvantaged industrial trainees, of Schrank's Air Force labeling study, and of our IDF experiments, as well as of other expectation-raising interventions proposed earlier, such as creating the Pygmalion effect. These approaches bypass the manager's awareness; he is told that something about the subordinates or something about the intervention program is the key to higher productivity. In contrast, in Pygmalion Leadership Training the manager is told that *he* is the key.

The success of the other interventions implies that managers already *possess* the requisite supervisory skills for getting subordinates to increase their productivity; raising their expectations gets them to *use* these skills more than they do when their expectations are lower. Conventional leadership training is useful for getting skills "into" managers; expectation raising is an effective way of "bringing out" the skills they already have. Hence, some of the costly investment in skill training can be saved by the inexpensive energizing of extant, underused managerial talent that results from raising managers' expectations of their subordinates.

In Pygmalion Leadership Training, as in the Pygmalion-at-Sea program, no attempt is made to bypass the manager's fully informed, active participation in creating SFP effects. Rather, the manager is invited to star centerstage in enacting the Pygmalion role willfully to create productive SFP. The managers are made aware of the hypothesized SFP effects by being informed about the entire process. They are taught a theoretical model designed to raise their expectations and are given workshop skill-training designed to change their supervisory behavior. Moreover, in addition to raising their expectations regarding their *subordinates'* potential to be high performers, Pygmalion Leadership Training also targets the supervisors' *self*-expectations for change. The supervisors are taught to expect that their subordinates can improve *and* to expect that they, the supervisors, have the capacity to lead their subordinates to higher levels of performance. Therefore, successful Pygmalion Leadership Training actually changes *two* supervisor expectations, as they come to expect more of their subordinates and more of themselves. This is coupled with skill training designed to change their supervisory behavior. Thus, Pygmalion Leadership Training explicitly targets both managers' expectations and their behavior for change. An assumption underlying Pygmalion Leadership Training is that managers who are made aware of SFP effects and rehearse the requisite skills can subsequently create such effects at will by treating all their subordinates as they naturally treat high-expectation subordinates. In this context, the existing body of SFP research serves as a didactic tool for teaching managers what the effective managerial behaviors are and convincing them that mastery and use of these behaviors on their part would be worthwhile.

In short, Pygmalion Leadership Training gives managers reason to believe that all or most of their subordinates can become more productive through the managers' own leadership efforts. It teaches managers to use the effective supervisory behaviors that have been found to characterize managers' treatment of high-expectation subordinates so that they can knowingly take the part of Pygmalion, the high-expectation supervisor, and effectively treat their subordinates as Galateas. The Pygmalion-at-Sea program evidently strengthened the optimism and confidence of both the commanders and their subordinates.

In chapter 2 we saw that King's five-minute expectation manipulation, which bypassed the managers' awareness, increased actual daily output by between 7 percent and 8 percent plantwide. In contrast, the Navy's eight-and-a-half days of full-disclosure expectation training at best raised supervisors' subjective assessments of a handful of subordinates' performance by a statistically significant amount. Thus, the evidence available from the two studies seems to indicate that King's five-minute expectancy raising had a much greater impact on productivity at a fraction of the cost of the Navy program. The less-than-candid five-minute manipulation appears to be the more effective.

However, despite the short-term cost ineffectiveness of the heavy investment required to conduct a skill-training intervention, it may nevertheless be the expectancy intervention of choice for many consultants. For one thing, whereas there are uncertainties about fade-out and repeatability with the five-minute expectation-only manipulation, the behavioral and attitudinal changes presumably produced by the more tedious Pygmalion Leadership Training are likely to lend this approach greater durability. Furthermore, it is repeatable and it deals with managers in a nondeceptive manner. In Pygmalion Leadership Training there is no attempt to convince the managers that there is something special inherent in *particular* subordinates, such as untapped potential or unique talents, that can serve as a pretext for supervisors' accepting higher expectations. It does not involve assigning positive labels such as "high aptitude personnel" or "high command potential" to some subordinates. Rather than being led to believe anything about the characteristics of (some of) their subordinates, managers are given reason to believe that all or most subordinates can become more productive through the managers' own leadership efforts.

Teacher Expectancy and Student Achievement (TESA) is a teacher skill-training program based on the Pygmalion concept. Originally developed for Los Angeles County schools, TESA trains teachers in the use of classroom behaviors found to be used frequently with high achievers but seldom with low achievers, and encourages more frequent use of these behaviors with the latter. Under the byword "Equal Opportunity in the Classroom," workshop discussion in the TESA program is focused on why some of the effective teaching techniques are not practiced as often with the "lows" as with the "highs." Kerman (1979) reported that this project achieved academic gains and reductions in absenteeism and discipline referrals. Wineburg (1987) cited a personal communication from Kerman according to which the TESA program is the most widely distributed in-service teacher training program in the United States, and it has been distributed in a number of other countries as well. Similarly, Project STILE (Student-Teacher Interactive Learning Environment) applies expectation training to get teachers to use those behaviors found to mediate the effects of high expectations (Banuazizi 1981; Greenfield, Banuazizi, & Ganon 1979; Terry 1985). Like TESA, STILE is based on the assumption that, if teachers increase the use of these behaviors, pupil learning will improve. The STILE program was derived from the Pygmalion concept and based on teacher expectation research. After the teachers are made fully aware of the teacher-expectation phenomenon, the STILE program invests considerable time in hands-on workshop skill training. There should be similar expectation training programs for managers.

Make Pygmalion Part of Every Training Program

> Being sent to Europe for a two-week training program during your first few months with the firm impresses the hell out of you. It makes you think: "This is a class outfit." It also both frightens you and gives you confidence. You say, "Boy, they must think I'm good if they're prepared to spend all this money on me." But then you worry about whether you can live up to it: it's very motivating.
> —A young professional's reaction to overseas training (Maister, 1985, 7).

Expectancy effects are part of every training program. The problem is that few people are aware of this. Most training specialists overlook the expectancy effect created by simply giving people access to company training. It is apparent from the reaction of the trainee that being treated as described resulted in highly elevated expectations. This may even explain a large measure of the training's effectiveness. To increase the likelihood that training programs capitalize on these expectation effects, training directors should make sure that training personnel know that expectation-raising is part of what they are expected to accomplish.

Besides the utility of dedicated expectation training as proposed in the previous section, *all training should be done with SFP in mind.* Whatever the learning goals of the particular training program, it would be more effective if the trainers were aware of expectation effects, used positive Pygmalion behaviors, and put their trainees into the Galatea role by raising their self-expectations. Pygmalion effects can improve the effectiveness of training in any specialty, including academic, business, and technical fields.

The modern-day Pygmalion concept was born in the classroom. Much of the research on expectation effects among adults has been conducted in training programs. Academic knowledge of these effects has been available for several years, and the scientific literature on training has begun citing the Pygmalion research and weighing its practical implications (Goldstein 1986; Wexley 1984). However, the practitioner-oriented training literature has remained unaffected by it. For example, despite its presumptuous title, *The Complete Book of Supervisory Training* (Lambert 1984) does not mention Pygmalion or expectation effects. Similarly devoid of any SFP-related concepts is the newest edition of Craig's (1987) encyclopedic *Training and Development Handbook,* a resource book used by many training professionals. The lapse extends even the chapter in the handbook titled *Classroom Instruction,* which states that "perhaps 95 percent of adult training is done in the classroom" (Broadwell 1987, 383). There is an urgent need to bring Pygmalion to the awareness of training professionals and training directors. The classroom, and training situations in general, are Pygmalion's home turf. Relying on the sagacity of trainees is chancy. There is always a danger that, wherever managers and instructors are unaware of interpersonal SFP, the Golem effect may fill the vacuum created by neglecting Pygmalion.

Guarantee a Good Start

The bulk of the evidence showing interpersonal expectancy effects in organizations has been gathered on members starting out in low-level entry positions. This warrants placing special emphasis on guaranteeing new employees an auspicious start, as Livingston (1969) recommended. New hires should be assigned to the best supervisors, who have demonstrated Pygmalion-like qualities in handling neophytes in the past. Giving managers the choice of which new employees are assigned to them would reduce the likelihood of Golem effects, since managers would not choose subordinates they expected to fail.

As this is the formative period of one's career, management should meticulously monitor each new employee to assess what SFP processes are taking place. If unreasonably low expectations are evident in the supervisor's attitude or behavior toward an employee, reassignment should be made forthwith to forestall the crystallization of a negative SFP process. The new employee should be given a chance to handle challenging problems that are within reach, and should be given a succession of ever more difficult tasks to foster a gradual growth in self-expectations, as the employee sees progression from success to success. Strong managerial intervention is called for in the event of both success and failure, to guide the employee in making the "right" attributions. Steering a new employee through a series of successes on the first job contributes to a high level of trait-expectancy, and stand the employee in good stead for a long time to come.

Success on the first job is too important to be left to chance.

Give Positive Feedback and Refrain from Destructive Criticism

So much has been written in support of positive feedback that little need be added here. For the recipient, positive feedback reinforces learning, encourages continues effort, and produces positive feelings, self-esteem, and self-confidence. Positive feedback also fosters open communication and relations of trust between the source and the recipient. Moreover, depending upon attribution, positive feedback boosts self-expectations for future performance. Thus, the Pygmalion model converges with the many other approaches to management that stress the importance of positive feedback.

Positive feedback creates these beneficial effects only when it has been earned—in the wake of good performance. It is not part of the Pygmalion Leadership Style to indiscriminantly hand around unearned positive feedback. Poor performance deserves, even requires, negative feedback. Phony positive feedback erodes credibility and dilutes the positive effects of positive feedback given when it *has* been earned. Negative feedback can be given in constructive ways that support the right attributions and nourish self-confidence, high expectations, and, consequently, good performance. Negative feedback should be administered thoughtfully with the aim of providing specific information about what was unacceptable and how to perform the job right the next time. Such negative feedback, being specific and considerate, helps people learn from their mistakes and improve their performance. Properly conveyed, negative feedback can also be used to boost expectations. "Now, I have no doubt that you are going to do a better job next time!"

Unfortunately, research by Ilgen and his colleagues (Ilgen, Fisher & Taylor 1979; Ilgen, Mitchell & Fredrickson 1981; Ilgen, Peterson, Martin & Boeschen 1981) has shown that negative feedback is rarely handled properly. Often, delayed negative feedback is provided by an angry boss making generalized comments attributing poor performance to internal causes in a sarcastic tone of voice. This is destructive criticism that fails to achieve the productive outcomes realized by immediate, specific, and considerate negative feedback. Most important for our present SFP context, Baron (1988) has demonstrated experimentally that destructive criticism causes people to expect less of themselves and to set lower performance goals. It is likely that a negative cycle of Poor Performance ──────▶ Destructive Criticism ──────▶ Poor performance is at the root of many Golem effects. Managers who enact the Pygmalion Leadership Style give subordinates positive and negative feedback when appropriate, and abstain from destructive criticism to prevent the destructive Golem cycle and create a productive cycle of Constructive Feedback (positive and negative) ———▶ Improved Performance ———▶ Constructive Feedback.

Immunize Potential Victims against the Golem Effect

Individuals who perform far below their ability because of the negative influence of their superiors' low expectations on their own self-expectations may be unaware of the process, and therefore defenseless. Special training or counseling could make such underachievers conscious of the debilitating SFP process, immunize them against it, and avert its recurrence. Immunization should have two focuses. One focus should be on what potential victims themselves can do, behaviorally, to raise the expectations of their superiors to prevent their superiors from treating them as Golems. If victims of low expectations could be helped to change their behavior so that they engage less in actions that reduce their supervisors' expectations, and more in actions that raise supervisors' expectations, negative expectation effects would be mitigated.

The second focus of immunization should be on the considerable power that the potential victims have to disrupt the SFP process by not responding to low supervisor expectations in a manner that turns them into Golems. This kind of inoculation entails conveying to potential Golems the following message:

> Now that you understand what SFP is and how it can influence both you and your supervisor, you can use this knowledge to protect yourself. You need not succumb to low expectations any longer. Even if you can't get your supervisor to treat you like a high-potential employee, and he persists in expecting little of you due to stereotypes, prejudices, your past record, or whatever, and treats you in a way that encourages you to perform poorly, you don't have to accommodate his expectations! If you know where those low expectations are coming from, maintain your own high expectations of yourself, and persist in trying to do the best job you can, you may break the vicious SFP cycle and succeed *despite* your supervisor's expectations. You can avoid becoming his Golem by being your own Pygmalion. If your supervisor deals with a bad hand by expecting you to fail, your own high self-expectations are your trump card that gives you immunity. In this way, you can master SFP and make the most of what you have.

This self-defensive orientation to SFP can be conveyed via specialized group training like the Pygmalion-at-Sea workshop training for low-performing sailors, or one-on-one by mentors in a coaching role. The populations that stand to benefit most from immunization are those which are most at risk for Golem effects, including known low performers, those stigmatized by blemishes on their record, and persons readily stereotyped as likely to fail.

Besides chronic low performers, individuals who have respectable records of past achievements may need immunization against imminent Golem effects as they naturally advance through stages in their careers and lives that arouse expectations that can precipitate negative SFP. One can only guess the number of productive workers who suffer debilitation because of widespread beliefs that certain responses must come "naturally" to certain situations that arise in life. For example, the general public has been bombarded with information, much of it exaggerated and even sensationalized, about burnout and about aging. Consequently, (mis)informed members of the workforce may come to expect personal and career crises as they approach midlife, and performance decrements as they approach retirement age. Such expectations may precipitate difficulties that would not have been experienced had they not been anticipated, and debilitating SFP results. Immunization through workshop training, counseling, or coaching could help prevent some types of harmful SFP.

Fight Negative Stereotypes

Stereotypes produce SFP because they involve expectations toward individuals on the basis of perceptions of their belonging to some social group or class. Those perceptions lead to differential treatment (Merton 1948; Snyder, Tanke & Berscheid 1977). Negative stereotypes produce Golem effects. When individuals are expected to perform poorly merely because of their race, age, sex, or any other ascribed characteristic not related to actual performance potential, a Golem effect is likely. The locations in organizations where counterproductive stereotypes are most likely to be operating are those staffed by racial and ethnic minorities, women, very old and very young employees, and others about whom stereotypes abound. The MEDKIT case described at the beginning of this chapter exemplifies a Golem effect based on a stereotype concerning persons of a particular ethnic origin and demonstrates how it can be profitably overcome. The use of epithets, such as "dirtbag" aboard the Pygmalion-at-Sea ships, and similar prejoratives, signals the operation of a negative stereotype. Termination of such stereotypes and the Golem effects they arouse deserves investment of management energy out of concern both for fairness toward the target and organizational effectiveness.

Not all stereotypes are negative. Positive stereotypes should not be discouraged. Belonging to a minority group that is stereotyped as industrious or intelligent can be a boon to individual members of that group because the resulting positive expectation effects can help make them more productive. There is no reason to deprive either individuals or organizations of this SFP-based blessing. An example currently being popularized in the American press is the scholastic achievement of Asian-Americans. This is a stereotype despite the fact that it is based on "a kernel of truth," and it is certainly not true of all young Asian-Americans in school. However, even individuals of average ability among this stereotyped group will benefit from the high expectations that others hold toward them because of the stereotype. Since we know that expectancy effects result also in better organizational outcomes, the company stands to gain as well. Why spoil a good thing?

Set Difficult Goals and Challenging Objectives

The goal-setting and management-by-objectives approaches converge in dealing more or less explicitly with performance expectations and in prescribing that performance goals and output objectives be high and difficult to achieve. "Objectives are statements of *expected output*" (Odiorne 1969, 20). Successful MBO may be interpreted as a special case of SFP. Challenging objectives are explicit expressions of high expectations. When a manager and a subordinate agree upon challenging objectives, they are setting the stage for double expectation effects—a Pygmalion effect on the manager's part and a Galatea effect on the subordinate's part.

Similarly, goal-setting experimentation has shown that difficult goals result in greater output than do intermediate or easy goals (Locke, Shaw, Saari & Latham 1981). Garland (1984) has revealed the manner in which expectations mediate the influence of goals on output, and Locke, Motowidlo, and Bobko (1986) have woven performance expectations into a revised theory of goal setting. Setting difficult goals raises expectations, which in turn spur improved performance. In other words, one evidently effective way to produce a Pygmalion effect is to set difficult goals, or, in MBO terminology, set challenging objectives. On the other hand, setting easy goals and/or low objectives produces a Golem effect because subordinates realize that little is expected of them and adjust their efforts downward accordingly.

Thus, MBO and goal setting are techniques for triggering SFP and owe their success to expectation effects. Both of these expectation-raising techniques share a limitation in that output must be specifiable, and preferably quantifiable, to define goals or objectives. This limitation is not shared by the other expectation-raising techniques proposed in this chapter. Raising expectations and setting difficult goals are so utterly compatible that one ought not to be considered without the other. Furthermore, both converge with MBO inasmuch as the central psychological variable that they activate in motivating workers to be more productive is expectancy. Appendix 6A proposes a model, based on SFP concepts, that integrates expectancy and goal setting and shows in greater detail how these two approaches to work motivation reinforce one another.

Clear the Record

Individuals who get off to a bad start in school, in a job, or in life in general often are locked into their past by an unforgetting—and unforgiving—record. More insidious even than the living memory of teachers, supervisors, and peers who have witnessed past failure, the written record remains as an indelible reminder that refreshes memories and contaminates—lowers—the expectations of persons who had no involvement in the original disgrace. Perusing a record rife with failures creates expectations for "more of the same." This is the negative version of the Matthew effect at work. Managers' access to the record contributes materially to low-performer recidivism through the operation of self-*sustaining* prophecy (Salomon 1981). Although the present manager had no part in *producing* the record, his expectations for future achievements *are affected* by the record. The manager is influenced by a record of poor performance to expect further failure. He therefore proceeds to treat the subordinate accordingly as a poor performer, thereby sustaining the subordinate's underachievement. There are undoubtedly multitudes of individuals scattered throughout society whose potential is never realized because they are victimized by the low expectations aroused by their past record.

This self-sustaining Golem scenario is widespread "in nature." The experimental expectation effect constitutes a self-*fulfilling* prophecy that does not simulate real life with complete fidelity because, in true experiments, randomization is used to assure preexperimental equivalence; in a randomized experiment the high-expectation subjects as a group have a past that is equivalent to that of the control subjects. However, in natural settings, managers do not get subordinates with equivalent records. Instead, managers form expectations of their subordinates in part on the basis of a record that may validly reflect past performance. However, the record often grossly underestimates potential performance, and thereby distorts expectations, particularly in the case of underachievers. In short, in most cases the manager does not *originate* positive or negative expectation effects; rather, he inherits them, *sustains* them, and passes them along to the next manager by adding his ratings and comments to the subordinate's record.

One practical implication of the distinction between self-sustaining and self-fulfilling prophecy is that *present managers should not be blamed for past Golem effects.* Ignoring self-sustaining prophecy and emphasizing only SFP imply that present managers are somehow at fault for their underachieving subordinates' poor performance. This implication naturally stiffens their resistance to corrective measures. For example, implied culpability was evident among teachers participating in a workshop designed to train them in the use of positive Pygmalion behaviors in the classroom. Banuazizi (1981, 48) reported that the teachers felt insulted because they interpreted what they were told about the Pygmalion effect as implying that they were doing things wrong in their classrooms. This made them quite defensive. In a similar vein, Crawford et al. (1980) wrote that in their supervisor workshops they had to deal with "considerable resistance on the part of some of the supervisors toward dealing with these issues . . . their reluctance to assume ownership of the problem was reflected by 'blaming' any of several factors that can contribute to their personnel problem. The recruiting system, recruit training, parents, and society at large were named as influencing low performance—factors that were well beyond the control of the supervisors" (p. 488). These teachers and supervisors were, of course, right.

It is therefore crucial for the success of any attempt to raise manager expectations that the consultant refrain from any accusatory words or tone. Empathy is called for here no less than in any other approach intended to aid beleaguered managers in coping with seemingly intractable problems. Particularly when it comes to raising the productivity of chronically low performers, the manager is being called upon to succeed where everyone else in society, including parents, teachers, and the clergy, has failed.

The second practical implication of self-sustaining prophecy is that we need to find ways of liberating individuals from the shackles of their records. This could be done by clearing the record of certain kinds of entries that are likely to arouse negative expectations in a new supervisor. Information retained in personnel files is often notoriously mistaken, ambiguous, and irrelevant (Laudon 1986). Stigmatizing labels, if they must be used at all, should be expunged at the end of a reasonable period of time. Like foodstuffs on the supermarket shelf and moving-violation points on a driver's record, a diagnostic, disciplinary, or evaluative entry in an employee's record should include an expiration date. Furthermore, a company could withhold the record of a new hire or a new transfer from the supervisor for an initial period of several weeks or months. During this time, manager expectations would be formed on the basis of direct personal experience rather than on the basis of the past preserved in the record. An obvious limitation to this kind of solution exists in companies in which it is easy for a manager to phone a new transfer's previous supervisor and obtain a quick evaluation. It is more applicable in very large firms, in companies that operate in multiple sites, and in the case of employees newly hired from outside the organization.

Organizations should install "worker protection programs," akin to the witness protection programs used by the FBI and Interpol to save the lives of criminals who turn state's evidence and then have to be obscured from the long arm of Mob vengeance. A worker with a bad performance record could be relocated in the same company or elsewhere, be given a new employee identity, and get "another chance" at a job free from the persecution of his own work history and the inevitable Golem effect it triggers each time anew. Such a move would block the recurrence of a destructive SFP and the worker's chances of using and developing his potential would be greater. Both the supervisor and the organization would enjoy the benefits of having a more productive employee. The upward mobility so characteristic of immigrant societies, such as Israel and the United States, might derive in part from the fact that generations of newcomers have found it relatively easy to leave a damning record behind and get a fresh start in their new environment. Once the past have been obliterated, the only thing that really counts is what the individual does "from now on."

To summarize, we need to invent new ways of enabling more people with unproductive records to become "organizational immigrants" with clean expectation slates and a chance to begin anew. We can disrupt the recurring cycle of poor performance producing more poor performance. Clearing the evidence of past failure from a record cluttered with stigmatizing information would reduce the frequency of unjust—and counterproductive—Golem effects.

Use Labeling Constructively

The effects of labeling run through our discussion of creating SFP in organizations. Although the only relevant evidence cited from an organizational study was that provided by Schrank (1968), clinical and educational psychology have given labeling its due place. In organizations we can deliberately use labeling to promote positive SFP. Livingston (1969) told how the label "super-staff" emerged in the Metropolitan Life Insurance Company, and described its positive effects. Without invoking the labeling concept, King (1971) used the label HAP (high aptitude personnel) to designate the trainees selected for the Pygmalion treatment. In the IDF experiments we used the label "high potential." Such labels can be generated in everyday situations and used to raise and maintain high expectations. Much inventiveness is invested in devising appropriate names for important projects and campaigns in organizations. Examples are "Operation Blastoff," "Zero Defects," and "Project Rainbow." Similarly, job titles are carefully chosen to bestow upon incumbents a sense of dignity, status, and self-respect, as when a garbage collector is dubbed a "municipal sanitation technician" and when employees who manage no one are given the title "assistant manager." Similar effort should be invested in inventing labels that convey high expectations of various groups of workers.

It is worth repeating that derogative and demeaning labels such as "dirt-bag" should not be tolerated by anyone in any organization. It is management's responsibility to inhibit Golem effects and to foster positive SFP by supplanting negative labels with positive ones. Providing an officially sanctioned label for an identifiable group of members will reduce the tendency of people to invent sarcastic labels. For example, chronically low performers could be relabeled "upward bound," "high potential," or something neutral.

Piggyback on Changes in Personnel and Organization

The endless changes in organizational structure, personnel assignments, product lines, work methods, and operating procedures provide managers and consultants virtually unlimited opportunities for raising expectations unobtrusively. This is not a mere restatement of the Lewinian conceptualization of the Unfreezing—Moving—Refreezing process (Lewin 1951). Rather, it is a call for the opportunistic use of the unfreezing of expectations wrought by organizational changes, whether "natural" or planned, for expectation-raising. Any nontrivial change unfreezes expectations, as members anticipate the repercussions that might positively or negatively effect their work and career. These vague moments of unclear expectations, when members are unsure what is in store for them, invite the alert manager or consultant to interject timely words of assurance, encouragement, confidence, and optimism, all varieties of positive expectations. When members are apprehensive because of their anticipation of an imminent turn for the worse in their situation, the optimistic words and deeds of a sanguine executive or consultant can reduce the suspense and avert a potential Golem effect as negative expectations are replaced by positive ones. The MEDKIT case illustrates how a nimble manager piggybacked on a naturally occurring change in personnel—the intake of a new group of workers—and opportunistically raised naturally low expectations, thereby successfully disrupting a recurring Golem effect.

There are countless examples of organizational changes whose success was augmented by positive expectations and changes that failed at least in part because of negative expectations. Even the classical Hawthorne experiments may have succeeded in boosting productivity by unwittingly raising expectations (Eden 1986). It is also possible that participative management, when it works, owes part of its success to SFP. Constantly "telling" subordinates in a directive manner what to do and how to do it implies a low opinion of their capability. Participation conveys positive regard for subordinates' opinions and potential to contribute. Participation enables individuals to take part in discussing the advantages and disadvantages of proposed changes and to influence decision making in the directions they deem appropriate. When participative decision making is implemented properly, participants will have higher postdecision performance expectations than employees who have not participated. Such expectation effects may contribute as much or more to the success of participation than the mediating variables commonly cited, such as psychological "ownership" of the decision-making process, acceptance of the resulting decisions, and improved information flow (Sashkin 1976). In a field experiment among retail sales personnel, Neider (1980) deliberately used participation to raise employees' effort-performance expectations. She found that, when combined with an incentive plan based on meeting sales targets designed to raise instrumentality, participation led to increased effort and productivity. It is likely that participation raises performance expectations in many instances of research and application, even when VIE theory and expectations are not on the agenda.

In their review of research on participative decision making, Locke and Schweiger (1979) provided indirect support for the argument that participation serves as a vehicle for the expression of manager confidence in subordinate competence. They concluded that subordinate expertise was the single most important determinant of the usefulness of joint decision making. Similarly, Leana (1987) found that the supervisor's perception of the subordinate's job capability was the best predictor of the supervisor's use of delegation. Therefore, the very acts of participation and delegation may be interpreted by subordinates as expressions of high-performance expectations on the part of the manager. Thus, expectations probably mediate the effects of participation on performance. The practical implication is that those managing participation, as other management techniques, should piggyback and use these opportunities deliberately to raise participants' expectations.

Ruinous debilitating effects can be wrought on any innovative program by individuals who harbor negative expectations toward it. Managers and consultants know that a strategically placed skeptic can doom a program by saying to peers and subordinates, "Those whiz kids up there have cooked up another one of their ingenious inventions for us; personally, I don't think it has a chance." The added thrust of the piggyback proposal is that even changes undertaken for extraneous reasons and changes initiated by *force majeure* should be seized upon by managers and consultants as opportunities for the deliberate creation of productive SFP. Telling people that the new computer system, the redesigned office layout, the revised procedures, the improved routing, the replacement engineer, the changes in the sources of raw material, the new software, the new warehouse forms, the weekend retreat, the divisional reorganization, the new chief of accounting, or any other change in how things are done, should be expected to improve productivity may make these changes more productive than otherwise. The cost of piggybacking is nil, and the potential payoff is appreciable.

An example of a piggybacking opportunity available in many organizations is the assessment center. Summarizing their evaluation of the validity of these centers, Turnage and Muchinsky (1984) wrote:

> It is conceivable that a primary function of an assessment center is to elevate individuals' expectations and self-esteem. That is, the candidates attribute their selection for assessment to their perceived worth to the company, and then they seek to perform both in assessment and later on the job at a level high enough to substantiate the lofty esteem in which they are perceived to be held. Thus selection into the assessment center may be the initiation of a subtle Pygmalion effect that generalizes beyond assessment. Therefore the

assessment center itself could be a source of constant error affecting both assessment and subsequent job performance, a source of error that may bedevil the researcher but delight the practitioner (p. 602).

Turnage and Muchinsky's appreciation of expectancy effects is exceptional. However, they stopped short of recommending the deliberate exploitation of assessment centers as an opportunity for raising employees' expectations. The assessment center is one good candidate for a naturally occurring organizational event on which it is practicable to piggyback and raise expectations to trigger productive SFP.

The proposal to piggyback expectancy-raising onto assessment centers, management training, and other organizational events and programs is not intended to relegate these other events to the status of mere convenient means to create SFP. Proposing that posh assessment programs or training junkets be lavished upon young professionals merely to raise their expectations would be absurd. No one would embark on a costly program of assessment or training with the sole intention of tricking individuals in the program into raising their expectations. But every assessment or training center that does not have expectation-raising on its agenda is wasting golden opportunities for the organization to gain the *additional* benefits of expectation effects. The marginal cost of piggybacking is negligible, and the payoff can be substantial.

Foster High-Expectation Culture: Create Positive Myths and Uproot Negative Myths

Changing an organization's culture is difficult. It requires macrolevel leverage over a pervasive, systemwide source of expectations. Therefore, not every manager can make major modifications in an organization's culture. If *anyone* is able to bring about major changes in organizational culture, it must be the chief executive officer or other top-ranking officers with very high visibility and credibility. Changing culture is a worthy task for those at the organization's pinnacle, for *"the unique and essential function of leadership is the manipulation of culture"* (Schein 1985, 317). When exercising the type of leadership called charismatic, visionary, or transformational, managers are changing the organization's culture, and the performance expectations that the culture implies. The consultant's role is to enlighten top executives as to their unique leverage over organizational culture.

Myth making is a promising way of influencing organizational culture. The impact of myths on expectations can be particularly insidious and persistent because, as part of the organization's culture, myths summarize complex, underlying beliefs and assumptions about the organization's capabilities and frailties, assumptions that have slipped out of awareness and become highly resistant to change. Boje, Fedor, and Rowland (1982) have proposed ways of intervening in the myth-making process in the interests of organizational effectiveness. They recommended building up the stock of myths that convey high performance expectations and rooting out negative myths that imply organizational impotence or helplessness. Consider the positive SFP that might flow from the widespread belief that "we are a can-do organization" or that we are "lean and mean" compared to the collective Golem effect generated by myths such as "Nothing ever gets done right around here," "Half the people in this organization are below average," or "We operate on Murphy's Law and the Peter Principle."

Myth making implies that middle managers can also make a cultural difference. After all, individual members are the medium through which culture is transmitted, and they can play a role in promoting, blocking, or changing it. Every manager should do his part to replace pernicious myths with positive ones. This includes refuting cynical stories and rumors that damage the fabric of organizationwide expectations.

Symbolic expressions of a high-achievement culture should be devised and enhanced where they already exist. Properly arranged props can be used to fortify performance-oriented leadership. Clinical psychologists are keenly aware of the effects of physical artifacts on client expectations and arrange them as props for maximal positive impact on client expectations. Coe (1980) has reviewed evidence showing the importance of the therapist's office location and decor and the therapist's dress and grooming. "Clearly, the physical surroundings and the therapist's appearance can have important effects. Alert therapists will recognize these effects and work to arrange (or rearrange) them in their favor" (p. 425). Coe then goes on to discuss how the clinician can make these arrangements under the heading "Techniques for Enhancing Expectation Effects."

In the management sphere, Peters (1978) described the manager's job in terms of the manipulation of symbols by use of "mundane tools." These tools are nothing more than the everyday, nitty-gritty behaviors that comprise the manager's job and how he "frames" them, including how, where, and with whom he spends his time, what gets onto his agenda, and the settings he chooses or creates as a symbolic backdrop for his actions: "Calendar behavior includes review of reports and the use of agenda and minutes to shape expectations" (p. 10). "The mundane tools that involve the creation and manipulation of symbols over time have impact to the extent that they reshape beliefs and expectations. Frequent, consistent, positive reinforcement is an unparalleled shaper of expectations—and, therefore, inducer of change" (p. 11). We all know some managers who are masters at manipulating furnishings, visual aids, schedules, and other environmental cues in ways that create and sustain high expectations. We need research on the effectiveness of various such arrangements and we need training programs to disseminate their use.

The IDF forward treatment center is an exquisite example of macroorganizational design features that foster a high-expectancy culture. By devoting meticulous attention to multiple sources of expectations in every conceivable aspect of an organization's impact on its members and immersing individuals in the resulting high-expectancy culture, SFP can be produced on an organizational scale. Designing high-expectancy culture requires hard work on the part of the would-be prophets. It requires top management's support and active participation in interventions in several aspects of the organization at various levels. The resulting SFP promises to pay off in huge dividends.

Undaunted by the elusiveness and intangibility of culture, some investigators are seeking to devise tools for quantitative cultural analysis so that researchers and practitioners can get a better grip on organizational culture. Cooke and Rousseau (1988) have constructed the *Organizational Culture Survey* for assessing culture in terms of the dominant norms and expectations in organizations and in their subunits. One of the twelve dimensions of organizational culture measured by their survey is "achievement culture," which is a feature of high-expectancy culture. Thus, in the future we may achieve a better grasp of the nature of organizational culture than its qualitative explorers have given us so far. This will make it possible to diagnose an organization's culture in terms of its potential for SFP and to spell out in more operational terms the SFP applications that target organizational culture.

Summary of SFP Applications

The foregoing applications are not the only ones conceivable. As more scholars consider the possibilities, more SFP innovations will be invented and tested. The various applications I've proposed do not contradict one another. The practitioner need not choose one to the exclusion of others. Several of the interventions and techniques can be applied in combination, provided they fit the particular circumstances. There are several general issues that cut across the various SFP applications. They are discussed next.

Creating Pygmalion Effects; Eliminating Golem Effects

The goal of the SFP approach to management is to change the work behavior of individuals, groups, or organizations to make them more productive. We may think of SFP applications in terms of Lewin's (1951) field theory concerning how social systems, individuals or aggregations, change. Every system exists in a field of forces that, when balanced, keep the system in a steady state called a "quasi-stationary equilibrium." A change in the force field results in a change in the system. Lewin distinguished between the "driving forces," which impel a system to move from its current quasistationary equilibrium toward a new state, and, opposing them, the "restraining forces," which resist change. Lewin postulated that creating change by eliminating or weakening restraining forces is to be preferred over the addition of driving forces, because adding driving forces increases the tension in the system, whereas removing restraining forces reduces tension. This part of Lewin's field theory give rise to the idea that management should seek to move organizations to new end-states by "overcoming resistance to change." Managers often try to make organizations more effective by using their hierarchical authority to impose productive changes on workers. This adds forces for change and increases the tension in the system. Being a staunch democrat, Lewin advocated participative decision making as the preferred means of reducing members' resistance to change without arousing undue tension.

In the spirit of the Lewinian tradition, we can draw a parallel between adding driving forces and removing restraining forces and sowing high expectations and eradicating low expectations, respectively. Raising expectations by producing the Pygmalion and Galatea effects, setting challenging goals, and creating positive myths, parallels the addition of forces driving toward a desirable new end-state of higher productivity. Eliminating low expectations toward stereotyped groups, clearing the record, and uprooting negative myths are ways of removing counterproductive restraining forces. It follows from field theory that it may be preferable to eliminate Golem effects than to create Pygmalion effects.

Moreover, improving the circumstances of those subject to Golem effects would be in the Lewinian tradition of egalitarianism. Negative SFP is patently unfair. One can embark on a program to fight the Golem effect with the sense of doing justice to victims by righting past wrongs. Many allies can be enlisted in this struggle to alleviate the deprivation among the victims of negative SFP. Helping those already doing well to do even better is harder to sell in some quarters.

The third reason for preferring to concentrate on the elimination of Golem effects is their ubiquity. Opportunities for countering negative SFP appear to be more bountiful in many organizations than opportunities to initiate positive SFP. In a retrospective commentary on his earlier article on Pygmalion in management, Livingston (1988) wrote that more attention should be focused on negative SFP effects because there are more "negative Pygmalions" than positive Pygmalions in U.S. industry. However, even Livingston expressed an understandable preference for dealing with the bright side of the Pygmalion effect, rather than with the negative Pygmalions, the "dark side" of SFP in management, which he finds "distressing." I share Livingston's sentiment. However, I suspect that tackling the distasteful negative effects is at least as important as the more delectable task of fostering positive effects. I also suspect that there are plenty of opportunities of both kinds. Therefore, for the practitioner, the best strategy is to assess the situation in

184 • Pygmalion in Management

terms of potential contribution to productivity, and then invest his energy in SFP effects, positive and negative, accordingly. If you detect costly Golem effects, try to eradicate them. If there are none, try to create positive Pygmalion effects by raising expectations using any of the proposals suggested in this chapter.

Merton's (1948) analysis of the operation of the Federal Deposit Insurance Corporation exemplifies one direction our thinking can take to devise innovative means of disrupting negative SFP. Banks were failing at a horrendous rate during the Depression because depositors, who lost faith in the banks—even solvent banks—and expected bank failure, panicked and precipitously withdrew their deposits in order to get out in time with their savings intact. This action by these "prophets of banking doom" created the kind of pressure that no bank, no matter how solvent, could withstand, and the prophecy was fulfilled as bankruptcy rapidly ensued in bank after bank.

The establishment of the FDIC has protected the banks and their depositors from this costly SFP by eliminating depositor anticipation of personal financial loss in the event of bank failure. No longer expecting personal loss in the event of bankruptcy of an FDIC-insured bank, depositors have little reason to panic and withdraw their funds. Hearing rumors of impending doom, they feel secure and sit pat, and the formerly commonplace SFP is averted.

We need to enrich the existing stock of management tools and consulting interventions with organizational inventions that will serve as FDIC-like blocks to negative SFP. Clearing employees' records of stale information about past failures and transferring employees as soon as low expectations are detected among their supervisors are proposals that can avert negative SFP. Getting people to attribute failure to external, ephemeral causes is another. Hopefully, more innovative blocks to destructive SFP at work will be devised.

When Pygmalion Fails at Sculpting Galatea

We have seen that not every research attempt to create the Pygmalion effect has succeeded. In the tougher world of practical application, there are bound to be failures. Not every manager will succeed adopting the Pygmalion Leadership Style or in conveying high expectations to subordinates. Not every program upon which one tries to piggyback will be effective. Most disappointing of all, not every individual subordinate upon whom special attention is lavished will blossom. It is these kinds of personal letdowns that contribute heavily to burnout among managers.

One way to handle these failures is to prepare managers for them in advance. Installing an SFP program or training managers in expectancy effects should include a segment designed to immunize managers against the psychological ravages of failure. This does not mean inducing *expectations* of failure, which would run counter to everything said above. It does mean that managers should be prepared to see results accrue gradually and unevenly, to remain undaunted by temporary reverses, and to recognize that ability does impose limits on what each individual can accomplish.

A systematic SFP program should be bolstered by a support group. In the group, managers can discuss problems in producing Pygmalion effects and share their successes and disappointments. They can learn from each other what has worked well, and they can dissipate some of their pent-up frustrations by sharing them with understanding peers. A useful composition for an SFP support goup is the same group that was trained in the Pygmalion Leadership Style. Maintaining that group as a Pygmalion support group would be a natural follow-up stage to facilitate applying what was learned.

Limitations

Discrepancy Effects

Throughout this book the reasonable boundaries of SFP effects have been stressed. This can be summed up by saying that expectations should be raised to a level that is high, difficult to attain, but realistically within the competence limits of the person or group of whose performance we speak. Writing about expectation effects in OD, Woodman and Tolchinsky (1985) similarly concluded that it is preferable "to establish high, but reasonably attainable, expectations among participants of a change program" (p. 485). They reached this conclusion after considering the potentially dysfunctional effects of achieving outcomes that differ from those expected. Suspecting that such "discrepancy effects" could be counterproductive, they invoked dissonance theory, contrast theory, and assimilation-contrast theory in weighing the implications of discrepancy effects of different orders of magnitude. Some of these theoretical implications concern participants' evaluations of, and satisfaction with, the program, rather than its productive outcomes. For example, Woodman and Tolchinsky reasoned that, according to contrast theory, initially understating the eventual outcomes of organizational change programs may lead to greater satisfaction with those outcomes. Such reasoning might lead one to conclude that initial expectations ought to be kept low. This would be a mistake.

Granting that postprogram affective byproducts are important in their own right, they are not as crucial to the change process as assuring success in the first place by establishing high initial expectations. For all the reasons stated in previous chapters, initially arousing high expectations for success should produce more success than lower initial expectations. However, discrepancy effects do imply a contradiction inherent in expectation-raising inasmuch as setting high initial expectations might be incompatible with long-term success when intermediate progress is assessable. Woodman and Tolchinsky's theoretical analysis indicates that when interim outcomes fall short of initial expectations, dissatisfaction and subsequent demotivation may result, to the detriment of continued progress. Thus, the high expectations that are helpful at the beginning of a program may come back to haunt the consultant in later stages. This is the apparent dilemma posed by discrepancy effects. Fortunately, there is a way out.

The manager has a crucial role to play in shaping subordinate reactions at critical junctions in the developmental process, when interim assessments of success and failure can be made. The consultant's role vis-à-vis clients is analogous to the manager's role vis-à-vis subordinates. When progress falls short of expectations, emphasis should be placed on how great an accomplishment it is to have progressed so far from where we started and to have come so close to a difficult goal. Competent attribution management on the part of managers and consultants can facilitate making interim outcomes—both success and failure—motivating for subordinates and clients. Skillful progress assessment and postprogram counseling entail helping subordinates and clients make attributions that prevent the erosion of confidence and build motivation to strive for better future results. Like the manager mentoring a subordinate, the consultant installing an organizational improvement program should channel attributions of success in meeting initial expectations to internal causes such as client ability and effort, and attributions of failure to unstable factors such as insufficient effort or bad luck. Such attributions set the stage for the next phase of development by energizing clients to sustain their efforts toward the goal of renewed success.

Opportunities for interim expectation-bolstering can be built into a development program by using a strategy of "small wins," described by Peters (1978) and elaborated on by Weick (1984). An ambitious, long-term project can be defined in terms of a series of small stages. One can build momentum toward eventual overall success by encouraging participants to savor the joys of successive small accomplishments that signal milestones along the way toward achieving more ambitious goals. Reaching each milestone justifies and reinforces high expectations. Failure in any particular stage need not be a devastating setback, since it can be interpreted as a surmountable delay in progress toward ultimate success, not total program failure. "The important tactic for dealing with the flops implicit in trying for small wins is to localize the disconfirmation of expectations" (Weick 1984, 48).

To illustrate the sophisticated motivational use of a "small win" on the road to achieving a difficult goal, consider the following statement made by a resident of Chatanooga in an interview broadcast over National Public Radio on March 31, 1986. The Enterprise Foundation was established by James and Patricia Rouse with the aim of revitalizing dilapidated housing in twenty-four American cities. The interviewee had been instrumental in bringing Mr. Rouse to Chatanooga with the goal of making all of the housing for the city's poor, estimated at ten thousand units, fit and livable within a decade. "If we only improve three thousand, or five thousand, or eight thousand homes for the poor, well then we'll just go on into the next decade. But what a wonderful failure, to have fallen a little bit short on an extremely ambitious goal!" Obviously, Enterprise in Chatanooga will not be stopped nor discouraged by not meeting the goal because whatever they do accomplish will be touted as a small win, and not such a small one at that!

To summarize, a strategy of "Small Wins—Big Success" circumvents the threat of discrepancy effects by simultaneously defining relatively easy short-term goals and more challenging long-term goals, and managing the attribution process accordingly. Different levels of expectations are established and fulfilled at different stages. Thus, although creating realistic high initial expectations can result in discrepancy effects, these effects can be handled in ways that either render them harmless or use them to increase motivation. The bottom line is still that high expectations yield the best bottom line.

Protect the Successful Golem

One particularly disturbing form of discrepancy effect warrants special attention. Rosenthal and Jacobson (1968) noted in their report on the original "Pygmalion in the Classroom" experiment that teachers developed negative attitudes toward high-achievement pupils in the control condition, concerning whom the researchers had not imparted high expectations. This was especially true of high-achievement pupils in the control condition who were also in the school's slow track. Tracking in schools, as well as in other types of organizations (such as "nontenure track," "unpromotable," "on probation"), is institutionalized expectation-setting. Discrepant high achievement on the part of individuals initially expected to do poorly may result in negative supervisor attitudes that impede further progress. Unanticipated high performance, which should come as a pleasant surprise and give cause for celebration, can be greeted instead with hostility. We need to be alert to potentially dysfunctional reactions on the part of managers who become frustrated when their negative prophecies are disconfirmed instead of fulfilled.

Managers and consultants should maintain their vigilance and try to detect this particular discrepancy effect and prevent its destructive consequences. Special organizational means may help. For example, unconfirmed negative consequences could be turned into a positive experience for all concerned by a program of special recognition for managers who salvage disadvantaged individuals and succeed in making them "employee of the year." Individual managers might change their negative reaction to successful Golems if the organization changed its approach to them.

Defensive Pessimism: An Exception

Defensive pessimism suggests another limit to the applicability of expectancy raising. Norem and Cantor (1986a, 1986b) have shown that, for some people, low performance expectations may be beneficial in terms of productivity, and that relieving them of the low expectations to which they cling may be deleterious to their performance. The expectancy strategy that these investigators dubbed *defensive pessimism* serves to aid highly anxious individuals in harnessing their anxiety and focusing their energy on performance. In these cases, low expectations serve as a means of raising motivation. For example, Norem and Cantor (1986b) cited the example of straight-A students who always expect to fail exams. The low expectations drive them to endless study, which contributes to their success. Such people "set expectations that seem considerably lower than what would be warranted by objective consideration of past base rates. These expectations do not, however, become self-fulfilling prophecies, nor does the anxiety, although real, lead directly to performance deficits. In fact, this strategy may be thought of as a method by which individuals are able to cope with their anxiety, in effect, change it from a debilitating to a motivational force" (p. 1209).

Norem and Cantor emphasized that the anxiety and expectations of which they speak are not the result of their experimental manipulation, but rather preexisting traits that people bring with them to the laboratory. They went on to demonstrate experimentally that individuals who use defensive pessimism as a strategy for handling their anxiety do not perform worse than do optimists of similar objective ability (measured in terms of grade point average) *unless* their pessimism is disrupted! Encouragement designed to raise their self-expectations served to strip these subjects of their defensive-pessimism strategy and impaired their performance.

These findings imply a limitation that any application of expectation raising must respect. It is likely that individuals who adopt defensive pessimism as a strategy for dealing with situations that challenge their competency are to be found not only in the experimental laboratory, but also in work organizations. Their personal style should be respected and not tampered with by someone bent on raising performance expectations indiscriminantly. There is no basis for estimating what proportion of the work force uses defensive pessimism as a strategy, but it probably is not very widespread.

No remedy is foolproof and no solution fits all problems. Besides defensive pessimism, psychologists may uncover other benefits of low expectations among certain types of individuals and in some circumstances. Care should always be taken to consider the uniqueness of the individuals involved, as well as the special features of the situation, before rushing in blindly to apply any procedure, including expectation raising. If performance is good *despite* low expectations, then it would be wise to leave well enough alone, particularly among highly anxious workers.

How Often Can Expectations Be Raised?

In addition to the limit on *how high* expectations should be raised, there is a limit to *how many times* expectation-raising can be implemented before losing its productive impact. Paraphrasing Honest Abe, in repeated attempts to create the Pygmalion effect using the deceptive experimental manipulation, 'you can fool many managers once or twice, but you won't be able to fool many of them more times than that.' Nevertheless, using different techniques each time, managers and consultants probably can raise expectations repeatedly without "wearing out" the approach. Varying the technique appears to be necessary. For example, the manager of the MEDKIT plant could not credibly tell his production manager that he had hand-picked every future cohort of new hires. Perhaps several serial successes would sufficiently weaken or terminate the stereotype that produced that particular Golem effect in the first place, and in that sense become a positive self-sustaining prophecy, obviating the need for repeated intervention. Also, several visible successes in creating productive expectation effects may meld into a positive SFP climate in the organization.

The question of the utility of repeatedly using SFP in practice does not arise with many of the applications proposed in this chapter. Pygmalion Leadership Training, clearing the record, FDIC-type blocking of negative SFP processes, and other applications that do not involve deception can be used repeatedly with no loss of potency.

Realistic Job Preview versus High Expectations

Raising performance expectations to realistically high levels does not contradict the need for realistic job preview (Wanous 1977; Premack & Wanous 1985). The realistic job preview is designed to prevent a faulty recruitment practice in which prospective employees are promised much more desirable working conditions, interesting job content, and opportunities for quick promotion than the organization is likely to provide. When it eventually becomes apparent to the new hire that the organization cannot make good on the overly optimistic picture painted at time of recruitment, the ensuing disappointment, frustration, and anger fuel the desire to look elsewhere. Realistic preview of what the future holds reduces this type of wasteful turnover.

The realistic job preview and the present prescription for high realistic expectations differ in several important respects. First, the expectations are for different things. The realistic job preview is geared toward creating realistic expectations for global features of the job such as authority and job scope, and rewards such as pay, fringe benefits, and opportunities for advancement. In contrast, in the Pygmalion context the expectations are for a level of future job performance. Second, realistic job preview is relevant at the recruitment stage only, whereas expectancy-raising is relevant throughout the job cycle.

Finally, the realistic job preview is designed to prevent overly ambitious recruiters from enticing overly greedy recruits into a commitment to enter the company's employ and to prevent subsequent turnover, whereas the aim of raising performance expectations to high levels is to boost productivity.

These differences render the two approaches compatible. Recruits should be given a *realistic* expectation of what their jobs will be like and of their prospects for future rewards, satisfaction, and advancement. At the same time, recruitment is an opportune moment of attentiveness on the part of recruits and should be used for raising performance expectations. The recruiter should be in the Pygmalion role and transmit *high* expectations regarding the recruits' likelihood of performing well in the company. Thus, the twofold expectancy mission of the recruiter should be to communicate realistic expectations about job conditions and to impart high, realistic expectations concerning the recruits' prospects for success in their new jobs.

Higher-Order Expectation Effects

The Consultant as Pygmalion

Wittingly or unwittingly, consultants also play the role of the prophet in SFP. High expectations on the part of a consultant who believes in the client's potential to improve cause the consultant to treat the client as a high-performance client, thereby triggering positive SFP. This may be dubbed a second-order Pygmalion effect. This is the naturally occurring field variant of King's high-expectation condition with the consultant replacing the experimenter as prophet. In parallel fashion, if a consultant harbors negative expectations about the client's capacity for improvement and does a poor job of concealing these low expectations, a negative SFP, or second-order Golem effect, is likely to result. Thus, consultants can unwittingly trigger expectation effects among their clients that are similar in kind to manager expectation effects.

The following statement about placebos could just as well apply to consultant expectation-raising interventions: they "should be equivalent to test procedures on all major recognized common factors. These might include induced expectancy of improvement; credibility of rationale; credibility of procedures; demand for improvement; and therapist attention, enthusiasm, effort, perceived belief in treatment procedures, and commitment to client improvement" (Critelli & Neumann 1984, 38). The therapist behaviors Critelli and Neumann listed build credibility for high outcome expectations, and therefore are instrumental in producing therapeutic placebo effects. The very same behaviors are appropriate for creating effective expectancy effects to aid in the successful implementation of *any* ameliorative program, including those undertaken by consultants in work organizations.

Therefore, the same caveats apply to consultants as to managers. A consultant who believes in the client's ability to improve will act toward the client in a manner similar to that in which physicians treat their patients when they produce a placebo effect. Treating the client as one who will most certainly improve conveys high consultant expectations that raise client self-expectations, initiating SFP as an auxiliary force that helps the organization achieve the improvements sought by the change program. Consultants who do not believe in a client's capacity to improve should disqualify themselves from working with that client, lest they produce an unintended Golem effect. Such consultants are false prophets. In short, consultants consult better for clients from whom they expect more. Woe is to the patient or the organization whose healer believes not in what he is doing.

SFP in consulting has an important practical implication for managers in the client role. If you detect in a consultant's words, intonation, or mannerisms any expression of cynicism, skepticism, sarcasm, or any other manifestation of disbelief in the capacity of members of your organization to improve, fire the consultant!

The Messiah Effect

The phenomenal success of some leading consultants and consulting firms may be in part a consequence of their ability to inspire high self-expectations among their clients. Some consultants may be unaware of this, but many are undoubtedly fully aware of what they are doing. The latter purposely use expectation-raising as a "secret weapon" whose power they know would be diluted by disclosure. In the case of famous consultants of high repute, their very arrival on the scene is sufficient to raise the expectations of key individuals in the organization that "things will certainly improve now." The resulting optimism causes these clients to redouble their efforts in getting on with what has to be done to revitalize the organization. The mobilization of extraordinary client energy and subsequent SFP brought about by the arrival of a renowned consultant is what I call the "messiah effect."

The messiah's power to relieve the client's woes is derived from the client's own optimistic expectations, sparked by the would-be redeemer's coming, and fueled by the client's eagerness to cooperate with the messiah in fulfilling his own expectations. Any organizational change of transformational proportions requires effective tapping of existing sources of human energy and the creation of new energies (Ackerman 1984; Bradley 1986). The arrival of a messiah expands the amount of energy available in an organization because of the high expectations that it arouses. The messiah comes endowed with no supernatural powers. He is as mortal and fallible as his client-followers. He derives his extraordinary powers from their belief in him. Thus, the messiah's real power is that given him by his clients, whose motivation to exert effort is boosted tremendously because of their expectations aroused by his arrival. This is how his prophecy "fulfills itself."

To illustrate the motivational impact of the arrival of a messianic consultant, consider again Rouse's Enterprise Foundation. In the National Public Radio broadcast cited earlier, Rouse said, "We set it up believing not that we were going to work at the problem, but that we were going to solve it." Said a local resident active in the "Chatanooga Venture" as Enterprise's project there was called, "You want the type of inspiration that he brings to a city. The same old local officials can't bring to a city what a James Rouse can bring." The Enterprise Foundation inspired people in Chatanooga to expend tremendous energy on the project. James Rouse knows how to fulfill the messiah role.

Playing the messiah role has its risks. When expectations get out of hand, it may be impossible to fulfill them, and the messiah's image, and his motivating power, may be tarnished. Deeper understanding of the underlying expectation processes at work in creating this kind of messianic zeal will further demystify SFP and turn it into a practical tool to be used by more managers and consultants.

*Third-Order Expectation Effects: The Impact of Our
Expectations on the Success of Organizational
Development and Management Consulting*

There are many "prophets" who voice expectations with regard to OD and consulting. Prophets of doom who expect OD to sink and be relegated to the stagnant backwaters of organizational science undoubtedly, and probably unwittingly, contribute to precisely that outcome. In a recent article in the Academy of Management's *OD Newsletter,* Michael Beer, long identified as a trendsetting OD theoretician and practitioner, wrote simply that "OD is dying" (Beer 1988). On the other hand, high expectations regarding the future contributions of OD to management and organization science will improve its chances of ultimately succeeding. In this sense we are all prophets. OD consultants have no *prima facie* claim to immunity from expectation effects.

Writing from a different perspective, Peters (1978) saw the seeds of pessimism in the concepts and theories that some of our leading management scholars invoke in describing organizational behavior and managerial decision making. Metaphors such as "garbage cans," "organizational seesaws," and "loosely coupled systems," and the idea that "optimizing" must give way to "satisficing," convey to the manager-reader the common message that the world is confusing, unpredictable, and perhaps unmanageable. Peters therefore proposed the management of symbols, patterns, and settings as a practical, mundane alternative to unrealistically complex prescriptions for how managers should deal with their problems. Making his "optimistic case for getting things done," Peters attempted to save his readers from the dire implications of the problem-oriented management literature.

Management scholars should be aware of their power as prophets. What we write may have more impact than we think. We can contribute to society-wide SFP—positive and negative. As many others in the prophet's role, authors of management books and articles are not necessarily aware of SFP and its constructive and destructive power.

A development that is particularly troubling in this context is an approach which, if misinterpreted, might legitimize failure in OD and weaken its effectiveness. Mirvis and Berg (1977) did consultants a great service by publishing *Failures in Organization Development and Change.* This book helped redress the imbalance inherent in a publication process that favors successful accounts and deprives readers of the potential learning from failure. However, treating failure *too* positively has its dangers. For example, Michael and Mirvis (1977) wrote, "*There is no need to expect that with the application of knowledge and skill things should always turn out right*" (p. 317). They encouraged practitioners "to free themselves and their clients of expectations that knowledge and skill guarantee successful change results" (p. 322). These authors coined the oxymoron "successful failure." In describing the benefits to be reaped as an organization increases its capacity for what they call "embracing its errors," Michael and Mirvis used the phrases "expect problems," "expect errors," and "lower their expectations."

Embracing failure so wholeheartedly is liable to produce unintended Golem effects. Learning from failure is fine up to a point. However, when we embrace failure too intimately and begin celebrating it, then it has gone too far. *Successful success* must remain the prize we seek. "Successful failure" is a booby prize. We must beware of the dangers of negative SFP as we dredge our failures for their golden nuggets of learning. Those who expect failure are more likely to fail, and failure further reduces expectations (Weiner 1980). Hopefully, those who read *Failures* learned and therefore strengthened their expectations of success. A proper approach to failure *can* nourish expectations of success and thereby sustain positive SFP. However, such an outcome cannot be taken for granted. Given what we know about how people respond to failure, even vicariously (Bandura 1986), negative SFP is an outcome of delving into failure that should not be ignored.

The Future of Self-Fulfilling Prophecy at Work

> When Pygmalion's Galatea, whom he had fashioned exactly after his dreams, endowing her with as much reality and existence as an artist can, finally came up to him and said: "Here I am," how different was the living woman from the sculptured stone.
> —Goethe, *Italian Journey*, 1962

After accumulating vast knowledge of Italy from books, the young Goethe journeyed there. In his diary, he repeatedly recorded his astonishment at how different the Italians in the flesh were from their literary images, which he had learned to know so well. In the above quote from his travel log, Goethe projected his amazement at the real Italians onto Pygmalion's putative surprise upon experiencing the voluptuousness of Galatea in the flesh, in contrast to her erstwhile stony qualities, which he had come to know so intimately before Aphrodite breathed life into her.

In life, too, preconceptions often pale next to reality.

Any topic removed from the confines of academic reflection to the rough-and-tumble world of managing organizations comes to life and assumes qualities unimagined in the ivory tower. Having pursued Pygmalion and other SFP processes in management for about a decade now, I'm overdue for my Aphrodite to advance my pursuit to its next, livelier stage, which is research on real-world application. The basic research so far has been fascinating, and I hope I've put some of the flavor of my own excitement into the pages of this book. Although there are still unanswered questions concerning the Pygmalion effect, I feel no more need to replicate the classical Pygmalion-in-the-classroom paradigm in work organizations. I look forward to field experimental work that will test ways of applying these ideas in actual management situations. Field work currently under way by my students and me promises to demonstrate the effectiveness of large-scale applications, especially Pygmalion Leadership Training. It is time to move on to research on the following issues.

Training Design. How should managers be trained in SFP? Which workshop designs get managers to internalize the Pygmalion Leadership Style most effectively? How should the subconscious aspects of the communication of expectations be handled? Is practice enough? Would a combination of role playing with videotaped feedback help managers root out nonverbal behaviors that convey negative expectations?

Acting Out of Concert With One's Expectations. Can managers be trained to act like Pygmalion toward subordinates of whom they really do not expect much? This would require extreme self-control and presence of mind. The manager would be called upon to be aware of the importance of expectancy effects, to be aware of their actual expectations toward their subordinates, and to stifle expression of their low expectations for the sake of productivity. Can they do this?

Besides the question of whether it is possible to train managers to act out of concert with their true expectations, another question is, *should* managers be trained to act contrary to their expectations to prevent Golem effects? The leaders who do this consistently are sports coaches. No matter how unfavorable the odds, I have never heard a coach in a pregame interview say that he expected his team to lose! Coaches know about the devastating motivational effects of low expectations. We should study athletic coaches more closely.

Business managers have a lot to learn from sports managers. Sports are a big business with a massive worldwide market. Sports are also part of the educational program at every high school and college and a major part of life on some campuses. Some athletics departments earn big money for their universities, and they do foster physical fitness. However, the educational justification for their existence as academic departments is that they contribute to student development by building character, competitiveness, perseverance, discipline, loyalty, commitment, teamwork, and sportsmanship, all presumed to be useful in their subsequent careers. This is undoubtedly what Arthur Wellesley, Duke of Wellington, had in mind when he said that the battle of Waterloo was won on the playing fields of Eton. In principle, fostering these traits in subordinates is part of managers' leadership role. Coaches lead individual athletes and teams to major achievements in competitive efforts watched by millions. Yet, management research has paid little attention to how they do this. Investigating how athletic instructors and coaches use expectancy effects might reveal some useful applications in the realm of business management in general, and Pygmalion in particular.

Pygmalion and Galatea. It is conceivable that we would get a stronger expectancy effect if we created both the Pygmalion effect and the Galatea effect simultaneously with the same subordinates. The combination of expecting much of oneself and perceiving high expectations from one's supervisor should be mutually reinforcing and have a multiplicative effect. However, in the IDF adjutancy experiment (Eden & Ravid 1982), we neglected to combine high instructor expectations with high trainee expectations to test the interaction. The only study that has crossed high supervisor expectations with high subordinate expectations was Zanna, Sheras, Cooper, and Shaw's (1975) field experiment in which some of the teachers were led to believe that some of their students had high ability and some of those students were also led to believe that they would perform well. They found two significant main effects but no significant interaction, meaning that raising either teacher expectations or pupil expectations had a positive effect on performance, but raising both did not. Zanna et al. interpreted their findings as perhaps indicating that raising expectations at both levels is too overwhelming for the positive effect to occur. We need replication among adults in work organizations to conclude whether raising both manager and subordinate expectations is worthwhile.

Galatea's Expectations of Pygmalion. How do subordinates' expectations toward their supervisors affect the supervisors' success? Is there any reciprocity between the expectations of managers and the expectations of subordinates? As Jones (1986) pointed out, those whom we commonly study as targets of expectations have expectations of their own. "They too play active roles in creating their social environment. In short, they are not the passive recipients of social influence in the service of confirming the perceiver's expectancies" (p. 44). One well-known teacher expectancy investigator has gone as far as to say that most of the relationships between teacher expectations and pupil performance in typical classrooms "are more accurately construed as student effects on teachers rather than as teacher expectation effects on students" (Brophy 1983, 634).

Despite this, the effects of the expectations of the targets have been almost totally ignored in SFP experimentation. Virtually all variants of SFP studied have involved the influence of expecters of higher status on the performance of expectees of lower status. Populations studied include teachers and pupils, instructors and trainees, experimenters and subjects, physicians and patients, managers and subordinates, and commanders and soldiers; almost without exception, high status versus low status, respectively. The only exception to date was a laboratory experiment conducted by Feldman and Theiss (1982) among college students who were assigned to teacher or pupil roles. The teachers were led to expect either high- or low-ability pupils, and the pupils were led to expect either a highly competent or a highly incompetent teacher. The results showed that teacher expectations affected pupil performance as predicted, but pupil expectations had no influence upon either teacher behavior or pupil performance.

Perhaps studies of expectancy effects have been top-down because SFP researchers have intuited some basic truth about human nature. Perhaps the status differential is essential for the expecter's expectations to have the required influence on the expectee's self-efficacy. However, it is possible that we have simply overlooked important effects because of a deeply entrenched, one-sided view of human relationships. Having been socialized in a world of hierarchical organizations, it is easier to see downward influence. Suppose the subordinates were led to believe that a new manager is highly competent. Would their positive expectations contribute to his managerial effectiveness? If trainees expect more of an instructor, does that make him a more effective instructor? Do subordinates with high expectations toward their managers draw out more effective managerial behaviors? A positive answer would seem reasonable. If confirmed by research findings, it could extend the SFP-at-Work model to include upward expectancy effects as well as the current downward effects. Lateral, or peer-to-peer, expectancy effects are also a possibility awaiting researchers' attention.

Expectancy Effects among Women. We need research on women in the role of Pygmalion and Galatea. There are not enough data available at this time to conclude anything. However, as we have seen, the evidence at hand gives us reason to be skeptical. Research should test expectancy effects among same-sex pairs, as well as among woman-boss-man-subordinate and man-boss-woman-subordinate pairs.

My life has been touched by several Pygmalions. I'm sure yours has, too. It is these personal experiences that really bring the topic to life for me, and probably for you, too. The data are there, and I've reviewed them to convince you scientifically. But on your journey to "Italy," you, too, will undoubtedly be amazed at how different, how much more exciting, it is "in the flesh." I am not a manager. But as I have found out trying to apply some of my own recommendations to bringing up my kids, these things are easier to write about than to implement.

One interpretation of the Pygmalion myth is that that lonely prince of Cyprus was striving to sculpt the perfect woman. His quest was unattainable, for perfection is not a human quality. Therefore, the merciful goddess put an end to his misery by bringing his statue to life. This book is at its end. Lacking divine intervention, it, too, lacks perfection. If it succeeds in drawing more researchers to the quest, and stimulates SFP applications in management, it will have been worth it.

Appendix 6A

Integrating Pygmalion and Goal Setting

In a previous discussion of the Pygmalion effect at work (Eden 1984), I suggested that setting difficult goals may be one of many effective ways to raise expectations and to trigger productive self-fulfilling prophecy in organizations. Recent goal-setting research and restatements of the goal-setting model have incorporated state-expectancy, usually in the form of self-efficacy, as an antecedent to performance (Locke et al. 1984; Locke et al. 1986; Taylor, Locke, Lee & Gist 1984; Wood & Locke 1987). These theoreticians sometimes mention expectancy and self-efficacy separately, and sometimes add one parenthetically. Convergent findings from research in the social learning theory tradition corroborate the importance of self-efficacy as a determinant (and byproduct) of performance (Bandura 1986; Bandura & Cervone 1986; Bandura & Schunk 1981). However, in the revised conceptualization of the goal-setting process, goal difficulty is still deemed to be the key causal variable, whose effects are moderated by the level of state-expectancy that subjects form on their own with no prompting from the experimenter beyond setting the goals. Although the direct impact of expectancy on performance has been found and acknowledged by goal-setting researchers, they have not earmarked expectancy for experimental manipulation and practical application. This is consistent with the goal setting's central focus on promoting specific, difficult goals as a means to raise productivity. However, the Pygmalion experiments reviewed in chapter 2 have shown that state-expectancy can be raised *directly* in the absence of deliberate goal setting, and that raising state-expectations in this way boosts motivation and performance. Of course, this does not preclude the possibility that subjects whose state-expectations have been raised consequently set difficult goals on their own. A theoretical model that included both raising state-expectations *and* simultaneously setting specific, difficult goals would integrate the compatible aspects of the Pygmalion and goal-setting approaches to work motivation.

Recent versions of the goal-setting model (Locke et al. 1984, figure 3; Locke et al. 1986, figure 3; Taylor et al. 1984) treat goal difficulty as being closest to performance. State-expectancy is posited as an antecedent of goal level; individuals who expect much of themselves tend to choose, accept, and be committed to, difficult goals. State-expectancy is also portrayed as having direct effects on performance. These models do not include the effects of goals on expectations. The notion that, in addition to their direct effects on performance, goals may have an indirect effect on performance that operates via expectancy or self-efficacy, does not appear in these statements of the model. However, Bandura and Schunk's (1981) experimental treatment manipulated goals and produced consequent changes in both perceived self-efficacy and performance.

Figure 6–1 presents an integrative model which is consistent with Pygmalion, social learning theory, and goal setting findings. It portrays trait-expectancy as antecedent to both state-expectancy and goal difficulty. The arrows from trait-expectancy represent the hypotheses that high trait-expectancy fosters high state-expectancy *and* makes difficult goals more acceptable. In turn, state-expectancy and goal difficulty are depicted as influencing each other and as affecting performance. The double-headed arrow connecting state-expectancy and goal difficulty represents the hypothesis that raising state-expectancy makes difficult goals more acceptable and the hypothesis that setting difficult goals raises state-expectancy. Thus, it is hypothesized that state-expectancy has a direct effect on performance and an

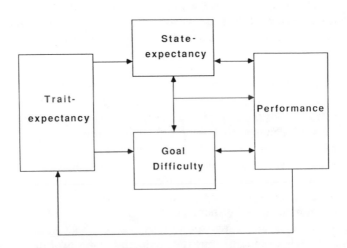

Figure 6–1. Model Integrating Trait-Expectancy, State-Expectancy, and Goal Difficulty as Determinants of Performance

indirect effect that operates via goal difficulty and, simultaneously, that goal difficulty has a direct effect on performance and an indirect effect that operates via state-expectancy. Thus, the model in figure 6–1 portrays state-expectations and goals as having mutually reinforcing effects on performance. Positioned equidistant from performance, state-expectancy and goals are hypothesized as having equivalently potent effects on performance. Both state-expectancy and goal difficulty are connected to performance by double-headed arrows to indicate that, apart from the effects of these two antecedents on performance, performance in turn influences its antecedents. Following success, state-expectancy rises and difficult goals are more acceptable, whereas in the aftermath of failure state-expectations sag and easier goals are embraced (Bandura 1986; Weiner 1974). Finally, the arrow from performance to trait-expectancy represents the hypothesis that repeated success or failure in time enhances or erodes trait-expectancy (Brockner 1988). Both state-expectancy and goal difficulty can be manipulated by experimenters and altered by managers. We need experiments that simultaneously manipulate both state-expectancy *and* goals to test both main effects and the interaction. The disproportionate boost in productivity that is hypothesized to result from the interaction of high expectations to achieve difficult goals awaits experimental confirmation. Meanwhile, the integrative model in figure 6–1 summarizes all the available evidence. For now, the best-informed practical advice to managers is to set difficult but attainable goals *and* to raise state-expectations to high but realistic levels.

Notes

Chapter 1. From Ancient Myth to Modern Reality: Rediscovery of the Power of Expectations

1. King wrote that the difference between the "high aptitude personnel" and the controls in picture preference was "surprising" and that it "dramatized" the "incredibly subtle" unintentional effect. In all this excitement he neglected to test it for statistical significance. Fortunately, the Fisher exact probability test (Siegel 1956) for the 2 × 2 table with frequencies of 5 and 0 for one group and 2 and 5 for the other is significant at the .05 level.

2. The tables in this chapter are simplified versions of those published in the scientific articles and papers cited. Readers interested in more detailed statistical information about these analyses should consult the sources referenced.

3. Reuven Stern was the military psychologist who conducted this experiment in the field and collected and analyzed the data under the author's supervision in partial fulfillment of the requirements for his master's degree at Tel Aviv University.

Chapter 3: Expectations, Motivation, and Performance: Why Do Workers Achieve What They Expect?

1. The model presented in this chapter is an elaboration of one originally published in the *Academy of Management Review* (Eden 1984). Some of the ideas about expectancy and motivation appeared in another article in the same journal (Eden 1988b).

Chapter 6. Managing Self-Fulfilling Prophecy in Organizations

1. A "jump-up" is a simple exercise in which a person begins in a standing position, bends his knees until his hands touch the floor, then kicks his feet back so that

his body is parallel to the floor supported by his hands and feet, and finally jumps back up to resume a standing position. Jump-ups are preferable to more strenuous exercises like push-ups for this demonstration because the number of jump-ups that a participant does is determined more by motivation than by muscular strength.

Bibliography

Ackerman, L.S. 1984. The flow state: A new view of organizing and managing. In J.D. Adams, ed., *Transforming work*. Alexandria, Virg.: Miles River Press.

Adams, J.D. 1978. Improving stress management: An action-research-based OD intervention. In W.W. Burke, ed., *The cutting edge: Current theory and practice in organization development*. La Jolla, Calif.: University Associates.

Adams, J.S. 1965. Inequity in social exchange. In L. Berkowitz, ed., *Advances in experimental social psychology*. New York: Academic Press.

Alker, H.R., Jr. 1969. A typology of ecological fallacies. In M. Dogan & S. Rokkan, eds., *Quantitative ecological analysis in the social sciences, 69–86*. Cambridge: MIT.

Allport, G.W. 1950. The role of expectancy. In H. Cantril, ed., *Tensions that cause wars, 43–78*. Urbana: University of Illinois Press.

American Psychological Association. 1982. *Ethical principles in the conduct of research with human participants*. Washington, D.C.: Author.

Atkinson, J.W. 1957. Motivational determinants of risk-taking behavior. *Psychological Review, 10*, 209–232.

———. 1964. *Motives in fantasy, action, and society*. Princeton, N.J.: Van Nostrand.

Atkinson, J.W., & Feather, N.T. 1966. *A theory of achievement motivation*. New York: Wiley.

Atkinson, J.W., & Raynor, J.O. 1974. *Motivation and achievement*. Washington, D.C.: Winston.

Babad, E.Y. 1978. On the biases of psychologists. *Behavioral and Brain Sciences, 3*, 387–388.

———. 1979. Personality correlates of susceptibility to biasing information. *Journal of Personality and Social Psychology, 37*, 195–202.

———. 1980. Expectancy bias in scoring as a function of ability and ethnic labels. *Psychological Reports, 46*, 625–626.

Babad, E.Y., & Inbar, J. 1981. Performance and personality correlates of teachers' susceptibility to biasing information. *Journal of Personality and Social Psychology, 40*, 553–561.

Babad, E.Y., Inbar, J., & Rosenthal, R. 1982a. Teachers' judgment of students' potential as a function of teachers' susceptibility to biasing information. *Journal of Personality and Social Psychology, 42*, 541–547.

Babad, E.Y., Inbar, J., & Rosenthal, R. 1982b. Pygmalion, Galatea, and the Golem: Investigations of biased and unbiased teachers. *Journal of Educational Psychology, 74,* 459–474.

Bandura, A. 1977. *Social learning theory.* Englewood Cliffs, N.J.: Prentice-Hall.

———. 1986. *Social foundations of thought and action: A social-cognitive view.* Englewood Cliffs, N.J.: Prentice-Hall.

Bandura, A., & Cervone, D. 1986. Differential engagement of self-reactive influences in cognitive motivation. *Organizational Behavior and Human Decision Processes, 38,* 92–113.

Bandura, A., & Schunk, D.H. 1981. Cultivating competence, self-efficacy, and intrinsic interest through proximal self-motivation. *Journal of Personality and Social Psychology, 41,* 586–598.

Banuazizi, A. 1981. An evaluation of the first year's activities of the National Demonstration Title II Project (Basic Skills Improvement Program) in selected elementary grades of Cambridge public schools. Unpublished manuscript, Department of Psychology, Boston College, Chestnut Hill, Mass., 02167.

Baron, R. 1988. Negative effects of destructive criticism: Impact on conflict, self-efficacy, and task performance. *Journal of Applied Psychology, 73,* 199–207.

Baron, R.M., Tom D.Y.H., & Cooper, H.M. 1985. Social class, race and teacher expectations. In J.B. Dusek, V.C. Hall, & W.J. Meyer, eds., *Teacher expectations,* 251–270. Hillsdale, N.J.: Lawrence Erlbaum.

Bass, B.M. 1985. *Leadership and performance beyond expectations.* New York: Free Press.

Beck, A.T. 1976. *Cognitive therapy and the emotional disorders.* New York: International Universities Press.

Beer, M. 1988. Towards a redefinition of OD: A critique of research focus and method. *Academy of Management OD Newsletter,* Winter, 6–7.

Beer, M., & Walton, A.E. 1987. Organization change and development. *Annual Review of Psychology, 38,* 339–367.

Bennis, W.G., & Nanus, B. 1985. *Leaders: The strategies for taking charge.* New York: Harper & Row.

Berlew, D.E., & Hall, D.T. 1966. The socialization of managers: Effects of expectations on performance. *Administrative Science Quarterly, 11,* 207–223.

Bernstein, D.A., & Neitzel, M.T. 1977. Demand characteristics in behavior modification: The natural history of a "nuisance." In M. Husen, R.M. Eisler, & P.M. Miller, eds., *Progress in behavior modification,* vol. 4. New York: Academic Press.

Boje, D.M., Fedor, D.B., & Rowland, K.M. 1982. Myth making: A qualitative step in OD interventions. *Journal of Applied Behavioral Science, 18,* 17–28.

Bowers, D.G., & Seashore, S.E. 1966. Predicting organizational effectiveness with a four-factor theory of leadership. *Administrative Science Quarterly, 11,* 238–263.

Bradley, G.W. 1978. Self-serving bias in the attribution process: A reexamination of the fact or fiction question. *Journal of Personality and Social Psychology, 36,* 56–71.

Bradley, R.T. 1986. *Transforming order: A study of charisma, power, and communion.* New York: Paragon House.

Brief, A.P., & Aldag, R.J. 1981. The "self" in work organizations: A conceptual review. *Academy of Management Review, 6,* 75–88.

Broadwell, M.M. 1987. Classroom instruction. In R. Craig, ed., *Training and development handbook,* 3d ed., 383–398. New York: McGraw-Hill.

Brockner, J. 1985. The relation of self-esteem and positive inequity to productivity. *Journal of Personality, 53,* 517–529.

———. 1988. *Self-Esteem at work: Research, theory, and practice.* Lexington, Mass.: Lexington Books.

Brophy, J.E. 1983. Research on the self-fulfilling prophecy and teacher expectations. *Journal of Educational Psychology, 75,* 631–661.

———. 1985. Teacher-student interaction. In J.B. Dusek, V.C. Hall, & W.J. Meyer, eds., *Teacher expectancies,* 303–328. Hillsdale, N.J.: Lawrence Erlbaum.

Burns, J.M. 1978. *Leadership.* New York: Harper & Row.

Campbell, D., & Stanley, J. 1966. *Experimental and quasiexperimental designs for research.* Chicago: Rand McNally.

Campbell, J.P., & Pritchard, R.D. 1976. Motivation theory in industrial and organizational psychology. In M.D. Dunnette, ed., *Handbook of industrial and organizational psychology,* 63–130. Chicago: Rand McNally.

Caplan, R.D., & Jones, K.W. 1975. Effects of work load, ambiguity, and type A personality on anxiety, depression, and heart rate. *Journal of Applied Psychology, 60,* 713–719.

Carter, K., Sabers, D., Cushing, K., Pinnegar, S., & Berliner, D.C. 1987. Processing and using information about students: A study of expert, novice, and postulant teachers. *Teaching & Teacher Education, 3,* 147–157.

Clark, K.B. 1963. Educational stimulation of racially disadvantaged children. In A.H. Passow, ed., *Education in depressed areas.* New York: Bureau of Publications, Teachers College, Columbia University.

Clymer, A. 1986, December 7, part 2. A Times poll of M.B.A.'s. *The New York Times Magazine, 22, 26, 28.*

Coe, W.C. 1980. Expectations, hypnosis, and suggestion in behavior change. In F.H. Kanfer & A.P. Goldstein, eds., *Helping people change: A textbook of methods,* 2d ed., 423–469. New York: Pergamon.

Conger, J.A., & Kanungo, R.N. 1987. Toward a behavioral theory of charismatic leadership in organizational settings. *Academy of Management Review, 12,* 637–647.

Cooke, R.A., & Rousseau, D.M. 1988. Behavioral norms and expectations: A quantitative approach to the assessment of organizational culture. *Group & Organization Studies, 13,* 245–273.

Craig, R.L., ed. 1987. *Training and development handbook: A guide to human resources development,* 3d ed. New York: McGraw-Hill.

Crawford, K.S., Thomas, E.D., & Fink, J.J. 1980. Pygmalion at sea: Improving the work effectiveness of low performers. *Journal of Applied Behavioral Science, 16,* 482–505.

Critelli, J.W., & Neumann, K.F. 1984. The placebo: Conceptual analysis of a construct in transition. *American Psychologist, 39,* 32–39.

Curtin, R.T., ed. 1976. *Survey of Consumers, 1974–75: Contributions to Behavioral Economics.* Ann Arbor, Mich.: Institute for Social Research.

Dansereau, F., Graen, G., & Haga, W.J. 1975. A vertical dyad linkage approach to leadership within formal organizations. *Organizational Behavior and Human Performance, 13,* 46–78.

Darley, J.M., & Gross, P.H. 1983. A hypothesis-confirming bias in labeling effects. *Journal of Personality and Social Psychology, 44,* 20–33.

Dawson, J.E., Messe, L.A., & Phillips, J.L. 1972. Effect of instructor-leader behavior on student performance. *Journal of Applied Psychology, 56,* 369–376.

Deal, T.E., & Kennedy, A.A. 1982. *Corporate cultures: The rites and rituals of corporate life.* Reading, Mass.: Addison-Wesley.

Dean, K., & Lewis, L.L. 1984. Structure of gender stereotypes: Interrelationships among components and gender label. *Journal of Personality and Social Psychology, 46,* 991–1004.

Dohrenwend, B.S., & Dohrenwend, B., eds. 1974. *Stressful life events: Their nature and effects.* New York: Wiley.

Duchon, D., Green, S.G., & Taber, T.D. 1986. Vertical dyad linkage: A longitudinal assessment of antecedents, measures, and consequences. *Journal of Applied Psychology, 71,* 56–60.

Dusek, J.B., Hall, V.C., & Meyer, W.J., eds. 1985. *Teacher expectancies.* Hillsdale, N.J.: Lawrence Erlbaum.

Dusek, J.B., & Joseph, G. 1985. The bases of teacher expectancies. In J.B. Dusek, V.C. Hall, & W.J. Meyer, eds., *Teacher expectancies,* 229–250. Hillsdale, N.J.: Lawrence Erlbaum.

Eden, D. 1982. Critical job events, acute stress, and strain: A multiple interrupted time series. *Organizational Behavior and Human Performance, 30,* 312–329.

———. 1984. Self-fulfilling prophecy as a management tool: Harnessing Pygmalion. *Academy of Management Review, 9,* 64–73.

———. 1986. OD and self-fulfilling prophecy: Boosting productivity by raising expectations. *Journal of Applied Behavioral Science, 22,* 1–13.

———. 1988a. Creating expectation effects in OD: Applying self-fulfilling prophecy. *Research in Organizational Change and Development, 2,* 235–267.

———. 1988b. Pygmalion, goal setting, and expectancy: Compatible ways to raise productivity. *Academy of Management Review, 13,* 639–652.

———. 1988 November. Industrialization as a self-fulfilling prophecy: The role of expectations in development. Paper presented at the International Symposium on Social Values and Effective Organizations, Taipei, Taiwan.

———. 1990. Acute and chronic job stress, strain, and vacation relief. *Organizational Behavior and Human Decision Processes,* in press.

Eden, D., & Daniely, S. 1979 September. Survey-based OD in the Israel Defense Forces: A field experiment. Paper presented at the meeting of the American Psychological Association, New York.

Eden, D., & Leviatan, U. 1975. Implicit leadership theory as a determinant of the factor structure underlying supervisory behavior scales. *Journal of Applied Psychology, 60,* 736–741.

Eden, D., & Ravid, G. 1981 December. Effects of expectancy on performance among male and female trainees. Paper presented at the International Interdisciplinary Congress on Women, Haifa, Israel.

———. 1982. Pygmalion vs. self-expectancy: Effects of instructor- and self-expectancy on trainee performance. *Organizational Behavior and Human Performance, 30,* 351–364.

Eden, D., & Shani, A.B. 1979 September. Pygmalion goes to boot camp: Expectancy, leadership, and trainee performance. Paper presented at the meeting of the American Psychological Association, New York.

Eden, D., & Shani, A.B. 1982. Pygmalion goes to boot camp: Expectancy, leadership, and trainee performance. *Journal of Applied Psychology, 67,* 194–199.

Erez, M., & Kanfer, F.H. 1983. The role of goal acceptance in goal setting and task performance. *Academy of Management Review, 8,* 454–463.

Erez, M., & Zidon, I. 1984. Effect of goal acceptance on the relationship of goal difficulty to performance. *Journal of Applied Psychology, 69,* 69–78.

Fallows, J. December 1985. Bad for business: The case against credentialism. *The Atlantic Monthly,* 49–67.

Feather, N.T. 1963. Mowrer's revised two-factor theory and the motive-expectancy-value model. *Psychological Review, 7,* 500–515.

Feldman, J.M. 1981. Beyond attribution theory: Cognitive processes in performance evaluation. *Journal of Applied Psychology, 66,* 127–148.

Feldman, R.S., & Theiss, A.J. 1982. The teacher and student as Pygmalions: Joint effects of teacher and student expectations. *Journal of Educational Psychology, 74,* 217–223.

Flanagan, J.C. 1960. *Test of General Ability: Preliminary technical report.* Chicago: Science Research Associates.

Frayne, C., & Latham, G.P. 1987. Application of social learning theory to employee self-management of attendance. *Journal of Applied Psychology, 72,* 387–392.

French, W.L., & Bell, C.H., Jr. 1978. *Organizational development: Behavioral science interventions for organization improvement,* 2d ed. Englewood Cliffs, N.J.: Prentice-Hall.

Freudenberger, H.R., & Richelson, G. 1980. *Burnout: The high cost of high achievement.* New York: Doubleday.

Galbraith, J., & Cummings, L.L. 1967. An empirical investigation of the motivational determinants of task performance: Interactive effects between instrumentality-valence and motivation-ability. *Organizational Behavior and Human Performance, 2,* 237–257.

Garland, H. 1982. Goal levels and task performance: A compelling replication of some compelling results. *Journal of Applied Psychology, 67,* 245–248.

———. 1983. The influence of ability, assigned goals, and normative information on personal goals and performance: A challenge to the goal attainability assumption. *Journal of Applied Psychology, 68,* 20–30.

———. 1984. Relation of effort-performance expectancy to performance in goal-setting experiments. *Journal of Applied Psychology, 69,* 79–84.

Gioia, D.A., & Sims, H.P., Jr. 1985. Self-serving bias and actor-observer differences in organizations: An empirical analysis. *Journal of Applied Social Psychology, 15,* 547–563.

Gist, M.E. 1987. Self-efficacy: Implications for organizational behavior and human resource management. *Academy of Management Review, 12,* 472–485.

Goethe, J.W. 1962. *Italian journey,* p. 116. W.H. Auden & E. Mayer, trans. New York: Pantheon Books. Original work published 1816.

Goldfried, M.R., & Robins, C. 1982. On the facilitation of self-efficacy. *Cognitive Therapy and Research, 6,* 361–380.

Goldstein, A.P., & Sorcher, M. 1974. *Changing supervisor behavior.* New York: Pergamon.

Goldstein, I.L. 1986. *Training in organizations: Needs assessment, development, and evaluation,* 2d ed. Monterey, Calif.: Brooks/Cole.

Good, T.L., & Findley, M.J. 1985. Sex role expectations and achievement. In J.B. Dusek, V.C. Hall, & W.J. Meyer, eds., *Teacher expectancies,* 271–302. Hillsdale, N.J.: Lawrence Erlbaum.

Graen, G. 1969. Instrumentality theory of work motivation: Some experimental results and suggested modifications. *Journal of Applied Psychology Monograph, 53,* 1–25.

———. 1976. Role making processes within complex organizations. In M.D. Dunnette, ed., *Handbook of Industrial and Organizational Psychology,* chap. 28. Chicago: Rand McNally.

Graen, G., & Cashman, J.F. 1975. A role-making model of leadership in formal organizations: A developmental approach. In J.G. Hunt & L.L. Larson, eds., *Leadership frontiers.* Kent, Ohio: Kent State University Press.

Graen, G., & Schiemann, W. 1978. Leader-member agreement: A vertical dyad linkage approach. *Journal of Applied Psychology, 63,* 206–212.

Green, S.G., & Mitchell, T.R. 1979. Attributional precesses of leaders in leader-member interactions. *Organizational Behavior and Human Performance, 23,* 429–458.

Greenfield, D., Banuazizi, A., & Ganon, J. 1979. Project STILE: An evaluation of the second year. Unpublished manuscript, Department of Psychology, Boston College, Chestnut Hill, Mass., 02167.

Hall, V.C., & Merkel, S.P. 1985. Teacher expectancy effects and educational psychology. In J.B. Dusek, V.C. Hall, & W.J. Meyer, eds., *Teacher expectancies,* 67–92. Hillsdale, N.J.: Lawrence Erlbaum.

Heckhausen, H. 1967. *The anatomy of achievement motivation.* New York: Academic Press.

Heilman, M., Simon, M.C., & Repper, D.P. 1987. Intentionally favored, unintentionally harmed? Impact of sex-based preferential selection on self-perceptions and self-evaluations. *Journal of Applied Psychology, 72,* 62–68.

Hersey, P., & Blanchard, K.H. 1977. *Management of organizational behavior: Utilizing human resources,* 3d ed. Englewood Cliffs, N.J.: Prentice-Hall.

Herzl, T. 1902. *Altneuland.* Leipzig: Hermann Seeman Nachfolger.

Hollenbeck, J.R., & Klein, H.J. 1987. Goal commitment and the goal-setting process: Problems, prospects, and proposals for future research. *Journal of Applied Psychology, 72,* 212–220.

Holmes, T.H., & Rahe, R.H. 1967. The Social Readjustment Rating Scale. *Journal of Psychosomatic Research, 11,* 213–218.

House, R.J. 1977. A 1976 theory of charismatic leadership. In J.G. Hunt & L.L. Larson, eds. *Leadership: The cutting edge.* Carbondale, Ill.: Southern Illinois University Press.

Huse, E.F., & Cummings, T. 1985. *Organization development and change,* 3d ed. St. Paul, Minn.: West.

Iacocca, L. 1984. *Iacocca: An autobiography.* New York: Bantam Books.

Ilgen, D.R., Fisher, C.D., & Taylor, M.S. 1979. Consequences of individual feedback on behavior in organizations. *Journal of Applied Psychology, 64,* 349–371.

Ilgen, D.R., Mitchell, T.R., & Frederickson, J.W. 1981. Poor performers: Supervisors' and subordinates' responses. *Organizational Behavior and Human Performance, 27,* 386–410.

Ilgen, D.R., Nebeker, D.M., & Pritchard, R.D. 1981. Expectancy theory measures: An empirical comparison in an experimental simulation. *Organizational Behavior and Human Performance, 28,* 189–223.

Ilgen, D.R., Peterson, R.B., Martin, B., & Boeschen, D. 1981. Superior and subordinate reactions to performance appraisal sessions. *Organizational Behavior and Human Performance, 28,* 311–330.

Jensen, A.R. 1969. How much can we boost IQ and scholastic achievement? *Harvard Educational Review, 39,* 1–123.

Johnson, J.T., & Judd, C.M. 1983. Overlooking the incongruent: Categorization biases in the identification of political statements. *Journal of Personality and Social Psychology, 45,* 978–996.

Jones, E.E. 1986. Interpreting interpersonal behavior: The effects of expectancies. *Science, 234,* 41–46.

Jones, E.E., & Nisbett, R.E. 1972. *The actor and the observer: Divergent perceptions of the causes of behavior.* New York: General Learning Press.

Jones, J.W., ed. 1981. *The burnout syndrome.* London: London House Press.

Jones, R.A. 1977. *Self-fulfilling prophecies: Social, psychological, and physiological effects of expectancies.* Hillsdale, N.J.: Lawrence Erlbaum.

Jussim, L. 1986. Self-fulfilling prophecies: A theoretical and integrative review. *Psychological Review, 93,* 429–445.

Kahn, R.L., Wolfe, D.M., Quinn, R.P., Snoek, J.D., & Rosenthal, R.A. 1964. *Organizational stress: Studies in role conflict and ambiguity.* New York: Wiley.

Kanfer, F.H. 1980. Self-management methods. In F.H. Kanfer & A.P. Goldstein, eds., *Helping people change: A textbook of methods,* 2d ed., 334–389. New York: Pergamon.

Kanfer, F.H., & Gaelick, L. 1986. Self-management methods. In F.H. Kanfer & A.P. Goldstein, eds., *Helping people change: A textbook of methods,* 3d ed., 283–345. New York: Pergamon.

Kanfer, F.H., & Goldstein, A.P. eds. 1986. *Helping people change: A textbook of methods,* 3d ed. New York: Pergamon.

Katz, D., & Kahn, R.L. 1966. *The social psychology of organizations.* New York: Wiley.

Kerman, S. 1979. Teacher expectations and students' achievement. *Phi Delta Kappan, 60,* 716–718.

King, A.S. 1970. Managerial relations with disadvantaged work groups: Supervisory expectations of the underprivileged worker. Ph.D. diss., Texas Tech University.

———. 1971. Self-fulfilling prophecies in training the hard-core: Supervisors' expectations and the underprivileged workers' performance. *Social Science Quarterly, 52,* 369–378.

———. 1974. Expectation effects in organization change. *Administrative Science Quarterly, 19,* 221–230.

Kirsch, I. 1985. Self-efficacy and expectancy: Old wine with new labels. *Journal of Personality and Social Psychology, 42,* 132–136.

———. 1986. Early research on self-efficacy: What we already know without knowing we knew. *Journal of Social and Clinical Psychology, 4,* 339–358.

Klineberg, O. 1984. Public opinion and nuclear war. *American Psychologist, 39,* 1245–1253.

Kluckhohn, F.R., & Strodtbeck, F.L. 1961. *Variations in value orientations.* New York: Harper & Row.

Komaki, J.L. 1986. Toward effective supervision. *Journal of Applied Psychology, 71,* 270–279.

Kopelman, R.E., & Thompson, P.H. 1976. Boundary conditions for expectancy theory predictions of work motivation and job performance. *Academy of Management Journal, 19,* 237–258.

Korman, A.K. 1970. Toward a hypothesis of work behavior. *Journal of Applied Psychology, 54,* 31–41.

———. 1971. Expectancies as determinants of performance. *Journal of Applied Psychology, 55,* 218–222.

———. 1976. Hypothesis of work behavior revisited and an extension. *Academy of Management Review, 1,* 50–63.

———. 1988. *The outsiders: Jews and corporate America.* Lexington, Mass.: Lexington Books.

Lambert, C. 1984. *The complete book of supervisory training.* New York: Wiley.

Larson, J.R., Jr. 1982. Cognitive mechanisms mediating the impact of implicit theories of leader behavior on leader behavior ratings. *Organizational Behavior and Human Performance, 29,* 129–140.

Latham, G.P., & Saari, L.M. 1979. The application of social learning theory to training supervisors through behavioral modeling. *Journal of Applied Psychology, 64,* 239–246.

Laudon, K.C. 1986. *Dossier society: Value choices in the design of national information systems.* New York: Columbia University Press.

Lawler, E.E., III. 1971. *Pay and organizational effectiveness: A psychological view.* New York: McGraw-Hill.

———. 1973. *Motivation in work organizations.* Monterey, Calif.: Brooks/Cole.

Leana, C.R. 1987. Power relinquishment versus power sharing: Theoretical clarification and empirical comparison of delegation and participation. *Journal of Applied Psychology, 72,* 228–233.

Lenney, E. 1977. Women's self-confidence in achievement settings. *Psychological Bulletin, 84,* 1–12.

Levinson, D.J. 1978. *The seasons of a man's life.* New York: Ballantine.

Lewin, K. 1935. *A dynamic theory of personality.* New York: McGraw-Hill.

———. 1951. *Field theory in social science.* New York: Harper & Row.

Liden, R., & Graen, G. 1980. Generalizability of the vertical dyad linkage model of leadership. *Academy of Management Journal, 23,* 451–465.

Likert, R. 1961. *New patterns of management.* New York: McGraw-Hill.

———. 1967. *The human organization: Its management and value.* New York: McGraw-Hill.

Livingston, J.S. 1969. Pygmalion in management. *Harvard Business Review, 47*(4), 81–89.

———. 1988. Retrospective commentary. *Harvard Business Review,* September-October, 125.

Locke, E.A. 1968. Toward a theory of task motivation and incentives. *Organizational Behavior and Human Performance, 3,* 157–189.

Locke, E.A., Frederick, E., Lee, C., & Bobko, P. 1984. Effect of self-efficacy, goals, and task strategies on task performance. *Journal of Applied Psychology, 69,* 241–251.

Locke, E.A., & Latham, G.P. 1984. *Goal setting: A motivational technique that works!* Englewood Cliffs, N.J.: Prentice-Hall.

Locke, E.A., Motowidlo, S.J., & Bobko, P. 1986. Using self-efficacy theory to resolve the conflict between goal-setting theory and expectancy theory in organizational behavior and industrial/organizational psychology. *Journal of Social and Clinical Psychology, 4,* 328–338.

Locke, E.A., & Schweiger, D.M. 1979. Participation in decision making: One more look. In B.M. Staw, ed., *Research in organizational behavior,* vol. 1, 265–339. Greenwich, Conn.: JAI Press.

Locke, E.A., Shaw, K.N. Saari, L.M., & Latham, G.P. 1981. Goal setting and task performance: 1969–1980, *Psychological Bulletin, 90,* 125–152.

Lucas, R.E. 1972. Expectations and the neutrality of money. *Journal of Economic Theory, 4,* April, 103–124.

McClelland, D.C. 1958. Risk-taking in children with high and low need for achievement. In J.W. Atkinson, ed., *Motives in fantasy, action, and society,* 288–305. Princeton: Van Nostrand.

McClelland, D.C., Atkinson, J.W., Clark, R.A., & Lowell, E.L. 1953. *The achievement motive.* New York: Appleton-Century-Crofts.

McGrath, J.E. 1976. Stress and behavior in organizations. In M.D. Dunnette, ed., *Handbook of industrial and organizational psychology,* 1351–1395. Chicago: Rand McNally.

McGregor, D. 1960. *The human side of enterprise.* New York: McGraw-Hill.

Mahone, C.H. 1960. Fear of failure and unrealistic vocational aspiration. *Journal of Abnormal and Social Psychology, 60,* 253–261.

Maister, D.H. 1985. The one-firm firm: What makes it successful. *Sloan Management Review,* Fall, 3–13.

Marks, M.L., & Schriber, J. 1988 August. Factors influencing employee expectations of an internal corporate merger. Paper presented at the meeting of the National Academy of Management, Anaheim, Calif.

Markus, H., & Kunda, Z. 1986. Stability and malleability of the self-concept. *Journal of Personality and Social Psychology, 51,* 858–866.

Martinko, M.J., & Gardner, W.L. 1987. The leader/member attribution process. *Academy of Management Review, 12,* 235–249.

Maslach, C. 1982. *Burnout: The cost of caring.* Englewood Cliffs, N.J.: Prentice-Hall.

Maslow, A.H. 1954. *Motivation and personality.* New York: Harper.

———. 1965. *Eupsychian management.* Homewood, Ill.: Dorsey-Irwin.

Matsui, T., Okado, A., & Mizuguchi, R. 1981. Expectancy theory prediction of the goal theory postulate. *Journal of Applied Psychology, 66,* 54–58.

Mento, A.J., Cartledge, N.D., & Locke, E.A. 1980. Maryland vs. Michigan vs. Minnesota: Another look at the relationship of expectancy and goal difficulty to task performance. *Organizational Behavior and Human Performance, 25,* 419–440.

Mento, A.J., Steel, R.P., & Karren, R.J. 1987. A meta-analytic study of the effects of goal setting on task performance: 1966–1984. *Organizational Behavior and Human Decision Processes, 39,* 52–83.

Merton, R.K. 1948. The self-fulfilling prophecy. *Antioch Review, 8,* 193–210.

———. 1968. The Matthew effect in science. *Science, 159,* 56–63.

Michael, D.N., & Mirvis, P.H. 1977. Changing, erring, and learning. In P.H. Mirvis & D.N. Berg, eds., *Failures in organization development and change: Cases and essays for learning.* New York: Wiley.

Miller, D.T., & Ross, M. 1975. Self-serving biases in the attribution of causality: Fact or fiction? *Psychological Bulletin, 82,* 213–225.

Miller, D.T., & Turnbull, W. 1986. Expectancies and interpersonal processes. *Annual Review of Psychology, 37,* 233–256.

Mirvis, P.H., & Berg, D.N., eds. 1977. *Failures in organization development and change: Cases and essays for learning.* New York: Wiley.

Mitchell, T.R., Green, S.G., & Wood, R.E. 1981. An attributional model of leadership and the poor performing subordinate. In B.M. Staw & L.L. Cummings, eds., *Research in organizational behavior,* vol. 3, 197–234. Greenwich, Conn.: JAI Press.

Mitchell, T.R., & Larson, J.R., Jr. 1987. *People in organizations: An introduction to organizational behavior,* 3d ed. New York: McGraw-Hill.

Mitchell, T.R., & Wood, R.E. 1980. Supervisors' responses to subordinate poor performance: A test of an attributional model. *Organizational Behavior and Human Performance, 25,* 123–138.

Morgan, G. 1986. *Images of organization.* Beverly Hills: Sage.

Morris, J.L. 1967. Propensity for risk taking as determinant of vocational choice: An extension of the theory of achievement motivation. *Journal of Personality and Social Psychology, 3,* 328–335.

Neider, L. 1980. An experimental field investigation utilizing an expectancy theory view of participation. *Organizational Behavior and Human Performance, 26,* 425–442.

Nicholsen, S. 1982. *Report on fieldwork: An evaluation of Project STILE on participants in the Cambridge public schools.* Cambridge, Mass.: Harvard Graduate School of Education.

Norem, J.K., & Cantor, N. 1986a. Anticipatory and post-hoc cushioning strategies: Optimism and defensive pessimism in "risky" situations. *Cognitive Therapy and Research, 16,* 347–362.

———. 1986b. Defensive pessimism: Harnessing anxiety as motivation. *Journal of Personality and Social Psychology, 51,* 1208–1217.

Noy, S., Solomon, Z., & Benbenishti, R. 1983. *The forward treatment of combat reactions: A testcase in the 1982 conflict in Lebanon.* Tel Hashomer, Israel: Research Branch, Mental Health Department, Medical Corps., Israel Defense Forces.

Nunnally, J.C. 1978. *Psychometric theory,* 2d ed. New York: McGraw-Hill.

Odiorne, G.S. 1969. *Management decision by objectives.* Englewood Cliffs, N.J.: Prentice-Hall.

O'Leary, V.E. 1977. *Toward understanding women.* Monterey, Calif.: Brooks/Cole.

Peters, T.J. 1978. Symbols, patterns, and settings: An optimistic case for getting things done. *Organizational Dynamics, 7,* 3–23.

Peters, T.J., & Waterman, R.H. 1982. *In search of excellence.* New York: Harper & Row.

Phillips, J.S. 1984. The accuracy of leadership ratings: A cognitive categorization perspective. *Organizational Behavior and Human Performance, 33,* 125–138.

Phillips, J.S., & Lord, R.G. 1982. Schematic information processing and perceptions of leadership in problem-solving groups. *Journal of Applied Psychology, 67,* 486–492.

Pinder, C.C. 1984. *Work motivation: Theory, issues, and applications.* Glenview, Ill.: Scott, Foresman.

Pines, A.M., & Aronson, E. 1981. *Burnout: From tedium to personal growth.* New York: Free Press.

Porter, L.W., & Lawler, E.E., III. 1968. *Managerial attitudes and performance.* Homewood, Ill.: Richard D. Irwin.

Premack, S.L., & Wanous, J.P. 1985. A meta-analysis of realistic job preview experiments. *Journal of Applied Psychology, 70,* 706–719.

Raudenbush, S.W. 1984. Magnitude of teacher expectancy effects on pupil IQ as a function of the credibility of expectancy induction: A synthesis of findings from 18 experiments. *Journal of Educational Psychology, 76,* 85–97.

Roethlesberger, F.J., & Dickson, W.V. 1939. *Management and the worker.* Cambridge, Mass.: Harvard University Press.

Rosenthal, R. 1963. On the social psychology of the psychological experiment: The experimenter's hypothesis as unintended determinant of experimental results. *American Scientist, 51,* 268–283.

———. 1973. On the social psychology of the self-fulfilling prophecy: Further evidence for Pygmalion effects and their mediating mechanisms. New York: MSS Modular Publications, Module 53.

———. 1976. *Experimenter effects in behavioral research: Enlarged edition.* New York: Irvington Publishers, Halstead Division of Wiley.

———. 1981. Pavlov's mice, Pfungst's horse, and Pygmalion's PONS: Some models for the study of interpersonal expectancy effects. In T.A. Sebok & R. Rosenthal, eds., *The Clever Hans phenomenon.* Annals of the New York Academy of Sciences, N. 364.

———. 1985. From unconscious experimenter bias to teacher expectancy effects. In J.B. Dusek, V.C. Hall, & W.J. Meyer, eds., *Teacher expectancies,* 37–65. Hillsdale, N.J.: Lawrence Erlbaum.

Rosenthal, R., & Fode, K.L. 1963. The effect of experimenter bias on the performance of the albino rat. *Behavioral Science, 8,* 183–189.

Rosenthal, R., Hall, J.A., DiMatteo, M.R., Rogers, P.L., & Archer, D. 1979. *Sensitivity to nonverbal communication: The PONS test.* Baltimore, Md.: Johns Hopkins Press.

Rosenthal, R., & Jacobson, L. 1968. *Pygmalion in the classroom: Teacher expectation and pupils' intellectual development.* New York: Holt, Rinehart & Winston.

Rotter, J.B. 1943. Level of aspiration as a method of studying personality, III. Group validity studies. *Character and Personality, 11,* 254–274.

———. 1945. Level of aspiration as a method of studying personality, IV. The analysis of patterns of response. *Journal of Social Psychology, 21,* 159–177.

Salomon, G. 1981. Self-fulfilling and self-sustaining prophecies and the behaviors that realize them. *American Psychologist, 36,* 1452–1453.

Sargent, T.J., & Wallace, N. 1976. Rational expectations and the theory of economic policy. *Journal of Monetary Economics, 2,* 169–183.

Sashkin, M. 1976. Changing toward participative management approaches: A model and methods. *Academy of Management Review, 1,* 75–86.

———. 1988. The visionary principal: School leadership for the next century. *Education and Urban Society, 20,* 239–249.

Sashkin, M., & Burke, W.W. 1987. Organization development in the 1980's. *Journal of Management, 13,* 205–229.

Sayle, M. 1982 November. The yellow peril and the red-haired devils. *Harper's,* 23–35.

Scandura, T.A., Graen, G.B., & Novak, M.A. 1986. When managers decide not to decide autocratically: An investigation of leader-member exchange and decision influence. *Journal of Applied Psychology, 71,* 579–584.

Scheff, T.J. 1975. *Labeling madness.* Englewood Cliffs, N.J.: Prentice-Hall.

Schein, E.H. 1985. *Organizational culture and leadership.* San Francisco: Jossey-Bass.

Schrank, W.R. 1968. The labeling effect of ability grouping. *Journal of Educational Research, 62,* 51–52.

Seiz, R.C. 1982. Pygmalion: Adrift at sea. *Journal of Applied Behavioral Science, 18,* 127–129.

Shapiro, A.K. 1971. Placebo effects in medicine, psychotherapy, and psychoanalysis. In A.E. Bergin & S.L. Garfield, eds., *Handbook of psychotherapy and behavior change,* chap. 12. New York: Wiley.

Shaw, G.B. 1957. *Pygmalion.* London: Longmans, Green.

Sherer, M., & Adams, C.H. 1983. Construct validation of the self-efficacy scale. *Psychological Reports, 53,* 899–902.

Sherer, M., Maddux, J.E., Mercadante, B., Prentice-Dunn, S., Jacobs, B., & Rogers, R.W. 1982. The self-efficacy scale: Construction and validation. *Psychological Reports, 51,* 663–671.

Siegel, S. 1956. *Nonparametric statistics for the behavioral sciences.* New York: McGraw-Hill.

Smircich, L., & Morgan, G. 1982. Leadership: The management of meaning. *Journal of Applied Behavioral Science, 18,* 257–273.

Snyder, M. 1984. When belief creates reality. *Advances in Experimental Social Psychology, 18,* 247–305.

Snyder, M., Tanke, E.D., & Berscheid, E. 1977. Social perception and interpersonal behavior: On the self-fulfilling nature of social stereotypes. *Journal of Personality and Social Psychology, 35,* 656–666.

Stedry, A.C., & Kay, E. 1966. The effects of goal difficulty on performance. *Behavioral Science, 11,* 459–470.

Stein, A.H., & Bailey, M.M. 1973. The socialization of achievement motivation in females. *Psychological Bulletin, 80,* 345–366.

Sutton, C.D. 1986. Pygmalion goes to work: The effects of supervisor expectations in a retail setting. Ph.D. diss., Texas A & M University.

Taylor, J.C., & Bowers, D.G. 1972. *The survey of organizations: A machine scored standardized questionnaire instrument.* Ann Arbor, Mich.: Institute for Social Research.

Taylor, M.S., Locke, E.A., Lee, C., & Gist, M.E. 1984. Type A behavior and faculty research productivity: What are the mechanisms? *Organizational Behavior and Human Performance, 34,* 402–418.

Terry, J.P. 1985 February. Student performance and school-related attitudes as a function of teacher expectations and behavior. Unpublished manuscript, Cambridge, MIT, Program for Science, Technology and Society.

Tinsley, H.E.A., Bowman, S.L., & Ray, S.B. 1988. Manipulation of expectancies about counseling and psychotherapy: Review and analysis of expectancy manipulation strategies and results. *Journal of Counseling Psychology, 35,* 99–108.

Tipton, R.M., & Worthington, E.L., Jr. 1984. The measurement of generalized self-efficacy: A study of construct validity. *Journal of Personality Assessment, 48,* 545–548.

Turnage, J.J., & Muchinsky, P.M. 1984. A comparison of the predictive validity of assessment center evaluations versus traditional measures in forecasting supervisory job performance: Interpretive implications of criterion distortion for the assessment paradigm. *Journal of Applied Psychology, 69,* 595–602.

Tversky, A., & Kahneman, D. 1974. Judgment under uncertainty. *Science, 185,* 1124–1130.

Van Maanen, J. 1985. *Tales of the field.* Unpublished manuscript.

Van Maanen, J., & Kunda, G. 1985 August. *"Real Feelings:" Emotional expression and organization culture.* Unpublished manuscript, Cambridge, MIT.

Vollmer, F. 1986. Why do men have higher expectancy than women? *Sex Roles, 14,* 351–362.

Vroom, V.H. 1964. *Work and motivation.* New York: Wiley.

Wanous, J.P. 1977. Organizational entry: The individual's viewpoint. In J.R. Hackman, E.E. Lawler, III, & L.W. Porter, eds., *Perspectives on behavior in organizations.* New York: McGraw-Hill.

Weber, M. 1947. *The theory of social and economic organizations,* T. Parsons, trans. New York: Free Press. Original work published 1924.

Webster's New Universal Unabridged Dictionary, 2d ed. 1983. New York: Simon & Schuster.

Weick, K.E. 1979. *The social psychology of organizing,* 2d ed. Reading, Mass.: Addison-Wesley.

———. 1984. Small wins: Redefining the scale of social problems. *American Psychologist, 39,* 40–49.

Weiner, B. 1974. *Achievement motivation and attribution theory.* Morristown, N.J.: General Learning Press.

———. 1979. A theory of motivation for some classroom experiences. *Journal of Educational Psychology, 71,* 3–25.

———. 1980. *Human motivation.* New York: Holt, Rinehart & Winston.

Weiner, B., Frieze, I., Kukla, A., Reed, L, Rest, B., & Rosenbaum, R.M. 1971. *Perceiving the causes of success and failure.* Morristown, N.J.: General Learning Press.

Weiss, H., & Adler, S. 1984. Personality and organizational behavior. In B. M. Staw & L.L. Cummings, eds., *Research in organizational behavior,* vol. 6, 1–50. Greenwich, Conn.: JAI Press.

Westman, M., & Eden, D. 1989a. Implicit stress theory: The spurious effects of stress on performance ratings. Unpublished manuscript.

Westman, M., & Eden, D. 1989b January. Job stress and subsequent objective performance. Presented at the Fourth International Conference on Psychological Stress and Adjustment in Time of War and Peace, Tel Aviv, Israel.

Wexley, K.N. 1984. Personnel training. *Annual Review of Psychology, 35,* 519–551.

Wineburg, S.S. 1987 December. The self-fulfillment of the self-fulfilling prophecy. *Educational Researcher,* 28–37.

Wood, R.E., & Locke, E.A. 1987. The relation of self-efficacy and grade goals to academic performance. *Educational and Psychological Measurement, 47,* 1013–1024.

Woodman, R.W., & Tolchinsky, P.D. 1985. Expectation effects: Implications for organization development interventions. In D.D. Warrick, ed., *Contemporary organization development: Current thinking and applications,* 477–487. Glenview, Ill.: Scott, Foresman.

Yankelovich, D., & Immerwahr, J. 1983. *Putting the work ethic to work.* New York: Public Agenda Foundation.

Zanna, M.P., Sheras, P.L., Cooper, J., & Shaw, C. 1975. Pygmalion and Galatea: The interactive effect of teacher and student expectancies. *Journal of Experimental Social Psychology, 11,* 279–287.

Zuroff, D.C., & Rotter, J.B. 1985. A history of the expectancy construct in psychology. In J.B. Dusek, V.C. Hall, & W.J. Meyer, eds., *Teacher expectancies,* 9–36. Hillsdale, N.J.: Lawrence Erlbaum.

Index

About the Author

Dov Eden (formerly Barry Fine) received his Ph.D. in organizational psychology at the University of Michigan and immigrated to Israel in 1970. He is currently associate professor of management at Tel Aviv University's Leon Recanati Graduate School of Business Administration, and is director of the Israel Institute of Business Research. His main areas of research include interpersonal expectancy effects, organization development, leadership, work motivation, training, job stress, group behavior, and team development. He has presented scholarly papers at scientific meetings of the American Psychological Association and the Academy of Management as well as at various meetings in Israel and international conventions. He has published articles in many leading journals on organizational psychology, organizational behavior, and management; including the *Journal of Applied Psychology, Journal of Applied Social Psychology, Academy of Management Review, Journal of Applied Behavioral Science,* and *Organizational Behavior and Human Decision Processes.* He is a member of the editorial review board of *Group & Organization Studies.* He has done executive development and management consultation with some of Israel's leading industrial and public-sector organizations.